D120Z373

COLONIAL AND ANTI-COLONIAL DISCOURSES

Albert Camus and Algeria

An Intertextual Dialogue with Mouloud Mammeri,
Mouloud Feraoun, and Mohammed Dib

Ena C. Vulor

University Press of America,® Inc.
Lanham · New York · Oxford

Copyright © 2000 by
University Press of America,® Inc.
4720 Boston Way
Lanham, Maryland 20706

12 Hid's Copse Rd.
Cumnor Hill, Oxford OX2 9JJ

Library of Congress Cataloging-in-Publication Data

Vulor, Ena C.
Colonial and anti-colonial discourses : Albert Camus and Algeria :
an intertextual dialoque with Mouloud Mammeri, Mouloud Feraoun,
and Mohhammed Dib / Ena C. Vulor.
p.   cm.
Includes bibliographical references and index.
1. Camus, Albert, 1913-1960—Knowledge—Algeria. 2. Algeria—
In literature. 3. Algeria—Colonization. 4. Camus, Albert, 1913-1960—Influence.
5.   Mammeri, Mouloud, 1917—Criticism and interpretation. 6.
Feraoun, Mouloud—Criticism and interpretation. 7. Dib,
Mohammed, 1920–Criticism and interpretation. I. Title: Albert Camus
and Algeria. II. Title: Intertextual dialoque with Mouloud Mammeri,
Mouloud Feraoun, and Mohhammed Dib. III. Title.
PQ2605.A3734Z92   2000   848'.91409—dc21   00-060709 CIP

ISBN 0-7618-1816-2 (cloth: alk. ppr.)

Dedication

To the memory of my father, Joseph Kwame Vulor, 1920–1999
To my mother, Delphine Vulor, and to my brothers and sisters.

*"Heureux vous qui pleurez maintenant, car vous
serez dans la joie."*

Luc 6. 21

Contents

Preface   vii

Acknowledgments   xi

Introduction   xiii

Chapter 1   **Algeria: A Socio-Political Appraisal, and Birth of National Consciousness and Literary Discourse**   1

Chapter 2   ***L'Ecole d'Alger***: **Universalist Humanist Dilemma, Mediterranean Myth and Colonial Malaise**   29

Chapter 3   **Camus, Mammeri, Feraoun and *L'Etranger*: Landscapes of the Absurd and Colonial Landscapes**   69

Chapter 4   **Albert Camus, Mohammed Dib and the Plagues of Colonialism: A Political Re-Reading of *La Peste***   121

Chapter 5   **The Dialogical Conclusion: A Breakdown of the Univocal Vision and Exile From the Kingdom**   157

Index   191

Selected Bibliography   193

Preface

Traditionally, Camus's work has been read as part of the French national literary heritage. My study departs from this tradition by suggesting that Camus's writings are viewed more productively within the Francophone literary tradition of his native country, Algeria. This work examines the ideological parameters—colonial history, French assimilationist practices, politics of citizenship, etc.—that provide a generative context for the writings of Albert Camus, Mouloud Mammeri, Mouloud Feraoun, and Mohammed Dib.

The work's strength and contribution to scholarship, specifically, to the growing field of postcolonial cultural critique, lie in its attempt to read the fictions of Camus from the perspective of a North African literary tradition as opposed to a French literary tradition. I bring his writings into a mutual dialogic interrogation with those of three North African writers, whose fictions articulate a state of cultural heterogeneity at the very moment when they confront the problem of Western—particularly French—hegemony.

As observed by his various biographers, notably Lottman, Camus grew up surrounded by the signs of Algeria's latent nationalism and subsequent bloody resistance to French domination. And his notoriety, surpassing that of any other French Algerian writer, grew and fed from this context of Algeria's colonial turbulence. I argue that despite the claim to articulating universal dilemma inherent in the Human Condition, Camus's work is nourished by the French colonial presence and by his own position vis-à-vis the history of French rule in Algeria. It cannot be dissociated from either the colonial discourse, or the Francophone North African literary discourse of the time. Moreover, although Camus and the three North African writers selected for this study have all sought to interpret Algeria's colonial culture, the fictions of Mammeri, Feraoun and Dib actually provide counter-arguments to Camus's field of vision. The works of the three indigenous writers not only help to recontextualize Camus's fiction on Algeria, but they also call into question his "universalist" humanist rhetoric which transcends the immediate actuality of colonialism.

By appropriating Camus's signature theme of "estrangement," Feraoun's *La Terre et le sang* (1953) and Mammeri's *Le Sommeil du juste* (1955) articulate a political malaise specific to Algeria, and point to the Arab's alienation (in its sociological implications), and his political and existential exclusion from the culturally dominant universe of the Settler minority group. The colonial discourse, repressed in Camus's *L'Etranger*, surfaces in their writings as oppressive and alienating. If Camus's Meursault is presented as an "outsider"—the estranged *persona* whose quest for metaphysical freedom is curtailed by the moral code of a paternalistic institution—within the conceptual lenses of the indigenous writers, however, the actual outsider becomes the Arab. In the Manichean universe described by these writers, the figure of "l'étranger" (the colonized) speaks a different "truth."

In *La Peste,* Camus seems to skirt once more the thorny question of French colonial domination, this time, by expunging the problematic figure of the Arab from the text altogether. Conversely, by recasting the theme of the "plague" against the Algerian colonial background, Mohammed Dib's trilogy, *La Grande Maison* (1952), *L'Incendie* (1954), and *Le Métier à tisser* (1957), exposes it as a process of "clochardisation" resulting from colonial domination. My study of the intertextual dialogue between these various texts points to the "narrative displacement," or a certain inbuilt blindness of Camus's mytho-poetic vision of the Absurd.

My theoretical approach to these works is socio-historical. The colonial society, as structured by the dynamics of relationships between colonizer and colonized, has been the subject of many theoretical speculations. Frantz Fanon, writing out of his years of experience in Algeria, points to the master/slave dialectics as characterized by exclusion and violence. The colonial machinery put in place (government policies, land appropriation, school system, disruption of pre-existing systems of values) creates a fundamental contrast and division—a compartmentalization (*Wretched of the Earth* 1963). Albert Memmi's forceful study of the rapports of "colonial subjects" provides further insights into the individual's relation to the field of colonialist discourses, revealing the complexity of such relations (*Portrait of the Colonizer and Colonized* 1965). Abdul JanMohamed sums up the colonial rapport as one of "power-and interest-relations [which] in turn provides the central feature of the colonialist cognitive framework and colonialist literary representation: the manichean allegory" (*Manichean Aesthetics* 1983). These theoretical formulations on the dynamics governing all colonial rapports, and the individual's response, provide a cogent analytical framework within which I propose to study the various literary exploitations of the colonial scene by both pied-noir and indigenous writers.

Acknowledgments

I would like to express my gratitude to Professor Gregson Davis of Duke University, and to Professors Susan Tarrow and David Grossvogel, both of Cornell University, for reading through the early versions of this manuscript, and for sharing with me their expertise, specifically in the areas of Francophone literature, the Maghreb, and Algeria.

I also wish to thank the Marietta College Faculty Development Committee for the 1996 Summer Professional Improvement Grant that enabled me to do preliminary work on this project. Over the years, many people have helped directly or indirectly with this book. My thanks go to my husband, Patrick Mensah, for his support and encouragement, and his willingness to read through my work and make corrections and suggestions. Thanks also to my children, Abi, Nana and Adjeiwaa, who have been my constant companions, and have put up with all my shortcomings. I extend heartfelt appreciation and thanks to colleagues and friends such as Carolyn Hares-Stryker, Richard Danford, Donna Bentley, Margaret Lutchmansingh, Ruth Berga, and Jane Schwendeman, for the wide range of help they have given me: professional advice, friendship, help with the children so I could get my work done. Being able to count on their support and encouragement has made my professional life here at Marietta College a lot easier than it would otherwise have been. To my friend Tarez Graban, I owe a debt of gratitude for her invaluable help in formatting and proofreading the manuscript.

Last, but not least, the author and publisher would like to extend our grateful acknowledgment to the following for granting permission to use copyrighted materials:

Introduction

> I have had a long affair with Algeria which will undoubtedly never
> end and which keeps me from being completely lucid about it . . .
> [Algeria] is my true country. (Albert Camus)

The emergence of written literature by Africans following Europe's
encounter with Africa has aroused a great deal of critical interest over
the last several decades. Such interest has been fueled and made more
complex by recent liberal critique of literary canon formation.
Considerable critical attention has also been given to what, in the wake
of Albert Memmi, came to be known as "tourist literature" on Africa
written by Europeans.

Tourist writers, as Memmi's designation suggests, were pilgrims
on a temporary voyage, for whom the mysterious African shores were
"a literary subject or locale, intriguing, inviting in their exotic
appeal."[1] Many were the French writers who crossed the Mediterranean,
leaving behind "the less vivid colors of Europe for a land of new
sensations."[2] As Maupassant enthusiastically put it,

> je me sentais attiré vers l'Afrique par un impérieux besoin, par la
> nostalgie du désert ignoré, comme par le pressentiment d'une
> passion qui va naître. [...] Je voulais voir cette terre du soleil et du
> sable en plein été, sous la pesante chaleur, dans l'éblouissement
> furieux de la lumière.[3]

> [I felt drawn towards Africa by a pressing need, by a nostalgia for
> the unknown desert, as by the premonition of a passion to be born.
> {...} I wanted to see this land of the sun and the sand in full summer,
> under the heavy heat, and in the furious glare of the light.][4]

From Théophile Gautier to André Gide and Henri de Montherlant, one finds the expression of similar enthusiasm. They all sought in this geographical space, not only a literary inspiration, but a physical escape from their own world. North Africa, the land most written about became thus, "un enrichissement accidental de leur palette et une terre d'évasion" (Memmi 1964, 12). For many, the "land of sunset" (Maghreb) provided "a therapeutic balm to spiritual discomforts" (ibid.).

The varying (mis)representations, which emerged from these transitory encounters with Africa, became the underpinning of a proprietorial European discourse that placed a great value on the exotic locale. It was within the framework of such discourse that tourist (or exotic) literature flourished, undergirded and nourished by various "preconceived notions and [a] cliché-ridden mythic vision [of North Africa]."[5] The colorful tableaux presented in these works exalted the natural beauty of the land while portraying its inhabitants, as part of the decor, or exalting them as "noble savages" who, in few cases, provided "transient thrills."[6]

With the rise to prominence of an entire new generation of French settlers and other European immigrants—a direct result of the French conquest of Algeria in 1830—there emerged a new form of literary discourse, reflected in the predominant view these new Algerians had of themselves as "insiders" in "a land to conquer, a frontier to settle and reshape" (Monego 1984, 13). With their political and economic emancipation came a certain awakening to a cultural otherness. The superficial curiosity of the tourist writers would be increasingly undermined by the colonialist discourse sustained by these new settlers. One prominent feature of these first representatives of an early colonial literature, Kirsch observes, "c'est leur patriotisme souvent tapageur. Ces gens-là se cramponnent à [leur] terre [l'Afrique du Nord] dont ils subissent le charme, et, dans une certaine mesure, la force d'assimilation" [It is often their loud patriotism. These people cling to {their} land {North Africa} whose charms they are subjected to, and to a certain extent, its strength of assimilation.] (Kirsch 1983, 131).

One prominent writer—a pioneer of a French settler literary tradition—to emerge from this new generation of French settlers, was Louis Bertrand, a French school teacher. He left France in 1891 to take up a post of school instructor in Algiers. Leaving behind a "stagnating [French] society," he found in Algeria an "energetic, robust Mediterranean race that fully embraced life" (ibid.). For half a century he would promulgate through his writings, his "pet theory of latinity," according to which the French occupation of North Africa was to be seen as a continuation of Roman civilization, which had been lying dormant under Arab rule. Speaking of French colonialism as a form of Latin

African "renaissance," he affirms that the French mission was simply to recuperate a lost Latin province.[7] Colonialist discursive practices, as Bertrand's endeavor indicates, were in full vigor during the dominant phase of French colonial rule. The underlying ideological agenda of such a discourse can be said to be threefold: the reintroduction of a mythical Roman heritage, the discursive approp-riation of North Africa as a land without a tradition, without a past, and most vital, the exclusion of the Arabs. All these sustained a myth essential, and intrinsic to the political period. With Bertrand, "one witnesses the interplay of the close affinities between politics and literature, propaganda and art. Overlapping, and serving each other, are two distinctive moves: the colonial adventure and the adventure of writing."[8]

Very little critical attention has been paid to this last category of writers who, obviously, witnessed directly the European expansionist era. Despite their colonist position, they did share a common ground with that first generation of Francophone North African and Sub-Saharan African writers whose works were a direct result of political circumstances generated by colonialism. For both groups, indigenous and non-indigenous, the colonies were the site of all the central experiences on which their literary works were based. As Memmi accurately points out,

> Il suffit de lire leurs textes [...] rapprochés pour apercevoir à quel point tous les écrivains d'Afrique du Nord, colonisateurs et colonisés, ont vécu, chacun à leur manière, la relation coloniale. Si les uns en ont vécu l'endroit, les autres le revers, c'était bien la même aventure. Page de frustration, de carence et de refus pour les uns, page de gloire et de privilèges pour les autres, dont ils se sentaient plus ou moins confusément fiers [ou] coupables. (1964:13)

> [One needs only to read their writings comparatively in order to realize to what extent all the writers of North Africa, colonizers and colonized, have lived, each in his/her own way, the colonial relationship. If the former have experienced one side, and the former the other, it was, nonetheless, the same adventure. Frustrations, lack and negation for one group, and for the other, glory and privileges of which they felt more or less proud or guilty.]

One reality, but two groups separated by racial, economic, political barriers. The same reality lived, apprehended differently depending on which side of the fence one stood.

It is within such a "compartmentalized world" that Albert Camus was born and bred, and eventually acquired his literary fame. As observed by his various biographers, notably, Lottman, he grew up surrounded by the signs of Algeria's latent nationalism and subsequent bloody resistance to French domination. It is, indeed, within the turbulence of colonial Algeria that Camus and his writings burst unto the international stage, seemingly, with instant success, a coup that no other French Algerian writer had ever achieved. However, as pointed out by Edward Saïd, "at the roots of the author's success lie, not the facts of, or any explicit involvement with the imperial actuality, but his own anguished preoccupation with global political and moral dilemmas that faced a whole post-war generation." His significance, Saïd pursues, "transcend[s] the immediate force of the colonial reality. What earned Camus his popularity were his political formulations on issues pertinent to the 1940s and 1950s: Fascism, the Spanish Civil War, [and] social injustices all couched within a socialist discourse."[9] Readers are also seduced by his limpid style of writing. Roland Barthes's *Dégré zéro de l'écriture* describes Camus's style as "l'écriture blanche." Concurrently Camus's philosophical pronouncements on man's exis-tential isolation and anguish echoed the pessimist mood prevailing in Europe at the time, earning him the reputation of a "universalist" humanist thinker and writer concerned with the plight of Man in a world bereft of both transcendental and immediate values. The philosophical thrust of his writings often led critics to mis/match him with Jean-Paul Sartre under the aegis of "existentialism," despite Camus's own protestation.

The recurrent coupling of the two writers as sharing similar philosophical ethics is not worth pondering over here. However, it can hardly be said that Camus ever developed a systematic method of inquiry into philosophical questions. As noted by Isaac, *L'Homme Révolté* (1951), his essay on the idea of revolt, is more of "a lyrical and meditative reflection than a rigorous philosophical treatise and does not readily fit within any identifiable school of thought."[10] In contrast to Sartre, whose ideas, in a way, could be said to fall within the tradition of Western Marxism, Camus's philosophical and political writings were "unanchored in the academic institutions within which most 'serious' theoretical discussions of politics have tended to take place" (ibid., 376). Thus, to classify Camus as belonging to a particular school of thought may appear ungrounded. However, the tendency of critics to associate him with existentialists, especially during the immediate post-war period, does have its own amount of justification; indeed, existentialism, an umbrella term for a general social malaise, became a fashionable garb for most young intellectuals. It was, Kellman notes, "a convenient catchall for a variety of attitudes, beliefs, and moods shared by a youthful, disillusioned generation. [...] [It] was the embodiment of a postwar zeitgeist profoundly cynical toward the shibboleths and values that had facilitated and camouflaged global catastrophe."[11]

Thus, in the face of postwar disillusionment, the task confronting the young intellectual was finding solutions to man's spiritual emptiness within the immediacy of our present corporate life without any appeal to metaphysical foundationalisms. Within such a mold, it was inevitable that the idea of the "absurd" expounded by Camus in *Le Mythe de Sisyphe* (1943) as an awakened consciousness to man's alienated condition, and re-articulated in *L'Homme Révolté* (1951) as "un passage vécu, un point de départ, l'équivalent, en existence, du doute méthodique de Descartes [qui peut et doit] orienter une nouvelle recherche," should be classified as a sub-variety of existentialism. [A lived experience, a starting point, the equivalent in existence of Descartes's methodical doubt, which could and should a new research.] Camus continues, however, to express his reservations with respect to existentialism as a philosophy, finding in it, as well as in various other speculative systems, the impossibility of providing adequately any positive guidance for human life, or of legitimizing human values.

Le Mythe de Sisyphe begins with the problem of suicide which, according to Camus, is the only serious philosophical question. The point is, once the meaninglessness of life has been understood and fully assimilated, does it make sense to go on living? Camus maintains that suicide is not an acceptable solution to the experience of absurdity, for suicide only suppresses one of the two poles—the human being and the world—that together produce the absurdity. The formu-lations on what this meaninglessness or "absurdity" really is, however, remain vague. At bottom, it seems it is the failure of the world to satisfy the human demand for coherence, and to provide a basis for human values capable of sustaining our personal as well as collective ideals, our judgments of right and wrong. With the decline, if not eradication, of the religious external supports on which the validity of moral ethics rested, Camus, O'Brien elaborates further, "insisted on the dangers inherent in the new secular religions, in particular Hegelian and Marxist historicism, that have attempted to tie human values to reality by means of a postulated schedule of historical development."[12]

L'Homme Révolté takes up further Camus's elaboration on the problem of suicide as a response to the absurd. Suicide is, however, replaced with the problem of murder, more specifically with the moral justification of political murder. Political action, Camus asserts, is essentially violent revolt that invariably leads to unjustifiable loss of lives; it raises the question of whether there is any justification for murder in the name of revolutionary ideals. The answer, Camus maintains, is that murder (in any form) is inconsistent with true revolt, since revolt asserts implicitly the existence of "a supraindividual value," the value of human life. The essay, however, fails to specify how the rejection of murder and the true revolt are to be interpreted in the light of specific revolutionary actions that were contemporary to his time.

Camus's play, *Les Justes* (1950), seems to convey an authorial approval of the Russian terrorist Kaliayev who murders the Grand Duke and insists on paying with his own life, apparently to affirm the inadmissibility of murder. Kaliayev's final act, the acceptance of his own death which is a form of suicide, stands in contradiction with the earlier views expressed in *Le Mythe de Sisyphe*. To substantiate his thesis further, *L'homme Révolté* reviews what Camus terms the historical follies of the past two centuries. Hegel and Marx are accorded a prominent position, apparently because of "their central role in the construction of a view of history and of the state that exempts man from all moral controls and proposes as the only valid ideal man's total mastery of his own fate."[13] The essay reviews mostly the French and Russian revolutions and Nazism to which Camus is reluctant to append the name of "revolution." Apart from the exaltation of a certain "pensée du midi" (Mediterranean solar thought that respects the limits of revolt) with which the essay ends, no attempt is made to evaluate other contemporary revolutions and struggles for human dignity which were irrupting in the colonies (Algeria, Indochina, Madagascar) at the time.

For Camus, the absurd stems from a confrontation of the mind with the world. Mind, in its encounter with the world, is alienated, resulting in a certain opaqueness. "Cette épaisseur et cette étrangeté du monde, c'est l'absurde."[14] The adventure of mind in the realm of the universe of nature, which is—according to Hegel—the very definition of history, is not necessarily a "principle of all becoming," nor that moving power propelling history ahead. It is at best a state of mind characterized by what he calls a lucid mind, "une indifférence clairvoyante" (ibid., 47) which finds its further elaboration in *L'Homme Révolté*. The acerbic criticism this last essay received was to have a lasting repercussion on Camus, aside from the break in his relationship with Sartre. The clamors varying only in intensity, ranged from "ineffectiveness of abstention" to "political impotence which ac-complishes nothing and consecrates injustice with its refusal to act" (Isaac 1989, 381).

As many critics have noted, Camus's opposition to the apocalyptic nature of the various revolutionary movements is in good part due to his inability to grasp the fact that the propelling basis of a number of modern social revolutions is not necessarily "the cosmic injustice of the human condition," but the much more concrete "evils" of historically conditioned injustices. Subsequently, Camus finds himself reduced to an ideal of "moral action" the kind undertaken by his fictional characters of *La Peste* (1947), Dr. Rieux and Tarrou in the face of the plague. Both characters, fully aware of their own limitations, struggle with the plague (symbol of all that is evil), not with the dream of total conquest, but with modesty, while also retaining their sense of humanity and their capacity for love and happiness. Tarrou's position, that of "a saint without God," echoing Camus's aspirations, seems to differ from traditional religious humanism mainly by virtue of the terminology of "revolt" appended to it, even though Camus has so thoroughly moralized his conception of revolt as to make it virtually non-applicable to any concrete political struggle.

Clinging to an ideal of human fraternity, the "brotherhood of man"[15] in its pure form, outside the entanglements of localized politics, ideologies and doctrine, Camus's attitude towards life appears at bottom, a moral integrity, with sympathy for fellow human beings, rendering the idea of revolt rather redundant. During his last years, as he increasingly withdrew from direct political action, he sought refuge in a strongly moralist humanism. His refusal to support the Algerian rebels during the French-Algerian war received bitter reproaches from left-wing politicians.

Réflexions sur la peine capitale written three years before his death in 1960 reiterates his earlier aversion to both political crimes, and capital punishment. Society, he argues, "has no right to put its criminals to death" (1957, 23). One is left to wonder in what circumstances, if any, Camus would have regarded the Algerian war and its catastrophes in human losses as morally acceptable.

While the bitter polemics generated by Camus's peculiar political vision in respect to his native land may have died down today, critical interest in the author has, however, picked up, fueled by the politics of civic unrest currently raging in Algeria, and also by the publication in 1994 of the manuscript (*Le Premier Homme*) found upon his body at the time of his death. This renewed interest—as evidenced by the September 1997 issue of the *Modern Language Notes* devoted entirely to the studies of Camus, and by the Fall 1999 issue of *Research in African Literature* which focused entirely on Algeria—has prompted me to re-open the political and literary debate with the purpose of re-evaluating Camus's "universalist" and humanist position, as it resonates within the colonial context of his native Algeria.

My reading of Camus within a historical-cultural context takes its roots partially, from Alec Hargreaves's seminal exposition (*The Colonial Experience in French Fiction*) of the colonial factor in the overall creative vision of three French men, Pierre Loti, Ernest Psichari and Pierre Mille; from the works of critics such as Conor Cruise O'Brien (*Camus of Europe and Africa*), Susan Tarrow (*Exile from the Kingdom*), and from Azzedine Haddour's study, "Camus: The Other as an outsider," to name a few. The latter's thesis which calls into question Camus's "liberal humanist position," is admirably sustained through an insightful analysis of the colonial climate that informs Camus's writings, thus, establishing a historical and literary context— Algeria—as a "hermeneutic field" in which to interpret the Camusian *oeuvre*. Both O'Brien and Tarrow, despite diverging assumptions, attempt to rethink the importance of Camus's native land as a context for the interpretation of both his political sensibility and his fictions.

Although O'Brien's study provides a thorough overview of the colonial situation of Algeria during Camus's rise to prominence, it fails to establish any possible connection between Camus's works and the imperial actuality. What we are left with is a juxtaposition of Algeria's colonial situation and Camus's fiction. Saïd, commenting on O'Brien's study, accurately points out that "despite the critical, tough-minded analysis of Camus's stance vis-à-vis the dynamic of colonial implantation and native resistance, O'Brien ultimately exculpates the author by pointing to him as "belonging to the frontier of Europe," and representing (unlike any other writer) a "Western consciousness [...] in relation to the non-Western world." There is, he continues, "a subtle act of transcendence, by which Camus is let off the hook" (1993, 172). O'Brien's notions of "frontier," "Western consciousness do not adequately render the facts of foreign implantation and the decolonizing drive of the period." Still on O'Brien's reading, Edward Saïd emphatically states that "Camus [is] not merely representative of so relatively weightless a thing as 'Western consciousness' but rather of Western dominance in the non-European world" (ibid., 173). Indeed, for the colonized Algerians and others under colonial rule, the im-mediate perception of their position as colonized subjects is not necessarily "a confrontation with an ahistorical Western consciousness" (1993, 173), but rather with concrete imperial practices such as land expropriation, destruction or disruption of existing social, cultural, economic structures resulting in mass cultural dispossession, and various other discursive ideological practices.

Any attempt to recuperate Camus's works within the Algerian colonial discourse (that is, the discourse of the colonizers and the colonized) involves a double thematic, namely the Francophone literary tradition of North Africa and the Algerian socio-political context within which I propose to ground my reading. As Emily Apter has demonstrated in a more recent study, it is "impossible to abstract Camus's writings from their Algerian backdrop, and more specially, from the current politics of civic strife."[16] Indeed, despite the claim to articulating universal dilemmas inherent in the Human Condition, Camus's work is nourished by the French colonial presence in Algeria and by his own position vis-à-vis the history of French rule. It cannot, therefore, be dissociated from either the colonial discourse, or the Francophone North African literary discourse of the time.

L'Algérianisme, L'Ecole d'Alger and *Littérature de Combat* constituted the colonial literary tradition in Algeria. The French politics of assimilation determined and indeed defined the literary practice as well as the political discourse of the three schools, caught in a cross-cultural dilemma. *L'Algérianisme*, which can be said to represent the orthodox French colonist position, came into existence formally, as early as 1921, disseminated later through *L'Afrique Latine* (1922–1938), a journal founded by Louis Bertrand. The latter insists, "nous sommes venus reprendre l'oeuvre de Rome en ces pays, que leur constitution géographique, leur voisinage et leur passé semblent placer naturellement sous l'hégémonie latine" (1922, 7). The idea of Algeria's "eternal" latinity which the school insisted upon carries both a supernatural significance and a historical resonance. The rhetoric, which sought to "eradicate existing cultural institutions and to mythologize history, constitutes a tremendous mobilizing force for colonial ideology, a particular stasis within change."[17]

L'Ecole d'Alger emerged primarily as a literary contestation bringing together French-educated Arabs and Berbers and French Algerians more open to an inclusive Algerian culture. It sprang amidst an increasing disenchantment on the part of the indigenous[18] population and a mounting wave of nationalism. Rather perceptible are a shift from "Latin" to a "Mediterranean" Algeria, and a much more conciliatory approach. Gabriel Audisio's work, *Jeunesse de la Méditerranée* (1935) marks not only the shift from the *Algérianiste* colonial rhetoric, but also the embryonic stage of a move towards a liberal humanist position. Assimilation of the indigenous group, as the ultimate solution to the Algerian colonial situation, was the political manifesto of its "spiritual father," Gabriel Audisio, and prominent member, Camus. *L'Ecole d'Alger* as Haddour points out aspired to an inaccessible reality (1989, 25). Not only is the idea of assimilation inaccessible, it had clearly become anachronistic. The movement developed thus, "dans le vide idéologique d'une période où l'idéologie assimilationiste a déjà fait la preuve de son échec."[19] Seeing in Algerian nationalism a sign of decadence, they insisted on the natural bonds which relate Europeans and Indigenes: the sun, the sea, the love of life and the certainty of death, and their human relations outside politics and history. These traits, they insisted, are the peculiarities of a certain "Mediterranean universe" topographically delineated as Algeria, Spain, Greece and Italy. Their cultural agenda, involved these writers in a attempt to "wedge Arabs and Europeans into a Mediterranean medley,"[20] disregarding the essential antagonism (compounded by political, economic, social factors) existing between the two conflicting cultures. Quilliot terms it "le souci de concilier la culture européenne et la culture indigène, de favoriser l'éclosion d'une civilisation méditer-ranéenne . . . et d'un collectivisme méditerranéen [...]." [The anxiety to reconcile European and native culture, to promote the dawn of a mediterranean civilization . . . and a mediterranean collectivism {...}.] He concludes that "on pourra juger ce patriotisme nord-africain plus sentimental qu'intellectuellement fondé" [this North African patriotism will be considered more sentimental than intellectually founded].[21] Such facile notions as "assimilation" and "fusion" of the races (Mediterranean culture), despite the humanistic perspective, were only "symptomatic of a half recognized problem" (ibid., 1317). JanMohammed, wisely, cautions that a more critical reading of these writers, however, must explore the basic dilemma of their "liberal consciousness" trapped between humanistic values and the highly antagonistic manicheanism of "colonial apartheid."[22]

These non-indigenous writers did share a number of political affinities with indigenous counterparts like M. Feraoun and M. Mammeri. The latter, like writers of *l'Ecole d'Alger* believed firmly in the emancipation of the Arab/Berber within the colonial structure, leading eventually to an interracial brotherhood. The idea of an independent Algeria crossed very few minds.[23] Ferhat Abbas, for instance, a strong believer in assimilation (during the 1950s, a belated convert to the *Front de Libération Nationale*), stated emphatically that the future of Algeria lay with France, because, to begin with, there had never been an Algerian nation. "I have looked into history," he declared, "I have questioned the living and the dead: I have visited the cemeteries. No one has spoken to me of an Algerian nation."[24] Naturally, this rather humorous statement undermined the nationalist drive, while substantiating and validating the colonial claim to a French Algeria. More important, however, Abbas's pronouncement is symptomatic of an entire generation of acculturated youth caught in the illusions of French assimilationist propaganda.

The fate of the French policy of assimilation upon which the indigenous elite built their hope is a well known story. Today, with the benefit of hindsight, and also in the light of present debate on multiculturalism predicated on cultural interconnectedness, differences and plural identities, the French project of assimilating, of dissolving Otherness—all reinforcing monoculturalism—underscores the contradictions. Assimilation is by essence a threat to French colonial domination. The indigenous elite, as well as the *pied-noir*[25] liberals such as Camus, failed to comprehend the contradictory terms contained in the French *mission civilisatrice*, with its "Jacobean ideals"—ideals which were simultaneously "imperialist and humanist, oppressive and egalitarian, selective and assimilating" (Haddour 1989, 45). As O'Brien points out, the "new" or "Mediterranean culture,"—a blend of French and Arab—sought for, is "an European one and in Algeria a French one" (1970, 9) The resulting "confused idealism" stemmed from the desire to reconcile "irreconcilable concepts which work against each other in colonial hegemony" (ibid.).

The political and cultural ambiguities, which I shall discuss in this study, stem from what is really "a monolithic politics of culture" (O'Brien 1970:9) which legitimized colonialism while advocating an impossible and problematic "free and equal association" between French and Arab. For these one time indigenous advocates of assimilation, the 1950s apparently marked a turning point. This period, which signaled the beginning of the French-Algerian crisis, also enacted a much stronger polarization,[26] during which these indigenous writers, owing to the necessity of a more radical stance found themselves grouped under a different political, and also literary umbrella: *Littérature de Combat, au service de la nation* (Dejeux 1978, 25). For these henceforth nationalist writers, a stronger anti-colonialist line was an imperative. Eventually, rather than assimilation, a complete political severance from the apron strings of France—a severance which meant the dissolution of French Algeria—became their demand.

These three distinct, yet continuous, discourses (*Algérianisme*; *L'Ecole d'Alger*; *Littérature de Combat*) have sought to reconstitute and interpret the experience of colonial Algeria, each bringing along its own distinctive ideological flavor. My study, conflating the literary positions of *L'Ecole d'Alger* and *Littérature de combat*, examines primarily the fictional writings of Albert Camus on one hand, and three indigenous writers, Mouloud Mammeri, Mouloud Feraoun and Mohammed Dib on the other, as both groups articulate the varying ambiguities inherent in their political stance, as strong advocates for the French assimilationist project. The historical and political contexts of their writings, which are analyzed in chapter one, point to a shared discursive field: that of a North African literary tradition inclusive of *pied-noir* writers. Borrowing Julia Kristeva's idea of a discursive and rational dialogue between literary texts, I shall insist on an intertextuality in the works of Camus and these other North-African writers, thus problematizing the rigid line of demarcation posited by critics between the writings of *L'Ecole d'Alger* and *Littérature de combat*. Intertextuality, according to Kristeva, is a patchwork, a fusion of allusions, for every text echoes another text. "Tout texte se construit comme mosaïque de citations, tout texte est absorption et transformation d'un autre texte."[27] The possibility of such a dialogical reading becomes thus an instrument of both "deconstruction" and "reconstruction," which enables me to position these early Algerian writers within the ideological setting of *L'Ecole d'Alger*, in order to bring out more clearly the ideological paradoxes they invariably shared with Camus.

The colonial and anti-colonial discourses gleaned from the works of Camus and other Algerian writers emerged from material and historical contexts. The vast majority of critical attention given to Camus's writings restricts itself by bracketing the importance of the Algerian colonial factor, or, at best, presenting it as accidental to the author's work. Both Albert Memmi's forceful study of the rapports of "colonial subjects" in *Portrait of the Colonizer and Colonized* (1965)[28] and Abdul JanMohamed's theoretical formulations of the manichean allegory governing all colonial rapports—*Manichean Aesthetics* (1983)—provide a cogent analytical framework through which one might apprehend these various exploitations of the colonial scene.

The title chosen for this study, namely, "Colonial and Anti-colonial Discourses: Camus and Algeria," poses one rather serious challenge. While the indigenous writers selected for this study, Mammeri, Feraoun and Dib, purposefully use their writings as vehicles for reflecting on the social and political malaise of the time, Camus's fiction on the other hand presents an initial dilemma: what various critics have referred to, one way or the other, as the writer's "novelistic silence" over both the cultural life of the native population, and the colonial situation of Algeria. Emily Apter, for instance, remarked that Camus's "literary style [...] white-washed the colonizer's shadow while neutralizing autochtonous subjects" (1997, 501). Camus, Saïd pointed out earlier, "is a novelist from whose work the facts of imperial actuality, so clearly there to be noted, have dropped away, [leaving behind] a detachable ethos suggesting universality and humanism, deeply at odds with the descriptions of geographical locale plainly given in the fiction" (1993, 172). Camus's narratives continue to be read today within a purely French literary tradition, as parables of the human condition. The choice of an Algerian setting appears almost incidental to the pressing issues of man's alienated condition. "True," Saïd observes, "Meursault kills an Arab, but this Arab is not named and seems to be without a history, let alone a mother and father; true also, Arabs die of plague in Oran, but they are not named either, whereas Rieux and Tarrou are pushed forward in the action" (1993, 175–76). Echoing Saïd's remarks, Kellman also states:

> It is extraordinary that a story [*The Plague*] set in Algeria's second largest city should have so entirely ignored a fundamental segment of its population. [...] Nowhere in *The Plague* is there a single characater who speaks Arabic. [...] Islam, which is now the state religion of Algeria, has no place in the novel. For those of Camus's characters who are religious at all, there is indeed one God; He is not Allah, however, but rather the Deity of the Roman Catholic Church. (1993, 76–77)

David Carroll, offering a more lenient perspective on Camus, invites us to see Camus's Algeria as "a construct or fiction which does not so much ignore or negate historical reality as recast or direct it. . . . Camus's Algeria thus represents an idea or fiction of community that was never actualized." [29]

One of the most prolific commentators—and also a contemporary— of Camus, Germaine Brée, tells us that "Camus describes, as none before him, not only the peculiar temperament, ethics, attitudes and language of the native Algerians, with whom he felt more at home than anyone else," but also "the working-class population of Belcourt [a mixture of Europeans, Arabs, Berbers—to which Camus belonged], [a working-class population] impervious to racial barriers. . . . The Berber and Arab never seemed 'strangers' to Camus." [30] This composite statement raises two important questions: first, what is Camus's representation of the Arab/Berber world, and second, what is the nature of relationship existing between the indigenous population and the European community? Commenting on the second part of Brée's statement, namely, racial harmony within the working population, O'Brien has this to say:

> A working-class population 'impervious to racial barriers' would be an unusual phenomenon. A population which could attain this condition when the barriers were not only 'of race' but also of religion, language, and culture, all reinforcing 'race'—as in the case

of the dividing line between European and Arab in Algeria—would be unique. (1970, 6)

Indeed, I would suggest that, as opaque as it is, the depiction of relationship between Europeans and Arabs, as in *L'Etranger*, and in some of Camus's short stories, "La Femme Adultère" and "L'hôte" for instance, does not reflect a harmony, but rather a division along racial lines that culminates in the murder of the Arab on a sunny beach, and in "La femme adultère," remains in its latent form. Having said this, the question still needs to be asked as to what the concrete colonial rapport as lived by *Pieds-noirs* and Arabs was. As illuminating as Brée's work is, her thesis rest on two assumptions: Camus's "accurate" representation of the colonial world and the unity prevalent in the colonial sub-universe of the working class. Both assumptions are inadequately problematized and unacceptable. They ignore the various material and discursive antagonisms between conquerors and natives, antagonisms that, more often than not, permeate all strata of colonial societies. Brée's interpretation puts into question Fanon's definition of the conqueror/native dynamics as a "Manichean struggle." As JanMohamed states, Fanon's analysis is by no means a "fanciful metaphorical caricature but an accurate representation of a profound conflict."[31] One would rather concur that the basis of the colonial catastrophes is not only "the co-existence of two populations with vigorous, radically distinct 'personalities,'"[32] but also, and more so, that disequilibrium engendered by colonialism. The colonial situation in Algeria presents the peculiar case of having a dominant minority pitted against a dominated majority—a situation analogous to that of defunct apartheid South Africa where, until very recently, a dominant minority held privileges at the expense of an oppressed majority. Such a "stabilized disequilibrium" can only generate disharmony. The colonial society as structured by the dynamics of relationships between colonizer and colonized "embodies" a rejection and counter-rejection. And I would adduce that one main factor which seems to have determined outlook and behavior of Europeans on a colony is the awareness that their own privilege is inseparable from the existence of a colonized/dominated indigenous population.

   Expounding further on Fanon's views on the disunity of colonial subjects, JanMohamed concurs that "[the colonizer] is [...] absolutely dependent upon the colonized people not only for his privileged social and material status but also for his sense of moral superiority and, therefore, ultimately for his very identity" (1983, 4). In Algeria's peculiar case, it could be argued that the assortment of European settlers could not by any stretch of the imagination be endowed with the traits or attributes of the colonizer. But, it might be pointed out that though the machinery of domination put in place (government policies, land appropriation, school system, disruption of pre-existing modes of production, etc.) may be solely in the hands of the colonial administration, its trappings permeate through to the bottom of the social ladder. It creates an overall awareness of a fundamental division between two collective groups, that fundamental distinction that Frantz Fanon, writing out of his years of experience in Algeria, posits and maintains between colonizer and colonized. Being an essential ingredient to both the existence of each group, and their co-existence, it is a division that has to be enacted anew on a daily basis. As Fanon insists, there could be no harmony—social, economic, or cultural—between colonized and colonizer. Contrast and division, being the two pillars upon which the colonial structure reposes, theirs is essentially a relationship characterized by exclusion and violence.

Indeed, we may not all subscribe to Fanon's "violent and Manichean" picture (O'Brien 1970, 10), or even to his subsequent invocation of violence as the sole means of liberation for the colonized, but "[he] does give a more realistic view of most colonial systems; and a point of view which ignores the possibility of this concrete colonial situation, may appear rather unrealistic, to the point of fantasy" (ibid., 11). Sartre, in his noted preface to Fanon's *The Wretched of the Earth*, warns us: "You need not think hotheadedness or an unhapphy childhood has given him [Fanon] some uncommon taste for violence; he acts as *the interpreter of the situation*"[33] (emphasis added). Such a "situation," the concrete colonial rapport is summed up for us in JanMohamed's noted essay, *The Manichean Aesthetics*:

> The dominant model of power-and interest-relations in all colonial societies is the manichean opposition between the putative superiority of the European and the supposed inferiority of the native. This axis in turn provides the central feature of the colonialist cognitive framework and colonialist literary representation: the manichean allegory. [...] The power relations underlying this model set in motion such strong currents that even a writer who is reluctant to acknowledge it and who may indeed be critical of imperialist exploitation is drawn into its vortex. (1983, 63)

JanMohamed's remarks not only point to actual colonial relationships but also to the complex nature of responses to colonial rule. The relation of the individual author to the field of the colonialist discourse could thus be one of involuntary participation. He "is tied to the legal and institutional systems that circumscribe, determine, and articulate the realms of discourses."[34]

In his theoretical speculation on the dynamics of relationships in the colony, Albert Memmi sums up Camus's stand within the concrete realm of politics, as that of the "colonizer who refuses" (1957, 40). His refusal to support Algerian independence, and his subsequent silence over the Franco-Algerian crises have been viewed by various left-wing critics as a tacit agreement with colonial structures. Memmi, however, generously affirms that Camus has the historical misfortune of being part of an oppressing group, and having to deal with the natural instinct to fight for the preservation of his own, the *pied-noir* culture. His is a position which "rebels against the ideology of the colonial system, while living its objective relations" (ibid.). Such a position, lacking clear-cut political aspirations, is characterized by "political ineffectiveness, not far removed from delusion or fantasy" (ibid., 41). Camus's stance, as opposed to that of the right-wing colonizer, is indeed an amorphous one. The latter, right-wing colonizer, "is consistent in his support of the colonial *status quo*, his cynical demands for more privileges and more rights at the expense of the colonized" (ibid.). Conversely, despite their ambiguous position, the political hopes and desires of the colonized seem relatively well articulated. Against these two groups, Camus presents the position of "no man's land" against the varied conflicts within colonialism (ibid.).

Assimilating the writer's plight to the existential malaise depicted in his best known work, Memmi again suggests that "*L'Etranger* n'est pas seulement un récit métaphysique, la relation d'une angoisse existentielle, c'est aussi Camus-étranger dans son pays natal" (1964, 14). Camus's eventual voluntary exile from Algeria reflects the destiny of the *pied-noir* society which failed to acknowledge, and open itself to historical changes. It also presaged the eventual demise of French Algeria.

Portrait of the Colonizer furnishes additional insight into Camus's position as the "colonizer of good will." Behind the myopically advocated fraternization of the races, Memmi insightfully saw the "implacable relationship of power" (1965, 38). As Memmi explains, the reconciliation sought for cannot but contradict the exploitation of colonial society. Left-wingers, such as Camus, live an illusion of "Mediterranean medleys and Spanish-Berber brotherhood." "No one" he says, "could doubt their generosity or their impotence; they live under the sign of a contradiction" (ibid., 39).

These various observations point to an inherent split within the author's thinking, producing what O'Brien refers to as Camus's "hallucinatory" position. Such a split, resulting in the author's own estrangement from the land he claimed as his own, forms the basis of Camus's entire life and being, and subsequently informs his literary production. This might also explain the polarization of critical perspectives on Camus's work. For many, Camus remains the celebrated "apostle of a global democracy" that acknowledges no political boundaries; faced with his uncertainties of the Algeria question, "[he] opted for an ethic embedded in a humanism distinguished by an [sic] generalized sense of justice and a universal commitment to human value."[35] Still, for a considerable number of readers and critics, his "models of cosmopolitical citizenship" are, not only at odds with colonial domination, but also predicated on a "moral double standards vis-à-vis Europe and North Africa" (Apter 1997, 500).

Within the framework of a postcolonial reading, Camus's fictional work reveals an overly conscious identification with the West, a "mental horizon" at odds with his universalist ethos. In *Lettres à un ami allemand* (1945) for instance, Camus is careful to identify himself as part of "we, free Europeans." Not surprisingly then—and contrary to Bree's insistence on "accurate description of Arabs" in Camus's fictions—the Arab world finds itself relegated to the periphery of the author's imaginative work. In *L'Etranger*, "the Arab is simply the 'Other'" (O'Brien 1970, 24). Recasting this last remark in a socio-political context, Apter observes that in *La Peste*, set in the Arab town of Oran, one notes a similar "systematic nullification" of Arab presence:

> Dissolving the contours of Algerian cities and coastal landscape into sibilant friezes or projection walls of the European mind, erasing the signs of precursory Algerian secessionism by recording not a trace of the protests and massacres at Sétif in the immediate aftermath of Liberation; and converting the site specificity of a soon-to-be imploding colonial war into a labyrinthine tectonics of European postwar melancholia, Camus presents colonial unease in a abstract landscape. [...] [Such] de-characterization carries serious political consequences; confirming the negation of a subject people at a time of colonial war (1997, 502–3).

Commenting upon the ideological images projected through Camus's fiction, Saïd insists that "it [the fiction] incorporates, intransigently recapitulates, and in many ways, depends on a massive French discourse on Algeria, one that belongs to the language of French imperial attitudes" (1993, 181). Camus's works, Saïd concludes, "draw on and in fact revive the history of French domination in Algeria, with a circumspect precision and a remarkable lack of remorse or compassion" (ibid.). Tarrow's study, however, which predates

Saïd's, maintains that Camus's attitude to the Algerian situation as well as his political views, are "not overtly expressed; [but] implied, [and] often distorted or dispersed by its passage through the prism of his creative imagination."[36]

Another critical position on Camus's representation of the colonial scene is that expressed by John Erickson, who asserts that "Camus disappoints the reader who seeks in his North African writings a telling encounter with the culture of the East, [for, despite] the engaging description of the physical landscape, nothing or astonishingly very little is said about the indigenous peoples, Berbers and Arabs."[37] Erickson argues that Camus's writings on North Africa present themselves as a discourse very much exterior to his place of birth, which is not surprising if one remembers that "Camus as a Frenchman born in Algeria (*a pied-noir*), undeniably inhabited a country within a country ("*Algérie française*"), and grew up within a culture and a language superimposed from without upon another already existing cultural-linguistic system" (1988, 75–76).

It would appear, then, that Camus's writing on Algeria not only falls within a discourse of exteriority, as observed by Erickson, but also reinforces what in the wake of Edward Saïd, has come to be known as the tradition of "French Orientalism." Can we indeed view Camus's fictional writings on North Africa as belonging to an extended discourse of one culture on another? A discourse that conveys not an insider's "truth" of another culture but simply a representation (or misrepresentation) of it from a position of exteriority? As Saïd intimated,

> Orientalism is premised upon exteriority, that is, on the fact that the Orientalist poet or scholar makes the Orient speak, describes the Orient, renders its mysteries plain for and to the West. He is never concerned with the Orient, except as the first cause of what he says. What he says and writes, by virtue of the fact that it is said and written, is meant to indicate that the Orientalist is outside the Orient, both as an existential and as a moral fact.[38]

In effect, Camus's *L'Etranger* (1942) for instance, simultaneously exploits and diffuses the Algerian colonial setting. Although the narrative appropriates the figure of the Arab, Camus sublimates what is clearly a colonial conflict to illustrate what purports to be a universal human dilemma. The Arab is thus evoked not in itself, but "only as an exotic background" (Erickson 1988, 76). Accordingly, the specific political problems attendant to the French Occupation of Algeria, which the novel explores, are suppressed through an opaque representation of the Arab on one hand, and on the other, through the narrative insistence on the protagonist, Meursault's innocence. The novel, by de-emphasizing Meursault's criminality, diffuses the political potencies of the narrative. The colonial malaise which is thus displaced persists, however, in Meursault's intercourse with the Arab. The narrative represses the setting's colonial history, a history which is nevertheless sedimented in the superstructure of Camus's text.

Interestingly, the appropriation of Camus's "signature theme of estrangement" (Apter 1997, 509) by Feraoun's *La Terre et le sang* (1953) and Mammeri's *Le Sommeil du juste* (1955) replicates the colonial malaise by pointing to the Arab's alienation (in its sociological implications) and his political and existential exclusion from the culturally dominant universe of the Settler minority group. The colonial discourse, repressed in *L'Etranger*, surfaces in their writings as oppressive and alienating. If Camus's Meursault is presented as an "outsider"—the estranged *persona* whose quest for metaphysical freedom is curtailed by the moral code of a paternalistic institution—within the conceptual lenses of the indigenous writers, however, the actual outsider becomes the Arab. In the Manichean universe described by these writers, the figure of "l'étranger" (the colonized) speaks a different "truth." The writings of Feraoun, Mammeri, and Dib give voice to what Abiola Irele has referred to as "the pathology of alienation as inscribed in [the] experience [of] a colonized people."[39]

In *La Peste* (1947) the plague, dissociated from its biblical origin, becomes a rich political allegory—what has been read as an allegory of German Nazism. Despite the political potency of the novel, Camus seems to skirt once again the thorny issue of colonial Algeria, this time, by expunging the problematic figure of the Arab from the text altogether. Conversely, Mohammed Dib's trilogy, *La Grande Maison* (1952), *L'Incendie* (1954), and *Le Métier à tisser* (1957), by recasting the theme of the "plague" against the Algerian colonial background, exposes it as a process of "clochardisation" resulting from colonial domination. Dib's writings establish an ideological context in which to unearth and reinterpret what is suppressed in *La Peste*'s politically selective vision.

The intertextual dialogue between these various texts points to the narrative displacement, or a certain disavowal in Camus's mytho-poetic vision of the Absurd. The Algerian perspective presented by Feraoun and Dib confronts the diamensions of colonial relationships denied by the Camusian narrative, or at best, cloaked with a "superstructure" which Sartre interprets as providing "the climate of the absurd." My reading, confronting two distinct perceptual tendencies (a claim to universality on the one hand, and a certain justifiable tendency towards parochialism, on the other), will reflect not only on the ideological paradoxes inherent in the liberalist position of *L'Ecole d'Alger*, as already stipulated, but also on the cultural ambiguities of the *jeunes évolués* writers. "Adoptive children" of French culture, and products of a "discursive coercion" or what JanMohamed terms "the hegemonic formation" (*Manichean* 1983, 8), they incarnate the contradictions inherent in the colonial theory of assimilation and the egalitarian ideals of the French colonial mission. Ashcroft, Griffiths and Tiffin in their essay, bearing the telling title of *The Empire Writes Back*, remark on the ideological framework within which literary endeavors by colonized subjects emerged. It is a dialectical framework of center and periphery. Writing by the indigenous authors becomes, thus,

> a mimicry of the centre proceeding from a desire not only to be accepted but to be adopted and absorbed [...]. It caused those from the periphery to immerse themselves in the imported culture, denying their origins in an attempt to become "more English than the English."[40]

The literary works of French-educated Arabs or Berbers, just like those of their counterparts under British rule, despite their latent subversiveness, betray their intellectual indebtedness to the central and controlling features of the French system of values and structures. The ideological portrait of these young elites epitomizes also Memmi's description of the acculturated Arab/Berber who, rejecting his cultural difference in order to penetrate the cultural universe of the colonizer, finds himself straddling (*à cheval sur*) two distinct cultural frames of reference. Memmi's terms point correctly to the abortiveness of the immersion sought for. This space of identity crisis, the overriding theme of many North and Sub-Saharan African writings, is elaborated in Cheik Hamidou Kane's celebrated novel, *L'Aventure Ambigüe*. The hero, Samba Diallo, "the archetype of the divided consciousness,"[41] clearly suffers from a cultural dispossession. His "dual nature" is marked by "a cleavage rather than an integration of its two frames of reference" (ibid.). The young hero, in summarizing what he calls "le complexe du Mal Aimé," asserts,

> Je ne suis pas un pays des Diallobé distinct, face à un Occident distinct, et appréciant d'une tête froide ce que je puis lui prendre et ce qu'il faut que je lui laisse en contrepartie. Je suis devenu les deux. Il n'y a pas une tête lucide entre deux termes d'un choix. Il y a une nature étrange, en détresse de n'être pas deux. (*L'Aventure* 1961, 163–4)

[I am not a distinctive Diallobe country, confronted with a distinctive Western world, appreciating with a dispassionate mind what I could take from it and give back in return. I have become the two. There is not a lucid mind caught between two terms of a choice. There is only a strange nature in distress for not being two.]

The "existential plight" of the *jeunes évolués* like Samba, found articulation earlier, within the works of Feraoun, Mammeri, Dib and others. Feraoun's *Les Chemins qui montent* (1957) gives voice to the double "déracinement" (uprootedness) of its protagonist, Amirouche, a child of a mixed marriage. The novel articulates the fundamental problem of the individual and his national identity, which for Amirouche, "le bâtard authentique" is concretized by his tragic inability to have a legitimate name, "a label" and to function within any cultural system. His suicide ultimately reflects his "spiritual and cultural demise." For lack of coherence, Amirouche is unable to relate to the Western world which remains illusive, and to his own traditional system of values which is increasingly becoming "a metaphor rather than a reality." (Irele 1981, 204)

Interesting here also is the notion of the "bastard" which is at the very basis of Maghrebian Francophone literary production. As pointed out by Marx-Scouras, "the first Maghrebine writers of the fifties and early sixties, having received the 'benefit' of a language and civilization of which they are not the legitimate heirs will experience the French language as a weapon, but also, and mostly as an exile."[42] As a bastard child of European colonialism (and an uprooted child of Arab/Berber Islamic tradition)—a "dominant metaphor" of earlier Francophone novels—the Westernized Arab/Berber, uncomfortable within the parameters of both systems of values, finds his identity faltering under the scrutinizing gaze of the two traditions he confronts. "The resulting condition of 'bastardy' of the young *évolués* will be sustained as a negative state, as an identity crisis" (Irele 1981, 204).

The writings of both groups, Camus and the Arab/Berber writers, duly articulate the malaise of their colonial society whose political demise is signaled in the growing hostility of an indigenous population. While the indigenous writers presented Algeria as a political context dominated by an oppressive colonialist ideology, Camus suppressed such a context, imaging Algeria—"l'éternelle méditerranée"—as a humanist empire, transcending historical and material specificities. Camus's "Mediterranean" utopia, an appropriation of the colonialist "latin" discourse of Bertrand and the *Algérianiste* movement, which not only evaded the colonial dilemmas, but also transformed its very specificities into a universal problematic, constitutes a refuge from the colonial malaise. The works of the three indigenous writers not only help to recontextualize Camus's fiction on Algeria, but they also call into question his "universalist" humanist rhetoric which transcends the immediate actuality of colonialism.

Camus's novelistic appropriation of the Algerian landscape wherein colonized Algeria becomes a sublimated context within which universal themes are tried out, seems to (re)enact the colonial vision of Louis Bertrand, a vision of colonial space as an empty Latin/Mediterranean space to be invaded, permeated with Western cultural values. As noted by Erickson, "Camus's representation of the indigenous culture as an adjunct of a mere topographical location, where the Arab assumes neither role nor subjectivity, replicates the monological power of the colonialist discourse, the ideological function of which was to effect a *mise-en-sac* of the cultural and social panorama of the colonized" (1988, 75).

As stated, my socio-historical approach to these various "colonial" texts proposes to delve into the political context that informs the works selected, assuming that there is such a reality beyond the texts. The cultural references which inform my reading should be seen as constituting a pole of reference. I am not considering these texts as mere social documents without aesthetic appeal; neither, I believe, am I giving in to what could be called a certain anthropologism, a "tracking down of anthropological details" (Irele 1981, 34). But I would like to assume that every piece of literature is a "living" entity, in the sense that every writing translates or reflects a world beyond itself.

A central problematic of my own reading that I am aware of is the necessity of having to negotiate the murky boundaries of fiction and reality. Man, we are told, is a "representational animal," *homo symbolicum*, "the creature whose distinctive character is the creation and manipulation of signs—things that 'stand for' or 'take the place of' something else."[43] There is, admittedly, a great deal of naiveté in assuming that there is a transparent relationship between literature and what it represents. The rise of an "Aesthetic Movement" made popular with Kant's *Critique of Aesthetic Judgment* (1790) validates writing as a "pure aesthetic experience," where the work of art becomes "the supreme value among human products," self-sufficient, with no claim to any aim beyond itself. This view of an inherent "autonomous" value in a work of art makes it absurd to take a writer to task for failing to give fictional voice to the geographical setting of his writing, or to applaud another for giving a "faithful representation" to the setting of his novels.

The issue here, if one were to rephrase it differently, is not that of representation or the lack thereof, but rather the ascription/inscription of subjecthood to colonized subjects. In the light of current postcolonial affirmation of subjectivity, Camus's mummified indigenous characters become both problematic and emblematic. Paul de Man refers to Camus's fiction on the whole as "a mask" behind which he hides. It could be argued that such "a mask" is a writer's prerogative. However, given Camus's involvement in public and political matters and his claim to expressing "conflicts that are typical of the historical situation in general," one is entitled to look for utterances [even in works of fiction] in which the true commitment [...] of the writer is revealed."[44]

Notes

1. Albert Memmi, ed., *Anthologie des écrivains maghrébins* (Paris: n.p., 1964), 12

2. Fritz Peter Kirsch, "Regards sur le Maghreb," *Franzosisch Heute* 3 (September 1983): 130.

3. Guy de Maupassant, Au Soleil (Paris: n.p., 1884), 10, quoted in Fritz Peter Kirsch, "Regards sur le Maghreb," *Franzosisch Heute* 3 (September 1983): 130.

4. All translations are mine, unless otherwise indicated.

5. Joan P. Monego, *Maghrebian Literature in French* (Boston: Tawyne Publishers, 1984), 13.

6. Kirsch writes: Dans leurs écrits, c'est bien souvent l'exotisme qui prédomine favorisant une écriture aux couleurs fortes, relatant des anecdotes savoureuses, exprimant l'émerveillement du touriste confronté à la "sauvagerie" pittoresques des autochtones." "Regards sur le Maghreb," *Franzosisch Heute* 3 (1983): 130.

7. Louis Bertrand, *Les villes d'or* (Paris: Favard, 1921), 9.

8. Jean Pommier, "Le mouvement littéraire français d'Algérie (Ce qu'il est. Ce qu'il doit être)," *La Grande Revue*, 11 juin 1923, 4.

9. Edward W. Saïd, *Culture and Imperialism* (New York: Alfred A. Knopf, 1993), 170.

10. Jeffrey C. Isaac, "On Rebellion and Revolution. Albert Camus's The Rebel Reconsidered," *Dissent* 36 (1989): 375.

11. Steven G. Kellman, *The Plague: Fiction and Resistance* (New York: Twayne Publishers, 1993), 4.

12. Conor Cruise O'Brien, *Albert Camus of Europe and Africa* (New York: The Viking Press, 1970), 72.

13. Frederick Olafson, "Albert Camus," *Encyclopedia of Philosophy*, edited by Paul Edwards (New York: Macmillan Company Inc., 1967), 17.

14. Albert Camus, *Le Mythe de Sisyphe* (Paris: Gallimard, 1943), 29.

15. Commenting on this "universal brotherhood of man," Immanuel Wallerstein observes that the phrase "belies itself, since this phrase is masculine in gender, thereby excluding or relegating to a secondary sphere all who are female." "The Ideological Tensions of Capitalism: Universalism versus Racism and Sexism." Etienne Balibar & Immanuel Wallerstein. *Race, Nation, Class. Ambiguous Identities* (New York: Verso 1991), 29.

16. Emily Apter, "Out of Character: Camus's French Algerian Subjects," *MLN* 112 (1997): 501.

17. Azzedine Haddour, "Camus: The Other as an Outsider in a Univocal Discourse" (Ph.D. diss., The University of Sussex, 1989), 24.

18. The word "Indigenous" is used here merely to distinguish Arab/ Berber writers from the French Algerians or *pieds-noirs*.

19. H. Gourdon, J. R. Henry, and F. Henry-Lorcerie, "Roman colonial et idéologie en Algérie," *Revue Algérienne des Sciences Juridiques Economiques et Politiques* 11 no. 1 (1974): 113.

20. Patrick McCarthy, *Camus, A Critical Study of his Life and Work* (London: Hamish Hamilton, 1982), 64.

21. Roger Quilliot, *Théâtre, Récits, Nouvelles* (Paris: Gallimard, 1957), 1316.

22. Abdul R. JanMohamed, *Manichean Aestheticst* (Amherst: University of Massachusetts Press, 1983), 9.

23. E.N.A. (Etoile Nord Africaine), founded in Paris in 1926 with Messali Hadj, was the only Nationalist party to have advocated very early, for full political independence for Algeria. The Party was viewed with suspicion by both the French and the Arab elites.

24. Qtd. in Patrick McCarthy, "The ambiguities of French Algeria," *Camus: a critical study of his life and work* (Great Britain: Hamish Hamilton, 1982), 64.

25. Term used by the Arabs in referring to the French, because of the black sandals they usually wore.

26. Commenting on the birth of a truly indigenous literature of protest, Jean Dejeux states: "À mesure que les 'évênements' politiques vont occuper le devant de la scène et polariser les esprits, ces écrivains [indigènes] vont se séparer non seulement de l'Ecole algérianiste, cela va de soi, mais encore de *l'Ecole d'Alger* [...] la guerre va obliger à clarifier les positions. Une littérature nationale voit le jour. [As political 'events' occupied more and more the public scene, and as minds became polalized, these writers [indegenous] would separate themselves, not only from the Algerianist school—that goes without saying—but also from *l'Ecole d'Alger* [...] the war would force them to clarify their positions.]" *Littérature Maghrébine de Langue Française* (Paris: Naaman, 1978), 25.

27. Julia Kristeva, *Séméotikè: Recherches pour une sémanalyse* (Paris: Seuil, 1969), 146.

28. Albert Memmi, *Portrait of the Colonizer and the Colonized* (n.p.: The Orion Press, Inc., 1965). Subsequent references to this work will appear under the shortened title *The Colonizer*.

29. David Carrol, "Camus's Algeria: Birthrights, Colonial Injustice, and the Fiction of a French-Algerian People," *MLN* 112 (1997): 518.

30. Germaine Brée, ed. *Camus: A Collection of Critical Essays* (Englewood Cliffs, N.J.: Prentice-Hall, 1962), 4.

31. Abdul R. JanMohamed, "The Economy of Manichean Allegory: The Function of Racial Difference in Colonialist Literature," *Critical Inquiry* 12 (1985): 63.

32. Germaine *Tillion, France and Algeria: Complementary Enemies* (New York: Alfred A. Knopf, 1961), 90.

33. Jean-Paul Sartre, "Preface," *The Wretched of the Earth*, trans. Constance Farrington (New York: Grove Press, Inc., 1963), 14.

34. Michel Foucault, "What is an Author," *Language, Counter-Memory, Practice: Selected Essays and Interviews*, edited by Donald F. Bouchard, trans. Bouchard and Simon (Ithaca, N.Y.: Cornell University Press. 1977), 130.

35. Lawrence D. Kritzman, "Camus's Curious Humanism or the Intellectual in Exile," *MLN* 112 (1997): 550.

36. Susan Tarrow, *Exile from the Kingdom: A Political Rereading of Albert Camus* (The University of Alabama Press, 1985), 11.

37. John Erickson, "Albert Camus and North Africa: A Discourse of Exteriority," *Critical Essays on Albert Camus*, edited by Bettina L. Knapp (Amherst: University of Massachusetts Press, 1988), 73.

38. Edward W. Saïd, *Orientalism* (n.p.: Vintage Books Edition, 1979), 20-21.

39. Abiola Irele, "In Praise of Alienation," *Présence Africaine and the Politics of Otherness 1947–1987*, edited by Valentin Y. Mudimbe (n.p.: The University of Chicago Press, 1992), 201.

40. Bill Ashcroft, Gareth Griffiths, and Helen Tiffin, *The Empire Writes Back. Theory and Practice in Post-Colonial Literatures* (London: Routledge, 1989), 4.

41. Abiola Irele, *The African Experience in Literature and Ideology* (London: Heinemann, 1981), 203.

42. Danielle Max-Scouras, "The Poetics of Maghrebine Illegitimacy," *L'Esprit Créateur* 26.1 (Spring 1986): 3.

43. W. J. T. Mitchell, "Representation," *Critical Terms for Literary Study*, edited by Frank Lentricchia and Thomas McLaughin (The University of Chicago Press, 1990), 11.

44. Paul De Man, "The Mask of Albert Camus," *Albert Camus*, edited by Harold Bloom (n.p.: Chelsea House Publishers, 1989), 10.

Chapter 1

Algeria: A Socio-Political Appraisal, and Birth of National Consciousness and Literary Discourse

Ici, l'intelligence n'a pas de place . . . Cette race [algérienne] est indifférente à l'esprit. Elle a le culte et l'admiration du corps. . . [C'est] un peuple sans passé, sans tradition, et cependant non sans poésie. (Albert Camus)

[Here, intelligence has no place. . . This (Algerian) race is indifferent to the intellect. It has the cult and the worship of the body. . . They are a people without history, without tradition, and yet, not without poetry.]

Introduction

The above passage furnishes a perfect instance of what has been referred to as "a discursive mytho-poetic position" whereby Algeria exits its socio-political realm to become "a cluster of symbolic, mythic structures" (Haddour 1989, 23). Correlatively, such symbolism suggests a certain vacuum, a void, analogous to Louis Bertrand's fictional and discursive appropriation of Algeria, as an empty space, "la cité de la mort" (*L'Église d'Afrique* 1930, 8), or Roman ruins, in need of reviving.

North African literary discourse—bearing in mind, my attempt at enlarging its hitherto restrictive frontiers—did not spring from the void. We must look to the interaction of historical events, sociological factors and political climate to explicate its genesis. As Merad rightly puts it, "s'il est un pays dont la littérature [...] ne peut être abordée que située dans son contexte politico-historique, c'est bien l'Algérie" (1976, 9). This apt assertion lays the ground for this chapter, the purpose of which is twofold. The first is to provide an overview of the "generative ambiance," to use JanMohamed's noted phrase, in which Algerian literature emerged. I shall seek to reconstitute the various important historical moments which shaped the "evolution" of North African writers, for they are essential to an understanding of the rise of Algerian nationalism and the formation of the various literary discourses. The second purpose is to trace the development of Algerian literary discourses within a politically defined context. The political and intellectual life of the 1920s and 1930s will be the focal point in this part. The French central doctrine of assimilation will be looked at within the context of its political and cultural ramifications. I shall endeavor to show that the doctrine not only constituted, politically and culturally, a "pole of colonial disjunction" within the colonial overall scheme, but it also manifested a duality of political aspirations, epitomized by the diverging interpretative stances of the *Jeunes Algériens* and the *Algérianistes* movements. Given the scope of this study, a logical starting point will be the onset of French colonialism[1] with its attendant co-optation of North Africa into the history of the European world.

Algeria: The Colonial Venture

Seen in the light of its peculiar onset, the French invasion of Algeria presented all the characteristics of an accidental and unforeseen event. A diplomatic dispute involving the French consul and the dey of Algiers—the notorious *coup d'éventail*[2]—barely constitutes a ground for a traumatic upheaval as that of colonialism. Such an encroachment makes sense only in as far as it is inextricably linked with the European expansionist movement; that era demarcated roughly by the closing decades of the nineteenth century, as the age of imperialism, where European states, through such methods as formal annexation, military occupation and protectorate treaties, extended their territorial claims at an unprecedented rate. The motives—economic, political— behind the European expansionist drive have since been analyzed by historians and literary critics. Talking specifically for France, Hargreaves sums the principal arguments as follows: "Firstly colonies were said to be vital for the economic well-being of the mother-land [France].   Secondly it was asserted that if she [France] failed to engage in territorial expansion, she would forfeit her status as a great power. Thirdly the nation was said to be carrying civilization to other races" (1981, 8).   Such expansionist policies did receive a great deal of criticism from "anti-imperialist" camps within the home country itself. Such oppositions were not necessarily inspired by an hostility towards the principle of imposing French rule on other races as such. They were motivated by much more pragmatic concerns, such as the high costs of conquering and administering colonies, and the fear of a weakening effect upon the continental power through massive exodus of French resources, including troops, into overseas adventures. It is clear though, that the priority concern for both camps centers around the protection and promotion of French power and interests. So in effect, "if new territories could be acquired without giving rise to excessive expenditure or international complications, few feathers would be ruffled."[3]

The third and most pernicious justification for the colonial enterprise, namely the French civilizing mission, held a lot of appeal, and did command a fair amount of support within France. The self-assigned historic role, that of imposing its civilization on a barbarous group, led to the perception of the conquest as part and parcel of *la grandeur de la France*. Such an outlook yielded an attitude of total uncompromising antagonism, cultural and religious. The two dimensions of the venture, namely, on one hand the antagonism and, on the other, the "humanitarian" mission constitute the composite elements of the ideology of the civilizing mission and account for the most dynamic trends within French colonial thought in Algeria. The most dedicated exponents of the French mission were the Christian missionaries, who it seems were themselves blindfolded to the inherent pitfalls of the idea. Monseigneur (later Cardinal) Lavigerie, appointed archbishop to Algiers in 1867 gave expression to the view held by many that "conversion to Christianity was the only way the Muslims could be [redeemed] from barbarism, and was therefore the only humane policy the French government could follow in Algeria" (Abun-Nasr 1971, 253). Stephen Neil, summarizing the "predicament" of Christian missionaries during the colonial period, explains:

> It is plain from the records that the primary concern of almost all missionaries was the well-being of the people whom they had come to serve. But human motives are never entirely pure and unmixed. All too often the missionary held that he could judge better the real interests of his people than they could themselves; his objectivity was blurred by a certain patronizing, and sometimes even contemptuous, attitude towards men whom he could never quite persuade himself to regard as grown up. (1966, 413)

Implicit here is a mild indictment of missionaries' patronizing attitude and unfounded conviction in their position as the best judges of the interests of potential converts. In effect, such is the underlying assumption of the missionary's mission; the latter is predicated upon the belief (implying a great deal of judgment) that the native's well-being lies solely with his conversion to the Christian faith. Algeria, it should be noted, in contrast to other colonies such as those of the Sub-Sahara, escaped to a greater extent, the Christian expansion, owing more or less to the peculiar nature of the French administration on the Algerian soil, and more so, to the challenging presence and role of Islam in social and religious legislations. However little impact it had on Algerian cultures, the underlying impulse of the missionary, a fundamental ingredient of the colonial outlook, is a certain ethno-centricity. By imposing new patterns of life and outlook that tore at existing mental structures, there is the claim, explicit or implicit that the new impositions are of a greater value than the existing life-style of the indigenous population. Coupled with this, is the general tendency to conceptualize the outside world in terms of the "Self" which is posited as the norm from which the "Other" deviates. Within such a conceptualization, other life-styles are regarded as abnormal or at best, exotic. France's self assigned role of "civilisatrice" will be dealt with later on, with its impact on the native Algerian population. I chose to touch upon it briefly here so as to give an idea of the weight of ideology that was brought to bear upon Algeria, when she was thrust into the Western world's scramble for power and dominion, and needless to say, material gains. One interesting aspect of the colonial venture—and also one that lends it weight—is the coupling throughout, of "Christianity" and "Humanism." One more example here, may suffice to illustrate further the manner in which Christian and humanist ideas concurred in the justification of colonialism—here that of Algeria, and by extension, other colonies. Commenting on the fall of Algiers, the Catholic d'Ault-Dumesnil declares:

> Yes, a big question was resolved: Algiers, whose name had until then imposed itself on the world; Algiers, this unreachable nest of proud and cruel robbers, Algiers, the capital of Islam in Africa [sic], the holy city, the warrior city, for so long the terror of the Christians, Algiers belonged to France. It was conquered to Christian freedom and civilization, it entered the large family of Christian cities. Thus fell, to the satisfaction of France and the applause of Europe and the world, this state whose existence was one insult to the rights of humanity, whose life was a deadly war against Christianity. Through this holy victory [...] we put an end to the White Slave Trade, to the exactions of all the shameful

tributes which Christian powers paid the Barbary regencies and to the insults [...] which European civilization had too long endured. The Mediterranean was free, the Barbary coast easy of access, the cross was planted anew in Africa. The glory of France had never been carried higher.[4]

Admittedly this is the view expressed by a Catholic, but it also rather succinctly summarizes the view of the period, namely the interchangeability of the causes espoused by "humanism" and Christianity. The initial French policy within Algeria was that of *occupation restreinte* (limited occupation). Such a policy never really progressed beyond its theoretical formulation,[5] for the very reason that it was incompatible with two dynamic elements in the Algerian situation: "the implacable hostility of Algerian Muslims to Christian rule, and the uncontrollable ambitions aroused in a technically advanced community having political control over a 'less advanced' society" (Abun-Nasr 1971, 240). This incompatibility set, right from the onset, the tone for relationships within the colony. An antagonism compounded further by the French legal system. In 1834 (?)[6], Algeria was officially annexed to France by virtue of which, the indigenous population is recognized as French nationals. A distinction is however established between French nationals, and French citizens, which clearly, the natives were not. Barrière's essay, "Le puzzle de la citoyenneté en Algérie," specifies that

[On] se posa la question de savoir si un musulman ou un juif algérien pouvait être considéré comme citoyen français. Le juge et le législateur répondirent par la négative. [...]
Le législateur fut amené à préciser le statut des indigènes d'Algérie par le sénatus-consulte du 14 juillet 1865. En vertu de ce texte, ils bénéficiaient de la qualité de Français et à ce titre ils pouvaient être appelés à un certain nombre de fonctions et emplois civils en Algérie. Mais ils n'étaient pas citoyens.[7]

[They wondered if a Moslem or an Algerian Jew could be considered a French citizen. The judge and the legislator replied in the negative {...}
The legislator was led to specify the status of the indigenous Algerians in a declaration of the consulate on July 14, 1865. By virtue of this declaration, the indigenous enjoyed the "French" status, and could, on that basis, be called to a number of public and civic functions and duties. But they were no citizens.]

What this meant, especially for Arabs, was that they were (I dare not say "protected"[8]) theoretically under French law, while allowed to remain under the jurisdiction of traditional religious (Islamic) law in litigation regarding personal matters. Algerians were ruled, so to speak, under special powers granted by the *Code de l'indigénat (le statut des indigènes)*. Under this, the colonial administration could, for instance, impose severe penalties on the native population for any forty-one specified offenses (including mere suspicion) without any legal procedure. Penalties ranged from detention without trial, to sequestration of properties.[9] The latter policy, sequestration of properties, was carried out for the purpose of settling new French emigrants in the rural districts.[10] For the indigenous population however, this meant the loss of their best lands through seizure, forced purchase, and the division of lands which were previously held by communities and families. The immediate effect of such an act on the Arab population may be understood in economic terms. Such a capitalist system of ownership, promoting the individual over the community, does go, however, beyond its economic repercussions. What is instituted here is a radical disintegration of ethnic groups, hitherto bound together by communally owned lands. Following this 1871 law, the indigenous population was left with no alternative but to attempt to live in a society whose political and economic structures were geared to serve solely the interests of the European community. The underlying explosiveness created by such structures needs not detain us here; suffice to note its pervasive presence, inevitable, in a situation where the dominance of a minority European population "made the Algerian Muslims a kind of 'minority-majority' in their own territory, in other words, a numerical majority enjoying only the rights of an oppressed minority."[11]

Constitutional and administrative policies within French Algeria served, then, to compartmentalize the Algerian population into a privileged European settler population and a suppressed indigenous community. Privileges, henceforth, resulted from "differences in political and civil rights, social outlook and organization, and economic opportunities" (Abun-Nasr 1971, 250) which kept the two communities separated. These various elements, made up of Arabs, Berbers, Jews, constituted the exploited population, and in terms of government and administration, largely the excluded people.

As the sociologist and writer Albert Memmi tells us, a European without privileges, living on a colony, is highly questionable. Using the term "colonial" (in contrast to "colonizer"), to designate "a European living in a colony but having no privileges, whose living conditions are not higher than those of a colonized person," he argues that such a colonial simply does not exist for "all Europeans in the colonies are privileged;—privilege [being] something relative, to different degrees, every European is privileged, at least comparatively so, ultimately to the detriment of the colonized" (*Colonizer* 1965, 11–12). Jean-Paul Sartre, perhaps one of the most vocal French liberals of his time, also denounces the colonial apparatus as positing and maintaining two distinct group of individuals: "one for whom privilege and humanity are one, who becomes a human being through exercising his rights; and the other, for whom the denial of rights sanctions misery, chronic hunger, or, in general, 'subhumanity.'"[12]

Not least of the paradoxes of French occupation is that, amid the various policies directed at political, economic exploitation and subjugation of the Arab population, France held on tenaciously to its "burden" of civilizing the Indigenes. As a result, the early twentieth century was to see a new category of Arabs/Berbers, the *évolués*; in other words, the few of the indigenous population to have benefited from the French educational system through France's policy of assimilation. The French educational system, however, only served to submerge the Arab-Muslim identity. In theory, the doctrine of assimilation meant that indigenous Algerians were to be transformed into "yellow-skinned Frenchmen" (Fanon 1963, 65) who could lead the same kind of life and enjoy the same rights as Whites. The policy, as generous as it was, never counted on the vehement opposition it received from the settler community to whom any emancipatory attempt having the Arab as recipient, became a threat. It was a violation upon the very being of the settler, caught in a master/slave dialectic. For the settler's status depended on the presence of the native as a colonized being. He, the settler, is dependent on the dominated native, "not only for his privileged social and material status, but also (...) for his very identity" (JanMohamed 1983, 4). The settler's response to a possible "cultural" and political emancipation of the dominated population betrays all the rigidity of "strict dichotomy with its identification of privilege with separation."[13] Within the settler's ideological context of colonial relation, such reformatory moves were perceived entirely as a threat to established privilege and thereby to French Algeria. More pragmatically though, the policy of assimilation died a premature death because very few serious attempts were made to implement it. The incongruity of the litany "our ancestors, the Gauls" (or its equivalent "La France est notre mère patrie"), and the Arab heritage was made more complex by the fact that for the Arab, it was without the accompanying birth rights. The Arab found himself at one point in a cultural limbo. In Dib's, *La Grande Maison*, Omar, the young schoolboy, asks: "Comment ce pays [la France] si lointain est-il ma mère?"[14] While native societies were dislocated by the colonial intrusion, they were never transformed into a carbon copy of metropolitan France. The "cultural limbo" created by the assimilationist project would be the basis for subsequent identity crisis of Algerian *Jeunes évolués*. If, from a Hegelian point of view, history is "a dynamic process through which a people *with a mission* fulfills itself," then one can understand the anguish of the Algerian, deprived of that very mission, yet caught in the "history making" of the Other; or "doing French history", to use Hélène Cixous's[15] laconic phrase. Novelists of the 1950s would devote much of their effort to the examination of this burning issue.

As Hargreaves puts it, critics of the colonial system " denied that the French ever seriously intended to make a reality of assimilation."[16] Indeed, assimilation while a "noble" justification for the French, would, if implemented, render the settler's foothold over the colony rather precarious, if not outright impossible (as stipulated earlier). Jules Ferry (representing a typical paternalistic position), at the head of a Senate commission to Algeria in 1892, denounced the European community as one permeated with long-established sentiments of a strongly anti-assimilationist nature. The blundering vocabulary used, in what purports to correct an erroneous attitude, makes it worth quoting at length:

> Il est difficile de faire entendre au colon européen qu'il existe d'autres droits que les siens en pays arabe, et que l'indigène n'est pas une race taillable et corvéable à merci. Je ne crois pas que le colon opprime l'indigène, au sens grossier du mot, qu'il le violente et le maltraite. [...] Mais si la violence n'est pas dans les actes, elle est dans le langage et dans les sentiments. On sent qu'il gronde encore, au fond des coeurs, un flot mal appaisé de rancune, de dédain et de crainte. Bien rares sont les colons pénétrés de *la mission éducatrice et civilisatrice qui appartient à la race supérieure*; plus rares encore sont ceux qui croient à une amélioration possible de la race vaincue. Ils la proclament à l'envi incorrigeable et non éducable, sans avoir jamais rien tenté cependant, depuis trente ans, pour *l'arracher à sa misère morale et intellectuelle*. (Colin 1898, 325–26; emphasis added).

> [It is difficult to bring the European colonist to understand that there exists other rights besides his in this Arab country, and that the native is not a race to be shaped and brought to task any how. I do not think that the colonist oppresses the indigenous, in the vulgar sense of the word, or that he abuses or maltreats him. {...} But if violence is not in his actions, it is, nevertheless, in the language, in the feelings. One still feels brewing up, deep in people's hearts, an ill-appeased stream of rancour, contempt, and fear. Very rare are the colonists who are filled with *the educational*

and civilizing mission that belongs to the superior race. Even more rare are those who believe in a possible amelioration of the conquered race. They declare them to be of incorrigible greed, incapable of being educated, without having ever tried in the last thirty years, *to pull them out of their moral and intellectual misery.*]

Ferry's words seem to ignore the vital necessity of the native's "incorrigible et non éducable" character to the existence of the colonists. By positing the native as "non éducable," the colonist acquires a justification for his own privileged status.

The pseudo scientific argument (inability to assimilate the native) and the necessity of maintaining the existing status quo soon gave rise to a new policy, which at best was merely a modification of that of assimilation. The theory of "association" which rapidly gained ground, far from bringing any substantial shift in colonial practice, simply provided an ideological confirmation of the non-assimilationist nature of the native. Hargreaves sums up the new doctrine as switching the spotlight "from grandiose pretensions of gallicising the overseas possessions to the more practical concern of Europeans and natives collaborating as 'associates' in the economic development of the colony" (1986, 12). Now, since the "economic development of the colony" is entirely predicated upon exploitation of the native population, for the benefit of both the metropolis and the settler population, one is at liberty to look at the new policy of "association" with as much suspicion. The term "associates" implies a partnership and, to varying degrees, equality, which the very structure of colonialism denies. Advocates of the policy deny the desirability and feasibility of natives to adopt *wholly* French way of life in place of their existing culture. This new and sudden emphasis on the native's way of life and professions of respect for the native culture (which would be subsequently synthesized in Camus's "La Maison de culture") provided theoretical justifications for the failure to admit the native into the French cultural city, as promised, and for the determination to withhold those aspects of French civilization—such as democratic rule—which would undermine the foundations of colonial rule. Albert Sarraut, one of such ardent associationsits, affirmed:

Au lieu d'adapter de force tous nos protégés aux conditions de la cité française, selon la vieille erreur assimilatrice, il faut se décider à comprendre enfin que leur évolution doit, *sous notre tutelle, se poursuivre dans le plan de leur civilisation, de leur tradition, de leur milieu, de leur vie sociale, [...] qu'il nous appartient d'améliorer, de vivifier par la pénétration intelligente de la nôtre, par l'infusion utile et sage des principes du progrès moderne,* mais que nous aurions tort de vouloir transformer ou bouleverser en leur imposant des 'décalques' de nos formes démocratiques, susceptible, parmi eux, de prendre figure de caricature beaucoup plus que des copies fidèles et heureuses du modèle. (emphasis added)[17]

[Instead of adapting by force our protégés to the conditions of French culture, following the old error of assimilation, we must bring ourselves to understand that their evolution, *under our tutelage, must take place within the context of their civilization, their tradition, their culture, and their social life, {...} which, it is our duty to improve, to give life to, through an intelligent penetration of our civilization, through a useful and wise infusion of the principles of modern progress.* It would be wrong on our part to want to transform and upset their way of life by imposing carbon copies of our democratic forms, which, with them, could become more caricatural than a faithful and happy replica of the model.]

The explicit desire here—to leave the pre colonial culture untouched—is undermined by the equally explicit desire to transform it: *améliorer, vivifier par la pénétration intelligente de la nôtre.* The immediate inference here is that of a double bind. In wishing to *améliorer, vivifier,* the colonialist structure presupposes that a Westernization of the indigenous culture at least to a certain degree can only be beneficial. Such an assumption is predicated upon an hierarchisation of cultures and upon the belief that the interests of others necessarily coincide with one's own objectives. On the other hand, such professions of respect for the native culture, also have as their only reality, the underlying motive: the cultural innovations proposed by assimilation were incompatible with the maintenance of French rule and the furtherance of French interests. The idea of an Arab, both culturally assimilated and subjugated, appears rather *contre nature.* The notion of assimilation, as I shall be arguing further in my analysis, interjects in effect a note of discord within the colonial structure.

Keeping, for the time being, to its political implications, let us note the underlying motive of the assimilationist drive as emphasized by Saraut, again in his attempt at defining the purpose of the colonial educational policy: "il importe" he states, "d'envisager, de prime abord, *l'utilité économique* de l'instruction de la masse" (1923, 98; emphasis added). In the light of the objectives thus defined, the mass of the indigenous population was denied access into the French cultural domain. After almost a century of French rule, Algeria counted around five hundred of the so-called culturally *évolués,* or, the culturally disrupted, who were to play a key role in the country's move towards decolonization.

The barely concealed reality beneath the colonial enterprise as underlined above, is—to paraphrase Hargreaves—that the venture as a whole was fraught with moral, social and political problems. At the roots of it all is "the issue of Self and others, which colonialism, with its confrontation between men from radically different cultures, raises in a particularly acute form" (1986:10). The colonial relationship, which is essentially an active phenomenon, raises vital questions of moral consciousness and responsibility. The double talk which permeated so much of colonial rhetoric reflected the difficulties which Europeans experienced in their attempts to construct a coherent rationale which would reconcile the various aspects of colonization into a morally and politically acceptable whole. Such tensions, as we shall see, naturally find their way into the fictional works of European writers, "stigmatized" by colonial experience. "The foredoomed attempt at constructing a rationale for an irrational phenomenon, inevitably creates tensions which disturb the fabric of creative works on the colonial theme, *sometimes with serious artistic consequences*" (Hargreaves 1986:10).

National Consciousness and Literary Discursive Formations

World War I and the Indigenes' participation in it were to alter drastically their perception of colonial reality. Algerian Muslims who had fought side by side with French, for France, emerged from the war with awakened political hopes. For one thing, having served on the continent, they had been exposed to both a higher standard of living and the democratic political concepts that seemed a way of life in France. Both of these were denied them at home. A small number of activists began agitating for reform of the legislative process where disproportionate representation gave the minority population of settlers, majority rule. By way of compensation for the natives' sacrifices and loyalty during the war, the *loi Jonnart*[18] was instituted, which increased representation within the Muslim assembly and dangled the prospect of naturalization, on condition that the colonized would renounce his Muslim status.

The period extending from 1920 to 1945 was marked by the emergence within colonial Algeria, in addition to the hitherto monopolistic colonialist position, of three political tendencies, all representing diverging and conflicting tendencies: *Jeunes Algériens*, the

Ulèmes, (Ulemas) and the *Parti Populaire Algérien* (P.P.A.). For the *Jeunes Algériens*, or lay reformists, the ideals of the French civilizing mission held tremedous appeal. The religious reformists, the *Ulèmes*, on the other hand, sought to reform Islam and to revive interest in Arabic language and culture which were felt to be in danger of disintegration. Their emphasis on the Arab-Muslim character of Algeria was a cautious rejection of assimilation. The P.P.A. which emerged from a previous Communist-affiliated party Etoile Nord-Africane (E.N.A.) was more radical in its demands for political autonomy. These three conflicting parties contributed to determine the colonial future of Algeria and influence literary practice. These various groups are worth looking at more closely in order to appreciate better their impact on literary formations.

Jeunes Algerians came into existence in the early part of the twentieth century on a "pro-naturalization" platform. A product of the French educational system, the group corresponded to Albert Memmi's portrait of the "acculturated who rejects his cultural difference to penetrate the cultural universe of the colonizer" (1965, 12). On the whole, The *Jeunes Algériens* movement sought for reforms within the ideals expounded by the colonial system. Explicit in its demands, was a will to appropriate a dominant (Western) ideology, which at least in theory permitted one to attain a political "humanity" and obtain its socio-economic advantages. But, its stance, it could be argued also, stemmed from a rather naive and uncritical acceptance of the theory of assimilation and the egalitarian ideals of the French civilizing mission. In seeking reforms within the existing colonial relationship, the *Jeunes Algériens* failed to note that the proponent and the opponent of indigenous Algerians' "emancipation" within, or into the French cultural city, were one and the same. For as, submitted previously, assimilation or emancipation of the native, must of necessity topple the colonial relationship. Under the "contemporary conditions of colonization," assimilation and colonization are essentially contra-dictory (Memmi 1963, 127).

Whatever the aspirations of the *Jeunes Algériens'* members were, it is apparent that they were not in tune with the socio-political situation of the times. Reforms instituted by the *Loi Jonnart* were elitist, to say the least.[19] Their restrictive nature-favoring, Pro-French attitudes excluded the majority of the indigenous society, namely the "vagrant emigrants, nomads hunting for temporary jobs from one place to the next." These vagrants (romantically dubbed nomads) were thus, "not only excluded from the French cultural city, but dispossessed from their civil and human rights as well" (Haddour 1989, 2). As naive as the aspirations of the *Jeunes Algériens* were, and as scanty as the reforms adopted were, both were to find their most ferocious contenders in the settlers, opposed as usual to any claim that could affect, at their detriment, the position and place of the native. The demands of the *Jeunes Algériens* were viewed suspiciously, as an anti-colonial propaganda impregnated with Marxist ideology (ibid., 3).

The religious reformists, the *Association of the Muslim Ulemas,*[20] whose stance appeared more scholastic than political, opposed the *Jeunes Algériens*'s pro-assimilationist position. Their initial efforts were mostly geared towards reforming the Islamic religion and reviving interest in Arabic language and culture, through the foundation of Koranic schools.[21] Despite the claim to an apolitical position, their preliminary declarations implied a necessary engagement in the political arena. Their first editorial *al-Muntaqid* (July 11, 1925) defining their framework, amounted to a political *prise de position*. The autochthonous population, they maintained, constituted a Muslim Algerian entity. Hence, as reformists, they pledged to safeguard the religious, moral, and cultural characters of their community; they aimed at promoting unity among the indigenous population, making the latter conscious of its national dignity. "Algeria cannot be French and does not want to be French" became their anti-assimilationist political slogan. The *Ulemas* describe their fight against what they call "cultural decadence" as an "ethnic nationalism", distinguishable from "political nationalism" of the P.P.A. Rather shrewdly, they defined "culture" which they sought to retrieve from the grips of colonialism in its broadest sense, i.e., religion, language, social life, and history, while "political nationalism" was "confined" to the colonial administration. The insistence upon this dichotomy may indeed reveal a great deal of simplistic assumptions (Haddour 1989, 3); but, it also reflects a certain foresightedness. In insisting on the cultural autonomy of the colonized rather than assimilation into French democracy, the religious reformists made it clear that the destiny of Algeria ought to depend more on a cultural decolonization. As problematic as a cultural recuperation was within the Algerian political context, the *Ulemas* were aware that it was a precondition of crucial importance to any meaningful political decolonization.[22]

However, these reformist tendencies—lay or religious—were represented by a numerically restricted intelligentsia, since the whole colonized mass remained overwhelmingly uninformed, the French civilizing project having failed in its mission for the various reasons already stipulated. The *Jeunes Algériens* movement sprang from a limited "handful" of French educated Arabs. That they advocated for a westernization of the colonized mass is hardly surprising. Their faith in the applicability of the ideals put forth by the French civilizing mission, however, raises questions. *Jeunes Algériens* limited its commitment to the political representation of the colonized and to assimilation as a means of emancipation within French culture. It considered neither the social nor the cultural implications to the mass of colonized Algerians. The crucial question of the indigenous cultural identity was completely ignored in the group's political scheme. Its francophonist position, espousing the idea of a French Algerian society, in accordance with the French "democratic" principle, provided a fertile "ideological terrain" for *Algérianisme* to launch its colonial campaign and to propagate the myth of Latin Algeria. As stipulated at various points in the study, the *colons* viewed the *Jeune Algérien* assimilationist aspirations with hostility, because they endangered the stability of the entire colonial system. Yet, as we shall presently establish, the *Algérianistes*, who were essentially spokesmen for an orthodox colonialist position, would appropriate the myth of assimilation, not in the same sense as the *Jeunes Algériens*, but to consolidate the colonialist stance at a time "when the indigenous elite entered into a political debate with France" (Haddour 1989, 6). *Algérianiste* discourse enables us to focus on a pertinent issue, central to this chapter, namely the interplay between aesthetic model and colonial ideology.

Algérianiste Discourse: The Myth of Assimilation and Search for Aesthetic Autonomy

On March 6, 1920, a handful of French Algerian writers, R. Hughs, L. Lecoq, J. Pomier, to name a few, met to discuss the "project of constituting a literary movement." Although his presence was not recorded at this inaugural meeting, the movement owed much of its structures to Louis Bertrand, commonly acknowledged as the "fountain" of French Algerian writing, and to Robert Randau. The latter's "philosophy of action" expressed in his work, *Les Algérianistes et les colons*, provides for the movement "an appellation and ideology which define its aesthetic framework."[23] It is a framework defined along a necessary interrelationship between aesthetic model and colonial ideology. Pomier's article, bearing the fitting title of "La Propagande et les Ecrivains," points to the close affinity between politics and literature, propaganda and art.[24] According to Pomier, politics, as a "practical reality" governing people in society, is projected within the "aesthetic." The immediate inference is that the "artist is an implicated party in the political arena. Within religious context, propaganda indicates the propagation of faith—the approach of a man who goes towards the Other with his beliefs, conviction and epistemology" (ibid., 3). Such propaganda, Pomier goes on, "informs all of men's interactions and initiates the conversion of the Other" (ibid.). So also in colonial discourse—at least as envisaged by the *Algérianiste* school—the term propaganda implies a diffusion of the colonizer's beliefs and ideas. Accordingly, "it behooved the *Algérianistes* to assume the clerical duty of propagating the colonial myth" (ibid., 7). Far from being damaging to art, the artist's involvement in colonial politics is seen as beneficial. Thus, the novel becomes at one and the same time an "aesthetic structure and a political propaganda [for] posing, ex-posing, and pro-posing Algeria" (ibid.). For the *Algérianiste* writers, art and politics are imbued with the same function and end.

Pour diriger les hommes, ce qui est du politique, comme pour les décrire, ce qui est de l'écrivain, il faut également connaître les hommes que l'on décrit ou que l'on dirige. Le politique et l'écrivain étudient donc l'un et l'autre l'individu et le milieu, et si, par cette scrutation le premier établit une méthode d'action, le second historie les aspects de cette action. L'un prépare l'avenir par la pensée, l'autre par des actes. Du politique, le peuple reçoit des normes; de l'écrivain, sa conscience d'art. Mais tous deux travaillent dans un même but d'harmonie, dont celui-là organise la poursuite, dont celui-ci évoque et suscite la beauté. (Pomier, "Politique" 1927, 3)

[To lead men, which is the task of the politician, or to describe them, which is the task of the writer, one must know the men that one seeks to lead or describe. The politician and the writer study then the individual and the milieu. And through this close study, one establishes a plan of action, and the other historicizes aspects of this action. One prepares the future through his thoughts, the other through his acts. From the politician, the people receive their norms; from the writer, their consciousness of art. But both work toward the same goal: harmony. One works at pursuing this harmony, the other evokes its beauty.]

This, as can be seen, is a formulation of a "politicized" aesthetic, a "littérature engagée" in the colonial propaganda. The writer—just as his counterpart, the politician engaged in political and economic affairs— sees to the construction of colonial consciousness and the diffusion of colonial ideology. The notion of solitary art contradicts the *Algérianiste* rhetoric and ideals, which were principally geared towards colonial conquest—"pénétrer le pays, avancer, conquérir" (Pomier 1928, 41). Confronted with such a task, Pomier argues that art, as defined by *Algérianisme*, cannot exist in solitude. The *Algérianiste* writer's duties, moral and political, are to consolidate the colonialist power, and require collective enterprise and effort (1927, 2–3).

Dejeux correctly asserts that the underlying aspiration of Algerianism is for an *"autonomie littéraire* de l'Algérie" (1978, 16; emphasis added). Quoting from Bertrand's *Le Jardin de la Mort*, Dejeux affirms:

> Le but de l'algérianisme est de constituer en Algérie une intellectualité commune aux races qui y vivent, de réaliser par là même leur union.[...] [Car] il doit y avoir une littérature nord-africaine originale parce qu'un peuple qui possède sa vie propre doit posséder aussi une langue et une littérature à lui.[25]

> [The aim of algerianism is to develop in Algeria an intellectuality that is common to the people who live here, and to promote their unity. {...} [For] there must exist an original North African literature because people in possession of their own lives must also possess a language and a literature.]

Clearly then, what is advocated here is not so much a political separation (*"autonomie"*) as a cultural one. As a distinct settler cultural identity crystallized, there was the need for an esthetically autonomous literature that would reflect this cultural distinction. The historical timing of the movement enables us to elaborate further. As we know, *Algérianisme* came into being in 1921, after the *Loi Jonnart*, giving more representation to the Arabs, and even the possibility of naturalization to those who would renounce their Muslim faith; the latter concession was in response to the *Jeunes Algériens's* first political claims. Thus, the Algerianist movement came into existence when a process of "decolonization" was already set in motion. Their objectives, explicit or implicit, were to fortify the orthodox French colonist position, the foundation of which was being undermined.[26]

The politics of "assimilation," as stated, determined and defined the literary practice as well as the political discourse of *Algérianisme*. However, the term assimilation took on here a connotation, different from that understood by the *Jeunes Algériens*. The concept, as appropriated by Algerianism, was much more in tune with the nineteenth century colonial objective, namely "the assimilation of property." This new dimension to the assimilationist endeavor provides the basis for Bertrand's writings, and plays a central role in the emergence of colonial literature. Bertrand's works reflects the modification in the French doctrine of assimilation. His work, as Gallup rightly sums it, marks "the closing of a debate" (1973, 313).

Indeed, it would seem that with Bertrand, the old debate involving all the ambiguities of the civilizing mission would find itself neatly resolved in an "unification of the doctrine and elimination of its contradictions, in accordance with one world-view: that of the settler" (ibid.). His book, *Le sens de L'ennemi* (1931), which was meant to be a summary of his position, opens with a five-fold exposition on his views. Let us simply retain two of them, because of their relative importance: 1. The need to adapt the colonial reality to a much more "modern world-view"; 2. The need for the new race to become barbarian (*se barbariser*). These undefined, seemingly illogical formulations, contain, however, an indictment against what he calls "a century of France's liberal attitude towards colonization" (1931, 314)

Taking as his point of departure the basic hostility underlying relationships between the settler and the indigenous, Bertrand vehemently opposed the humanitarian aspects of the colonial mission, which he regards as a French intellectualism, backed by a seeming belief in the humanist values of France's ideals. This is clearly an inconsistency, "[an] ideological and sentimental rubbish perpetrated by French intellectuals, the schools and universities, [thereby preventing] a practical vision of reality and a method of action" (1931, 312). As the title of his book suggests (*Le Sens de l'ennemi*), the Arab is essentially an enemy. This awareness must be kept in the forefront, for only then can the new race awaken to a constant vigilance. He diagnoses France's "mania" for civilizing and assimilating the native, as a "democratic-humanitarian virus" with a debilitating effect on the colonial system.

Contrasting French society (France) with the European society of Algeria, he finds the former seriously debilitated by contradictions arising from its humanitarian ideas within a colonial structure, while the latter (the settler society) exhibits all the signs of health. Algiers for Bertrand is the "melting pot" of the races. It is a society which lives with a daily awareness of the enemy "un ennemi qui n'a rien oublié, rien pardonné et qui ne désarme pas." Keeping this in mind, the settler holds on to the land in which he is now rooted, laying the foundation for a new race with all the virile healthy instincts of uncorrupted youth. The latter is endowed with the task of "remaking" Algeria, but an Algeria only as a rejuvenation of France and Rome: a Latin Algeria. Bertrand, Dejeux affirms, "était possédé par le démon de la latinité" (1978, 14). This concept of *latinité*, which constitutes the core of Bertrand's doctrine, is nothing new. It is a reworking and bringing to a logical conclusion, of an old ideological theme deeply rooted in French thought, namely the belief in religious (Christian) precedence. The novelty, however, in Bertrand's appropriation of the scheme, is that the concept for consolidating a colonialist/settler culture.

Thus, within the myth of Latin spirit, and finding expression within it, are the settlers' feelings of a distinct, different identity, even "a superiority over metropolitan France" (Gallup 1973, 316). The supposed superiority of the settler race over the French is due to an acquired "barbarism." This, originally a characteristic of the Indigenes, is described as a natural, healthy vigor that contrasts sharply with the degeneration of the French "owing to an overly sophisticated culture." The latter is called upon to "adopt the qualities of a healthy barbarism" (ibid.)—that of the North African Europeans—a direct result of the settler's contact with the Arab. The doctrine of "rebarbarization" (*se rebarbariser*) which Bertrand extrapolates from his observation of the settler community is fictionally illustrated in *Pépète et Balthazar*, a novel set in the petit bourgeois milieu of Algiers, where his European (Spanish) hero lives, endowed with the various character traits usually attributed to the Arabs: indifference, violence, cruelty, sensuality, jealousy, etc. By a stroke of the pen however, these traits lose their habitual negative aspects. The very characteristics which condemned "l'indigène incivilisable" to an unchangeable inferiority are revalorized to become positive features in the European personage. These features become a source of virility and energy for the European. This reverse assimilation (barbarization) is due not so much to the Arab, but to the North-African landscape. The transformation of the Indigenes' negative traits into creative forces in the European is contingent upon the physical geographical milieu; the sun, the wind, the endless desert. As Bertrand puts it, it is "the climate, the heat of the African sun, which hasten in the Latin settler the birth of faculties which had remained at an embryonic state in his native village (France/Europe)."[27] The North-African sun is a recurrent theme in colonial literature, reflecting no doubt, its importance in the life of the average North-African settler. Georges Joyaux talks of a "fervent and lyrical cult that the Mediterranean pays to the sun, the light. . . ."[28]

One parodoxical result of Bertrand's attempt at constructing the new Algerian persona, a synthesis of Latin and barbarism, is that political and economic justifications used for the colonial venture are transformed into a Latin prerogative. This, in turn, serves to create a distinctive colonial situation, with an outlook and behavior radically different from the much more paternalistic position of metropolitan France. Bertrand's vituperation against the French "democratic-humanitarian virus" is symptomatic of a consistency in his own position in respect to colonialism. Such a position points, however, to the fact that a colonial antagonism between foreign cultures and peoples has, by and large molded a distinct colonial society, within which the French civilizing mission definitely receives its "modern" garb: elimination of all humanitarian motives, and French effort reduced to the most basic claim of the crusade: the (re)appropriation of Roman territory, with the rejection of Islam outside the realm of European consciousness.

The *Algérianistes* perhaps better than any one else understood the racial conflicts (again, the telling title of Bertrand's book, *Le sens de l'ennemi*, would suggest this). Their efforts to create a French Algerian culture in exclusion of the disturbing presence of the Arab culture, became a way of resolving cross-cultural, cross-racial problems. One problematic and contradiction of their approach, however, stems from the necessity of positing Algeria as a *tabula rasa*—or a Roman site, a notion which by definition negates the existence of the problem—the presence of the Other.

The attempt by the *Algérianistes* (faced with the bankruptcy of the colonial mission in Algeria) to consolidate the colonist minority position, must be viewed as a move to re-conquer an Algeria that had already entered the arena of radical politics. For the *Algérianiste* to successfully do so, he sought a return to the 19th century ideal of assimilation, which was essentially a colonizing motive.

However, much more than the *Algérianiste* effort, the global political and economic crises of 1919 to 1939, which affected the colonies as well, were to determine to a greater extent the future of the colonial venture. Algerian economic crisis, worsened by the world economic calamities, thwarted the expansionist move of the colon community, with far-reaching negative effect on the agricultural life of the colonized. The economic malaise, compounded by political instability in the colony, became a commonplace reality that France could not deal with. The expansion of the colonist community—an attempt to correct the demographic imbalance (through resettlement of new colons)—failed to produce the desired result, emigration having lost the initial tempo owing to economic stagnation. Confronted with the demographic growth of the indigenous population, which was miraculously able to thrive on poverty, the settler population faced more and more its own numerical weakness. The settler felt threatened by the impoverished and expanding indigenous society. A budget deficit, coupled with pressures on the Algerian bank not to invest in land, dealt a final blow to the colonial project predicated upon land possessions and settlements. One immediate result was that Algeria witnessed a human movement from the rural to the urban centers, thus completing a cyclical repercussion on agricultural life. This rural exodus itself was to bring the settlers (*petits colons*) and the indigenous population into a new level of antagonism, what Haddour refers to as "politics of Trade Unionism and strikes" (1989, 13). The native's contact with the city would activate further the rise of nationalist pressures. Mohammed Dib's *Le Métier à tisser* (the concluding part of a trilogy) underscores the ideological role of the city in developing anti-colonial sentiments in the native. The sudden descent upon the city (Tlemcen) of rugged beggars, vagrants who had drifted in from the countryside in search of food, not only disrupted but inserted a discordant note within the notion of the "French cities" as a Latin heritage.

The city in its newest dimension could not be ignored. The European community, composed of various segments (French, Italians, Spaniards), was juxtaposed against a large hostile indigenous society, a situation which Pomier sums up rather astutely as follows:

> L'Algérie n'est pas la France, n'est pas le prolongement de la France [...], non parce qu'il y a des Espagnols, des Maltais, des Juifs, des Berbères, des Mozabites, des Italiens et des Arabes; [mais parce que] l'Algérie n'est pas encore une patrie. Ici, les races sont coude à coude, mais non fondues. Les religions sont encore des fanatismes presques médiévaux. ("Prélude à l'exposition coloniale" 1931, 4–5)

> [Algeria is not France, nor the extention of France {...}, not because there are Spaniards, Maltese, Jews, Berbers, Mozabites, Italians, and Arabs; [but because] Algeria is not yet a unified nation. Here, the races live side by side; they do not mix. Religions are still, almost, at the stage of medieval fanaticism.]

Evidently, assimilation failed to subsume these "hybrid" elements into one French entity (*L'Algérie n'est pas une patrie*). The later part of Pomier's statement (*les religions sont encore des fanatismes presque médiévaux*) was an explicit criticism of Islam, for the latter, more than any thing else, constituted a major barrier to the "sociological osmosis" sought for by the *Algérianiste* school. For Pomier "Islam fanatique, exclusif, comme toutes les religions sémites" (Gouverner 1926, 1), was responsible for the failure of "moral" progress in Algeria. Unlike Latinity and Catholicism (which were considered by the *Algérianistes* as "two unitarian and converging forces") Islam and the French colonial administration were in constant ideological conflict. There is on the one hand, an "Orient, statique morne de l'âme," and, on the other, an "Occident cinétique joyeuse, dynamisme lyrique, vie" (Pommier 1926, 2). It seems that the only force capable of retrieving Algeria from its backwardness was that of the Occident (the West). The legitimacy of the colonial duty is thereby given impetus. The threat of

Islam remained, however, paramount in the *Algérianistes*'s consciousness. The paranoia created by the vital presence of Islam was at the basis of *Algerianistes'*s objection to the *Ulemas*'s claim for religious and cultural autonomy from the colonial state. The malaise generated by the *Ulemas*'s demand, is now best understood in the light of Western ideal of separation of State from Religion as one of the important prerequisites for Western secular society and democracy. Naturally, Islam, freed from French colonial domination, posed an even greater threat: that of facilitating the mounting wave of nationalism. The *Algérianistes* were certainly not unaware of the role of Islam as an important infrastructure for Algerian nationalism. Randau presents the threat of Islam within this political frame:

> L'Islam cherche à se regrouper et à rétablir sa suprématie politique en même temps que l'intégralité de la croyance à la fois religieuse et sociale. [...] Il veut reconstituer une culture arabe et par là faire cesser le conflit. Le nationalisme musulman se rendra indépendant, par la religion, des entreprises européennes. Le nationaliste ne boira plus à la coupe empoisonnée. Obéissant à la voix de ses oulemas, qui sont des érudits, mais non des penseurs, car l'Islam a épuisé [...] toutes les possibilités de l'esprit, et il n'est plus besoin de penseurs, il reprendra son rôle traditionnel, qui est de soumettre à la loi les peuples infidèles ou de les convertir, et d'établir le culte de l'Unique sur terre.[29]

> [Islam seeks to regroup and to establish its political supremacy, as well as to bring about the integration of religious and social belief. {...} It seeks to reconstitute an Arab culture, and in so doing, end the conflict. Through religion, Islamic nationalism will become independent of European endeavors. Islamic nationalism will no longer drink from the poisoned cup. In obedience to the voices of its ulemas who are learned men, but not thinkers, Islam will regain its traditional role, which is to subject infidels to the law, or to convert them, and establish the worship of the Only God on earth.]

The *Ulemas*'s cultural and religious nationalism threatened not only the *Algérianistes*'s cultural mission ("créer une âme algérienne"), but their political interest—to consolidate a colonist position—as well. The separatist demands of the *Ulemas*, the nationalist manifestations of the P.P.A., the demand for "cultural emancipation" of the *Jeunes Algériens* generated in the *Algérianistes* a fearfulness, and suspicion to any reformist activities.

The threat posed by these three groups to the Algerianist movement can be understood in its political implication. On a cultural level also, their very presence threatened the Latin myth, central to the Algerianist cultural maneuvers. Evidently, the Algerianist movement as an aesthetic model could not boast of a cultural foundation in the colony, hence the insistence on the myth of Latinity. The myth would play a central role in defining the Algerianist literary structure. Bertrand's *Le Sang des races* (1899) would go a long way in crystallizing a literary life in Algeria. The writings of these earlier pioneers stemmed from a contestation of the tradition of tourist writers who had so far held the monopoly of representing Algeria in French literature. These tourist writers were viewed suspiciously by the new emerging group as incapable of comprehending the alien cultures of the colony. Their "post-card" writings only scratched at the exotic surfaces. Algerianists reacted against this touristic literature whose emphasis on the "picturesque" generated a great deal of distortion. Their impressionist and superfluous descriptions, the French settler contended, replicated invariably a preconceived metropolitan vision of the Orient. "In pursuit of the exotic image, the tourist writer invented it when none existed, thus conforming to metropolitan stereotypes and imagination."[30] Reacting against the outdated aesthetic formulae of Romanticism, the Algerianist proposed to depict life (Pomier 1926, 9). The underlying cause of the protest however, is that the representation of the colonial life as exotic thwarted colonial progress, since exotic literature by essence posits and recognizes the presence of the Other, albeit the Other as an object of colonial gaze and desire. In the Algerianist colonial scheme, it was mandatory that the colonized be seen not as a distinguishable "Other" but as "Same" (read "invisible") subsumed into colonial culture. As superficial as it is, the recognition that touristic writings accord the indigenous Arab tradition devalues the ideological basis of Bertrand's presentation of the colonial space as Latin. The myth of the Algerian setting as Roman ruins, "empty" space, was, at the political level, essential to the Algerianist discourse, since it served to legitimize colonialism as a recuperation of a Latin heritage. "En d'autres termes, l'Afrique française d'aujourd'hui c'est l'Afrique romaine qui continue à vivre, qui n'a jamais cessé de vivre, même aux époques les plus troubles et les plus barbares" (*Les villes d'or* 1921, 6). However, in idealizing the colonial landscape as "les villes d'or (golden cities)" and in excluding the indigenous culture, Algerianism replicated the romanticizing tendency of tourist writings. This tendency acquired here a political function, which was that of valorizing "the eternal Latin" heritage of Algeria, for the establishment of colonial hegemony. The political significance of the Algerianist discourse, in other words, was that through its vision of a "Latin" Algeria, it strove to reinforce the colonial process at a time when the French colonial mission entered its death throes.

To recapitulate then, the central issue of assimilation within the political and intellectual life of the 1920s enacted a polarization of political aspirations. The *Algérianistes* saw in assimilation a potential to disarm ideologically a "hostile" colonized population by destroying its predominant Islamic tradition, the one tradition to have posed the most serious challenge to the colonial mission of assimilation. This they strove to achieve by refuting the Algerian cultural panorama. Such a stance, as noted above, maintained a stasis threatened by historical changes. For the *Jeunes Algériens*, assimilation was an opening to the French city of human rights, "the widening of [their] political horizon, and the end of repressive laws instituted by colonial hegemony" (Haddour 1989, 17).

The two movements interpreted the concept of assimilation differently and according to "two distinct political realities." Whereas the *Algérianiste* movement sought in assimilation a way of perpetuating colonialism, the *Jeunes Algériens* perceived it as a means to espousing Western values. They insisted that France implemented her ideals of "equality and fraternity," which never went beyond their theoretical formulation. As Camus would remark a few years later, the *Jeunes Algériens*'s conceptualization of assimilation, "a rencontré en Algérie même, et principalement auprès des colons, une hostilité qui ne s'est jamais démentie."[31] (*Essais* 1977, 951). The 1936 boycott of the Blum-Violette Bill—a belated attempt at implementing French assimilation policy—introduced by the Front Populaire, was in itself a logical *dénouement*. The bill was to confer civic rights and the suffrage upon 60.000 Moslems. "Les grands Colons," Camus wrote, "opérèrent une telle contre-offensive que le projet ne fut même pas présenté devant les chambres" (ibid.). The political failure of the bill marked a turning point in the assimilationist stance of the *Jeunes Algériens* who henceforth moved from their former tepid demands for equality-integration, to insist on a complete political autonomy. Ferhas Abbas, advocating for "neither assimilation, nor new master," contended in his *Le Manifeste du peuple algérien* that the formation of a single people under the same paternalistic government had failed, because "the European bloc and the Muslim bloc remain separated from each other, without a soul in common."[32] The sudden impetus to the hitherto latent nationalism signaled the failure of the *Algérianiste* movement in its political and cultural mission of reconquest, and establishment of a Latin kingdom. It also brought into the cultural and political arena, a "new literary" movement. *L'Ecole d'Alger*, with its emphasis on a "humanist empire" based on the same colonial theory of assimilation, sought to reconcile contradictions in colonial culture.

To dissipate colonial malaise arising from the various antagonisms, *L'Ecole d'Alger* (which will be looked at in our next chapter) proposed a certain collectivism, by positing a Mediterranean myth. Such a Mediterranean utopia turned out to be a refuge transcending colonial specificities. The new humanism was evasive of colonial dilemmas, transposing them into a universal problematic. However, the process of decolonization, which signaled a movement away from the colonial "eldorado" to an era of exile, rendered the assimilation of the colonized into a Mediterranean culture, an anachronistic solution to the political problems of the 1940s.

Notes

1. It has been stated that the Maghreb entered "modern history" at this very period, which seemed to have been characterized by a proliferation of written materials (public and private archives, diplomatic and political records, legislative and administrative texts, etc), thus engendering a certain positivist and scientific historigraphy based on dated events. Abdallahi Laroui, in his essay on the history of the Maghreb warns against such "scientific" appraisal, for, "the clarity that seems to result is misleading" owing to the cleavage between "true history" (that of the conqueror) and "subhistory" (that of the conquered). The former, he says, is "recorded and analysed in detail [while] the latter is ignored. The motives of the [conquering forces] are examined under the microscope, while the problems of the Maghribis, the transformation of the countryside, the social disintegration and spiritual uprooting are treated as undecipherable enigmas." (*The History of the Maghreb*, Trans R. Manheim [New Jersey: Princeton, 1977] 291.)

2. Jamil Abun-Nasr, *History of the Maghrib* (Cambridge: n.p., 1971), 236. Abun-Nasr reports that "on 29 April 1827 the dey of Algiers, Husain, struck the French consul Pierre Deval on the face with a fly-swatter. This insult to the representative of France (...) started a crisis in relations between the two countries as a result of which the French government stumbled upon one of its most important colonial ventures." 236.

3. Alec G. Hargreaves, *The Colonial Experience in French Fiction* (New York: The Macmillan Press Ltd., 1981), 9.

4. Christian Schefer, *La Politique coloniale de la Monarchie de Juillet. L'Algérie et l'Evolution de la colonisation française* (Paris: 1928), 64. Quoted by Gallup "The French Image of Algeria: Its Origin, Its Place in Colonial Ideology. Its Effect On Algerian Acculturation" (Ph. D. diss., Los Angeles: University of California, 1973), 231.

5. Gallup writes that, "the impossibility of limited occupation was recognized and a new plan developed, accepted by parliament in May 1937.

Control of the whole country was now the official goal, yet it was to be attained gradually through infiltration, persuasion and negociation." (229). The explicit suggestion here of a people willingly surrendering to foreign invasion through "persuasion" and "negotiation" was as un-realistic as it was naïve, as events were to prove. The numerous hostilities, expressed through rebellions, resistance, uprising, which littered the history of the French conquest speak for themselves. It became apparent soon enough that the French conquest must by necessity be a military conquest.

6. Two conflicting dates are recorded for the formal annexation of Algeria. For instance, Menego sets the date at 1834 *Maghrebian Literature in French* (Boston: Twayne Publishers. 1984), 7; and 1870 according to Abun-Nasr, *History of the Maghreb* (Cambridge: n.p., 1971), 253. However, official implantation of France in Algeria dates back to 1830.

7. Cf Barrière's essay for an overview of the various modifications that were made to the statut des indigènes, prior to 1945, all in an attempt to give the Arab/Berber and Jews full French citizenship rights. Augustin Barrière, "Le puzzle de la citoyenneté en Algérie," *Plein Droit* no. 29–30 (1995): 92.

8. In 1863, Napoléon, by the Sénatus Consulte Law declared Algeria a kingdom with its people under his protection, and their lands safe from sequestration. cf. David Gordon, *The Passing of French Algeria* (London: Oxford University Press, 1966) 15.

9. The early period of the French occupation was marked by a systematic appropriation of tribal lands which by customary law were not transferable. During the governorship of Randon for instance (1851–1858) the acquisition of such lands was carried out within a policy of cantonment, whereby lands which in the governor's estimation were not needed for the use of a tribe, usually the most fertile, were taken away.

10. It is estimated that between 1853 and 1863 some fifty-one concessionaries received about 50,000 hectares of land and state subsidies for the purpose of establishing agricultural villages for European settlers. Most of them did not fulfill their obligations, and instead had the lands cultivated on their account by Muslim farmers. For more detail of French land policy in Algeria, see Abun-Nasr, *History of the Maghreb* (Cambridge: n.p., 1971), 248–249.

11. Joan Gillespie, *Algeria: Rebellion and Revolution* (New York: n.p., 1960), 5.

12. Jean-Paul Sartre, "Introduction" in Albert Memmi, *The Colonizer and the Colonized*, xxv.

13. Dorothea M. Gallup, 1973 "The French Image of Algeria: its origin, its place in Colonial Ideology. Its effect on Algerian Acculturation" Diss. Los Angeles: University of California (1973), 441.

14. Mohammed Dib, *La Grande Maison* (Paris: Seuil, 1952), 20.

15. Hélène Cixous and Catherine Clément, *The Newly Born Woman*, trans. Betsy Wing (University of Minnesota Press, 1986) 71. "I was born in Algeria [...] .My brothers by birth are Arab. Where are we in history? I

side with those who are injured, trespassed upon, colonized. I am (not) Arab. Who am I? I am 'doing' French history." Cixous's account of the Arab plight within French history is paradigmatic of the "crise d'identité" bewailed by many francophone évolués who emerged directly from colonial rule.

16. Alec Hargreaves, "Caught in the Middle: The Liberal Dilemma in the Algerian War," *Nottingham French Studies* 25 no.2 (1986):11.

17. Albert Saraut, *La mise en valeur des colonie françaises* (n.p.: Payot, 1923), 104.

18. Cf. Charles-Robert Agerdon, "Les réformes algériennes de 1914 à 1919," in *Les Algériens Musulmans et la France: 1871–1919* (Paris: Presses Universitaires de France, 1968), 1190-1225.

19. To obtain citizenship, for instance, the indigenous must be 1. monogamous; 2. less than 25 years of age; 3. must show proof of having resided for at least two years in an Algerian constituency; 4. must provide a certificate of good behaviour issued from the tribunal of his constituency. Cf. A. Nouschi. *Le Nationalisme Algérien* (Paris: Minuit, 1962), 53–54.

20. This movement takes its roots in the Salafiyya ideology propagated in Egypt at the end of the nineteenth century by Muhammad 'Abduh who argued that the Islamic religion of the early forefathers (Salaf) was a religion of progress, that the backwardness and superstition of Muslims was due to the corruption that Islam underwent over the centuries. Islam in its "pristine purity" was compatible with the adoption of European technology and methods of political organization. So, in effect, the original movement was a Muslim response to the challenge of European superiority. (Cf. Abun-Nasr 320).

21. By 1954, there were about 200 such schools in operation. Their established curriculum placed emphasis on Arabic.

22. A.T. Ibrahimi, De la décolonisation à la révolution culturelle (Alger: SNED,1981), quoted by Haddour, "Camus: The Other as an Outsider in a Univocal Discourse" (Ph.D. diss., The University of Sussex, 1989), 5. Ibrahimi argues that the Algerian cultural revolution does not start with political independence in 1960, but in the late 1920s, with the Ulema's cultural reformism.

23. F. Yahioui's *Roman et société coloniale dans l'Algérie de l'entre-deux-guerres* (Bruxelles: ENAL-GAM, n.d.), which focuses mainly on the work of L. Lecoq, provides an apt study of the Algerianiste school. Cf. also, J. Pomier "Algériennement," *Afrique* 1 (1924) 1.

24. Jean Pommier, "Politique et littérature," *Afrique* 31 (1927): 2.

25. "Le mouvement littéraire dans l'Afrique du Nord," *Les Belles Lettres* no. 17 (novembre 1920) 350–380. Quoted by Dejeux, *La Littérature Algérienne Contemporaine* (Paris: Presses Universitaires de France, 1975), 16.

26. One important clarification is called for here: the colonialist position which the movement seeks to strengthen, is not that represented by the metropolis (France), but that of the French/European settler living in

the colony (I shall elaborate further on this distinction later in my analysis).

27. L. Bertrand, *Le Jardin de la Mort* (Paris, 1921) ix–x. Quoted by Gallup, "The French Image of Algeria: its origin, its place in Colonial Ideology. Its effect on Algerian Acculturation" (Ph.D. diss., Los Angeles: University of California, 1973), 319.

28. Georges Joyaux, "Albert Camus and North Africa," *Yale French Studies* 25 (1960): 10.

29. R. Randau, "Un tableau d'ensemble de l'Islam moderne," *Afrique* 133 (1937), quoted by Haddour, "Camus: The Other as an Outsider in a Univocal Discourse" (Ph.D. diss., The University of Sussex, 1989), 15–16.

30. R. Lebel, *Histoire de la littérature coloniale en France* (Paris: Larose, 1931), 80.

31. Albert Camus, *Essais*, edited with Introduction and Notes by Roger Quilliot (Paris: Gallimard, 1965), 951.

32. Quoted by D.B. Marshall, *The French Colonial Myth* (New Haven: Yale University Press, 1973) 157.

Chapter 2

L'Ecole d'Alger: Universalist Humanist Dilemma, Mediterranean Myth and Colonial Malaise

> Dans toutes les capitales de l'Europe et du monde, des millions d'hommes, à la même heure, hurlaient la même joie. [...] Ce qu'ensemble ils célébraient, c'est la conscience de leurs droits et leur amour forcéné de l'indépendance. (Camus, *Combat* 9 mai 1945)

> [In all the capitals of Europe and the world, millions of men, at the same hour, cried out the same joy. {...} What they all celebrated together, was the awareness of their rights and their ingrained love of independence.]

Introduction

These lines taken from Camus's editorial of the Resistance clandestine news paper, *Combat*, give an indication of Europe's unanimous reaction to the fall of Hitler. For France, it was the end of the German Occupation a period which undermined the very democratic principles it had come to stand on since the French Revolution. The euphoric response to "the end of oppression" was quite understandable.

Across the Mediterranean, in a small town of Algeria, aspirations to a similar liberation received an entirely different response. On May 8, 1945, the town of Sétif witnessed what continues to be an embarrassment to France today, namely, the most atrocious massive government reprisal against an entire town. While Europe celebrated the end of the war, groups of Moslems in at least eleven cities of Algeria resorted to demonstrations. In Sétif, mobs cried out for

Messali's[1] release from prison and for Algerian freedom. The cries of "Vive Messali" and the "illegal" banderoles carried by the demonstrators incited the police to open fire. The death toll was estimated at 45,000.[2] Camus's immediate reaction to the events in Sétif was the publication of *Crise en Algérie*.

My attempt to juxtapose the two historical events is neither trivial nor gratuitous. It brings home forcibly Camus's keen interest in the political life of both his country of adoption, France, and his native country Algeria. The juxtaposition enables me to posit a certain directional framework for this chapter, which will be greatly informed by what critics have referred to as the dichotomy between Camus's beliefs within the context of Western thought, his political vision within the Third World in general, and his native country, in particular (Erickson 1988, 86). Within the latter context, the prevalent issue, one that generated a great deal of controversy, centered around the writer's silence over the Algerian war—one of the bloodiest and most ruthless colonial wars—which broke out in 1954 and ended in 1962, two years after his death.

One question invariably crops up. Was his silence that of "a man unwilling to contemplate fundamental political changes in Algeria" (Hargreaves 1986, 80)? One reason given by Camus himself was that in a conflict where opinions are polarized, the role of the true intellectual is to maintain the middle ground, which according to him was becoming increasingly non-existent. On a more personal level, we may say that Camus was understandably hesitant to say anything that might trigger terrorist reprisals against his own people. Asked by a British journal that he speak out on the French repression of the Arab rebels as vehemently as had done on the Soviets' crushing of the Hungarian revolt,[3] Camus insisted that the Hungarian and the Algerian situations were not in any way analogous. According to him, to view both in the same light amounts to overlooking "a significant historical fact":

> [T]here was not in Hungary, installed for more than a century, more than a million Russians (of whom 80% are ordinary folks) whose lives, whose rights the Hungarian revolution menaced [...]. The Hungarian problem is simple: the Hungarians must be given back their liberty. The Algerian problem is different: there, it is necessary to assure the liberties of the two peoples. ("Letter from Camus" 1957, 68)

To ignore one component of the Algerian drama (i.e., the fate of the French) would amount not only to a betrayal in the principle of effort towards a "humane solution" but to a "nihilistic political romanticism of the most irresponsible variety."[4] Sartre and Camus's dissension over the Algerian war and over the violent and mostly inhumane measures adopted by both parties, is well known. For Sartre, the Algerian conflict was nothing but an anti-colonial struggle in which the indigenous militants were simply "threading the tortuous but glorious path of history toward socialism and freedom." Accordingly, he saw the use of extreme violence both comprehensible and justified. It was nothing but a long-suppressed outburst in response to the systematic and daily economic, social, and political oppression that the French in Algeria had inflicted upon the indigenous population for over a century. As Sartre saw it, the rebels' violence was "nothing else but the violence of the colonial; there was never any other violence."[5] Condemning the rebels' acts in the name of formal, "abstract" principles, amounted to an implicit sanction of that other form of violence represented by political and economic oppression inherent in a colonial structure.

Camus was acutely aware that his arduous effort to point and to adhere to the "narrow path of humanity" in the midst of violently clashing forces met with a great deal of incomprehension, derision and even hostility. At a press conference in Stockholm, following the award of the Nobel Prize (1957), he was harassed by an Algerian student who accused him of condoning colonial injustices, by refusing to support Algerians' demand for independence. "Je crois à la justice," he replied, "mais je défendrai ma mère avant la justice." This rather impulsive replique quickly acquired a notoriety of its own.[6] Indeed, it could, and has been, interpreted in various ways. If one wishes to trivialize it, the statement could indeed reflect his understandable anxieties over his mother, still living in Algiers.[7] It could also be read in the light of his own critique of "abstraction," which according to him, was the tendency to single out a principle (even a noble one as "justice" or "freedom") and endow it with supreme value. More generally though, Camus's statement has been interpreted as a kind of "Freudian slip," revealing that "when the chips were down, Camus would if necessary side with the *pied-noir* community if it was a question of choosing between their interests on the one hand and justice for the Muslims on the other" (Hargreaves 1986, 80). If indeed, Camus's anti-colonial feelings ran as deep as it was generally assumed, it seems legitimate to ask whether an open support for the Arab cause might not have been more consistent with his theoretical position. From a certain critical perspective however, the whole argument regarding Camus's stance in the Algerian war for political independence is irrelevant, unless it can be viewed within the writer's "existential political morality."

Willhoite, in *Beyond Nihilism, Albert Camus's Contribution to Political Thought*, contends that Camus's stance in relation to the crises which ravaged his country, is the best example of his principles concerning social and political changes. These principles taken in isolation are themselves meaningless. He argues that

> No political thinker of any consequence can be understood simply through an examination of his views on governmental institutions and policies. Marx's critique of government, and his premonitions of the character of a truly communist society, cannot be grasped without an initial effort to comprehend his views of man's alienated conditions and of the nature of human history. [So also,] Camus's distinctly political ideas cannot assume the meaning and significance he intended for them unless we first explore his views on man's nature and condition (1968, 17).

This chapter adopts a reverse approach from that of Willhoite. I shall not be concerned with Camus's "philosophical theories" per se, but with his political position which underlies such theories. In other words, I shall locate Camus's "metaphysical apparatus" within a socio-political context. The central critical claim of this chapter is that Camus's writing is informed by his political vision. The combination here of the author's "literary" and political positions confer a certain hybridity on this chapter. I will attempt to bring to light both the immediate socio-political realities (mostly analyzed in my previous chapter) and Camus's own various political thoughts which impinge upon his literary creation, disrupting what purports to be purely aesthetic.

Given the multi-purposiveness of this chapter, a certain break down is necessary. I have divided the chapter into four main parts. The first section establishes a certain "genealogy" of Camus's Mediterranean cult, insisting here on the influence of writers such as Audisio and Grenier upon Camus. In section two, I look at Camus's own appropriation of the Mediterranean, within an ideological vacuum. I will highlight here the various colonial politics that pervade such a scheme. Section three provides a political re-reading of Camus's absurd sensibility. I will explore here Pierre Nora's reading of metaphysical alienation (the absurd) as a political malaise. The last part of this chapter will deal with the central issue of Rebellion. I shall insist here on the historical problematic of such a concept, within colonial violence. To give myself a certain perspective, I would like to begin by situating Camus within the literary circle, designated as *l'Ecole d'Alger*, a movement which emerged from the failures of the previous *Algérianiste* group analyzed in the previous chapter.

As has been established previously, the *Algérianistes*, confronted with the mounting wave of Algerian nationalism, sought to consolidate culturally, if not politically, the colonial structure, by insisting on the settler's Latin right. This was a regressive move to block the dynamics of history being activated by Algerian nationalism. The Latin myth, predicated on decay/death, both symbolizes and reflects a society (that of the pied-noir) on the brink of suicide/death, back-looking into a Latin dominion, drawing on a dead glory (history) to thwart the future (Algerian nationalism) which threatened its existence. The Latin heritage, central to *Algérianiste* discourse, served to evacuate the colonial space, to erase the Arab and his cultural panorama. In political terms, it was an attempt to legitimize colonization as the recuperation of Latin heritage, and, faced with the threats of the nationalists' demands, to re-enact the colonial processes being undermined. The Latin myth, reflecting a stasis, if not a regression, was ultimately an instrument of imperialist ideology. Although one underlying impulse of the movement was to seek a kind of aesthetic autonomy from French literary circles, it remained faithful to the imperialist motives of the mother country, with an added element, namely the rejection of all humanitarian ideals of the colonial enterprise. Characteristically, then, the *Algérianistes* opposed both the French assimilationist political repertoire, and the nationalistic feelings of the colonized, expressed either by the lay reformists, *Parti du Peuple Algérien* (P.P.A.) or the religious reformists, the *Ulèmes*. However, aside from their objections, the feasibility of the assimilationist policies was itself undermined by various political and cultural contradictions inherent in the French colonial project.

If Algérianist discourse proposed Algeria as Latin, in order to revive a dead Roman (European) hegemony, *l'Ecole d'Alger* following chronologically from *Algerianisme*, saw Algeria as a direct descendant of Greece. Emerging in the heat of political rivalries between colonizer and colonized, *l'Ecole d'Alger*, better than any group, reflects the "existential problem of the pied-noir culture" threatened by the process of decolonisation taking place, and colonial violence emanating from nationalism and colonial antagonism. The new literary movement[8] reacted vehemently against the former's ideological rhetoric. Intrinsically though, the two schools remain twin movements. As pointed out correctly by a perceptive commentator,

> [l'École d'Alger] s'oppose [aux] conceptions [algérianistes] sans parvenir à leur substituer une parole neuve. Elle ne déplace pas le lieu de la parole: à travers elle, c'est toujours la colonie de peuplement qui parle; mais la parole n'est plus cynique ou conquérante, elle est devenue malheureuse ou hanteuse sous la pression des contradictions objectives. (Gourdon 1974, 88–89)

[[École d'Alger] is opposed to Algerianist conceptions without managing, however, to replace them with any substitute discourse. It does not displace the position of speech: through them, it is still the settler colony which speaks; but their discourse is no longer cynical or conquering; it has become miserable and haunting under the pressures of objective contradictions.]

Both *l'Algérianisme* and *l'Ecole d'Alger,* then, appropriated a myth (Latin/Mediterranean) for diverging purposes. While the Latin myth was used politically, to attempt to entrench the colonialist position, that of the Mediterranean served to transcend colonial specificities. Within both perspectives, however, colonial Algeria emerges more often not in any socio-political context, but as a mythic structure, or at best, a space where myth and reality coalesce. Myth, as Eliade defines it, is first and foremost constructed to provide a genesis. "[C'est] le récit d'une 'création': on rapporte comment quelque chose a été produit, a commencé à être."[9] The power of myth becomes thus, a vital requirement for instituting and constituting any given establishment, whether sacred or secular. Naturally then the role of fiction and the power of creation in both the *Algérianistes* and *l'Ecole d'Alger*'s discourse on Roman or Latin Algeria cannot be overstated.

Two distinct myths find articulation within *l'Ecole d'Alger*: *L'éternelle méditerranée,* heralded by Gabriel Audisio and Albert Camus; and *l'éternel Jugurtha* promulgated by the Berber writer, Jean Amrouche. They aspire to two different types of humanism. While the latter [Amrouche] and his subsequent followers, indigenous writers, presented Algeria as a political context dominated by an oppressive colonialist ideology, Audisio's humanism sought to subsume the colonial situation into a universalist problematic. In the literary circle of *l'Ecole d'Alger,* Amrouche—to counter the Algerianist Latin mythologies—introduced Jugurtha, both a legendary and a historical figure who (supposedly) destroyed the Latin edifice, the cities of Roman domination, to represent colonial Algeria as a ground of constant conflict. A forerunner of *Littérature de Combat,* Amrouche's "l'Eternel Jugurtha" marks the embryonic stage of a subversive and anti-colonial literature. Amrouche suggested that any literature specific to North Africa, must incarnate the spirit of Jugurtha, which is one of division. In his essay, *L'Eternel Jugurtha—propositions sur le génie africain,* written in 1943, and published in 1946 in *L'Arche,* Amrouche insists that, concerning the "génie africain," there is a "faisceau de caractères premiers" that concurs to produce "un tempérament spécifique." "Jugurtha," he goes on, "représente l'Africain du Nord, c'est-à-dire le Berbère, sous sa forme accomplie: le héros dont le destin historique peut être chargé d'une signification mythologique."[10] Camus, however, viewed Amrouche's endeavors as a gesture of bad faith, "coming from an ungrateful intellectual who lived on the cultural fruit of France, and yet appropriated anti-colonial metaphors."[11]

Putting aside Camus's contentions, it is clear that for Amrouche, the portrait of Jugurtha, "prenant toujours le *visage d'autrui, mimant à la perfection son langage et ses moeurs,*"[12] (emphasis added) represents the state of mind of the colonized évolués, impregnated with French culture, and suffering the inevitable consequences of a "cultural split." The duplex nature of Jugurtha embodies the ambiguities of the young indigenous intellectuals who identified with both the French culture and their own tradition without feeling at home in either one of them. The ensuing cultural alienation (emanating from a "double identity"), will find more prominent articulation within the *littérature de Combat*. Feraoun's *La Terre et le sang* and *Les Chemins qui montent*, are two instances of novelistic thematization of Amrouche self-division: "En moi le trouble et la division. Non point la révolte stérile ou l'ingratitude. Mais l'angoisse . . . Comment éteindre cette soif, satisfaire cette faim de communion dans l'identique qui tenaillent tous ceux qui furent coupés de leurs racines?" (1946, 92) Amrouche, throughout his writings, never lost sight of the psychological effects of colonialism— the native's suppressed dignity; the native *évolué*, that "cultural monster," that "historical error"; a mimic, through constant imitation of the French; the cultural stagnation or worse cultural genocide, etc. . . . These various effects, Amrouche argues, are the deep causes of the Algerian Revolution. In his analysis of events, he insists that "France and Algeria had never been married, and so no one could speak of [the revolution as] a 'divorce,' as some French commentators did. Algeria had simply been violated."[13]

Within the context of *L'Ecole d'Alger*, Audisio and Camus on the other hand, extrapolate from the Mediterranean landscape a unversalist discourse. "[Ils] refuse[nt] la problématique 'régionaliste' et colonialiste au profit d'une problématique universaliste et humaniste." I shall limit myself to examine here primarily the ideological scheme of the mediterranean myth as propounded by Audisio, and taken up by disciples such as Camus.[14] By positing Algeria—*l'éternelle méditerranée*—as a humanist empire, *l'Ecole d'Alger*, as I shall insist, suppressed the Algerian problem. The eternal Mediterranean character attributed to Algeria, and very akin to the previous Latin heritage, also perhaps unwittingly perpetuated colonial domination. As I shall be arguing in this chapter, *l'Ecole d'Alger*'s "aesthetic of the sun" obfuscated the mounting nationalist sentiments of the indigenous population.

By silencing anti-colonial polemic, the new movement failed to offer any substantial solution to the Algerian political situation. Humanist ideals of equality under one sun put forward by the school prove to be problematic. *l'Ecole d'Alger*, strong French assimilation advocatesm subsuming both early indigenous elites and liberal pied-noir, ignores the contradictions inherent in the guiding principle of the French civilizing mission which reposes on a set of binary contradictions: imperialist/humanist; oppressive/egalitarian; and elitist/assimilating. The colonial venture, riding on the wings of capitalism, and therefore overexploitation of a majority by a minority, contradicts any humanist claims.

These various contradictions were, however, overlooked by the new literary circle. The initial impulse at harmonizing conflicts was soon reduced to assimilating the Algerian landscapes, from which the "variegated human populace" was excluded. Their depiction of passive landscapes without the human factors became an open hermeneutic field against which humanist ideals could be tried out. Within such a scheme, the vagrant colonized finds himself located outside the open "tableau."

Gabriel Audiso: l'éternelle méditerranée

Audisio, as he admits himself, was an adherent of the *Algérianiste* school. In *Sel de la Mer*, he confesses, "L'Afrique latine, j'avoue que j'y ai d'abord cru un peu, comme tout le monde, et que j'avais suivi avec sympathie le mouvement qui s'était développé en Alger, sous l'influence de M. Louis Bertrand, voici quelque quinze ans."[15] The political upheavals of the 1930s forced Audisio to abandon the Algerianist scheme. His *Jeunesse de la Méditerranée*, which established formally his disagreement with the former school, appeared shortly before the failure of the Blum Violette Bill (1936) to carry out the assimilationist program advocated by the *Jeune Algérien* movement. The book would subsequently gain a certain popularity with the disgruntled jeunes évolués. This work can be considered as a landmark in the Francophone literary tradition. With Audisio, emerges for the first time the idea of a "unité méditerranéenne."

Que l'on nous fasse grâce de la trop facile latinité! La politique la littérature, le sentiment, se la disputent. On sait avec quelle allégresse [...] M. Louis Bertrand, supprime les douze siècles d'Islam qui ont pesé sur le Maghreb, avec quelle foi il fait appel à la conscience latine des musulmans nord-africains. Je n'ai guère

d'indulgence pour les autres généralisations qu'on impose à ma mer;
l'hellènique, la byzantine, ou la phénicienne [...] ne sont que des
"moments," des aspects transitoires de l'éternelle Méditer-ranée.[16]

[Spare us this facile notion of latinity! Politics, literature, feelings,
everything contests such a notion. We know the alacrity with
which {...} Mr. Louis Bertrand eliminates the twelve centuries of
Islam that have weighed on the Maghreb, the faith with which he
appeals to the latin conscience of North African Moslems. I have no
patience for all the other generalizations that are being imposed on
my sea: Hellenic, Byzantine, or Phoenician, {...} they are all but
transitory moments of the Eternal Mediterranean.]

Jeunesse de la Méditerranée, articulates the author's opposition to
his predecessor's myth of Latin Algeria. According to Pomier's review
of the book, it was a "poem of life" and beauty, a lyrical work in which
humanism could resolve racial and national conflicts, a refreshing
contrast to a divided Europe faced with racial and national oppositions.
It is also, according to Pomier, a praise of Man, the universal,
transcending national, ethnic frontiers, social and cultural barriers.
Despite the universality of Audisio's celebration of Man and life, his
discourse obviously, emanates from colonial specificities: *l'éternelle
méditerranée* is a colonialist metaphor. Pomier, following his initial
positive response to *l'Ecole d'Alger*, would undergo a *volte-face*,
pointing to the ideological similarity between the new "school" and
the *Algérianiste* movement. He argues that if the *Algérianiste* usurped
the myth of Latinity to designate the so-called "new race" occupying
the Algerian passive landscape from which the Arab is excluded, *l'Ecole
d'Alger*, on the other hand usurps the Mediterranean myth, to posit the
universal man, and by so doing, overlooks the Algerian reality, its
specificities, i.e., distinct moral, cultural and historical variants that
shape the lives of Algerians. Although, Audisio opposed Greece to
Rome, erecting a Mediterranean genius (Ulysses) against the tyrannical
rule of ancient Latin, ideologically, his discourse is not far removed
from that of his predecessors, because basically he also sought a moral
legitimization, if not justification to the French colonial mission in
Algeria. If Bertrand's metaphor of the Latin, or that of "le sang des
races" was loaded with racist assumptions, Audisio would find himself
appropriating the same ideal (le sang des races), but while insisting on
their mixture. The physical and mental climate of Algeria becomes thus
metaphorized into a mixture of different bloods, or what Audisio
himself will later term as "la chimie des globules."

Encore que la fusion des races ne soit qu'à son début, l'Algérien a
déjà conscience de sa particularité ethnique et mentale. Il croit au
climat et à l'influence du milieu, parfois il n'hésite pas à trouver en
soi-même quelque-chose de Berbère (on pourrait aussi dire quelque
chose d'Arabe [...] mais le Berbère habille mieux, on a pour lui le
préjugé favorable.) Il sait qu'il est un mélange spécique. Il faut
toujours en revenir à la fameuse réponse de Cagayous: "Etes-vous
Français?"—"Algériens, nous sommes."[17]

[Although the fusion of the races is only beginning, the Algerian is
already conscious of his ethnic and psychological particularity. He
believes in the climate and influence of his surrounding; often, he
does not hesitate to find within himself something of the Berber
(one could also say something of the Arab {...} but the Berber suits
him better; one is better disposed towards him.) He knows that he is
a special blend. One needs to recall the famous response of
Cagayous: "Are you French?"—"Algerians we are."]

Two vital contradictions find articulation within Audisio's
universalist scheme: the very movement of incision, or exclusion that
informs Audisio's text, and on the other hand the very insistence upon
a "particularité ethnique et mentale" which negates the universal.
Fifteen years after this initial impetus, Audisio will realize that in this
composition of races sought for, the races remain essentially unmixable.
Writing "Tête d'Africa ou le génie de l'Afrique du Nord" out of his
own disappointment, he admits to what is really a truism: that
different ethnic groups, Berbers, Arabs, Jews, Blacks, and Europeans,
cohabitated, without much hope of ever mixing. Despite this
observation, Audisio clings to the notion of an "essence" peculiar to
the North African. North Africans, be they Arab, Berber, Jews or
European, do share the same spirit; he insists that "le génie d'un pays
ne parle pas seulement par le sang de ses peuples, mais aussi par
l'esprit. Et l'esprit est au delà de la chimie des globules."[18] On the
rebound, then, Audisio would transform what was really a set-back in
his universalist scheme, into a positive image: a spirit of ambivalence,
essential characteristic of the North African. Audisio posits Ulysses as
the prototype, the embodiment of the North African spirit. Ulysses, the
homo duplex, the man of two faces, two hearts, in short, the man of
duplicity, typifies the notion of doubleness, essential to the North
African spirit. This move in a way, usurps the essential trait of
Jugurtha. But where Amrouche privileged the inalienable division as
the North African spirit, Audisio sees a ground for harmonization.
Audisio insists that his mythic construction reflects much more the
Algerian reality. "Le Mensonge et la Vérité, [...] la Mer et le Terroir,
la Bravoure et la Peur, la douce Mort et la Mort détestée. [Lie and

Truth, {...} Sea and Land, Bravery and Fear, Sweet Death and Loathsome Death.]" (*Le Génie d'Oc* 1943, 273) This because the dualism or ambivalence personified by Ulysses was an essential component of the Mediterranean genius. North Africa, where the races never mix, but remain in latent antagonism to one another, illustrates, more than any other geographical location, this genius.

> Aussi loin qu'on remonte dans le temps on voit cette Afrique du Nord marquée par le signe du dualisme et de ses conflits. Sous nos yeux, celui de l'Orient et de l'Occident est assez apparent pour qu'on n'y insiste point. [...] Pour parler avec un historien de métier: "pays à double vocation, indifféremment agricole ou pastorale . . . Nomades et sédentaires, base éternelle de la dualité d'âme du Maghreb" (Amrouche). Son âme à la double vocation, il faut donc que le génie nord-africain la cherche sans cesse entre deux pôles contradictoires. Et d'abord entre la barbarie et la civilisation, entre l'instinct et la raison, entre la jouissance et l'ascetisme. (*Le Génie d'Oc* 1943, 439–40)

> [As far as one can go back in time, one sees this North Africa marked by the sign of dualism and conflicts. Under our very eyes, the case of the Orient and the West is apparent enough for us not to dwell upon. {...} As a historian stated, "a country of double vocation, indifferently agricultural or pastoral, nomadic or sedentary, the eternal base of the duality of the Maghrebian soul" (Amrouche). The North African genius must seek his soul of double vocation between two contradictory poles. Primarily, between barbarism and civilization, between instinct and reason, between pleasure and ascetism.]

Obviously, Audisio's scheme, privileging the contradictions, the abortive mixture between East and West, goes against the *Algérianiste* school's earlier rejection or disregard of the Arab settings of Algeria.

The promulgation of this essential division (dualism) into a prominent feature of the Mediterranean, however, emerged from efforts to solve a political dilemma. The East and the West, two extremes co-habitating the Algerian landscape, was a political problem, arising from a colonial system. From political situation to a metaphysical problem there is a gap. Yet, in Audisio's program what is primarily a result of a historical situation is obliterated in a mythic construction. In viewing the political conflict between colonizer and colonized, as a humanist problem, Audisio distances himself from colonial politics, from "the apparent conflict between colonizer and colonized, [from] the confrontation of 'barbarie' and 'civilisation'" (Haddour 1989, 39). The essence (division, contradiction) which Audisio insists upon as "le génie nord-africain" or "l'éternelle méditerranée," was in effect a political situation, generated by a colonial structure. He, like, Bertrand (as indicated by his *Le sens de l'ennemi*), was not unaware of the colonial drama unfolding on the Algerian soil, as he himself affirms.

> Moins que personne, je n'ignore [pas] la complexité des problèmes qui se débattent entre ces peuples et nous, entre leurs idées et les idées d'Europe, entre leurs classes et les nôtres, entre l'Islam et l'Occident, si l'on veut réduire les énoncés du drame à des antinomies faciles. Mais je les tiens plus apparentes que réelles. Comme les pays, les problèmes sont d'abord les hommes qui les incarnent, et le drame universel se ramène toujours au drame des comportements de l'homme devant l'homme. ("D'homme à homme" 1947, 371)

> [Less than anyone else, I am not ignorant of the complexity of the problems at issue between these people and us, between their ideas and the ideas of Europe, between their classes and ours, between Islam and the West, if one wishes to reduce the drama to a set of facile oppositions. But I believe them to be more apparent than real. Problems are, like countries, formed primarily by the men who embody them, and the universal drama always boils down to the drama of men's behavior towards men.]

Present within both the Algerianist project and that of *l'Ecole d'Alger*, is, one would say, a certain tendency towards a harmonization of cultural antinomies, the unification of colonized and colonizer in a social synthesis. The approach however varies. In their quest for social syntheses, the *Algérianistes* had eliminated the indigenous cultural presence. Audisio, on the other hand, never lost sight of the conflicting cultures, but transcribed the colonial division unto a universalist plane, thereby transcending colonial dilemma. His was an attempt to present a mythic Algeria as a microcosm of the universe, grouping different, culturally conflicting races. Such a position by necessity dissipates colonial conflict and resolves human contradictions in a certain permanent notion of humanism. By insisting on the Algerian problem as primarily "un drame de comportement de l'homme devant l'homme," the colonial dilemma exits the political realm, to take on metaphysical assumptions. Also, one would note, the myth presented by Audisio as depicting the North African dualism, is Western cultural specific, reflecting yet again a failure to interpret the Algeria in its totality. Despite Audisio's attempt at creating a universal context, Algeria as an imaginary construct was restructured in such a way that contradictions are dispelled. Audisio's universal humanism, which paradoxically insisted on the "non-disjunction" of opposites (and this within a colonial setting!) summarized in a nutshell the precarious ideological position of *l'Ecole d'Alger*, seeking to construct a new Algeria, where men of good faith could work at erasing the essential antagonism between opposites.

L'Ecole d'Alger, L'éternelle Méditerranée: A Political Metaphor

In this section, I shall attempt to unearth the various problems (cultural and political) which impinge upon Camus's appropriation of the Mediterranean motif as an "apolitical" metaphor. Camus, like the spiritual founder of *l'Ecole d'Alger*, Audisio, saw in the Mediterranean a potential harmonization of "barbarie" and "civilization." His barbarie, is not that posited by Bertrand previously to glorify the colonial ideal, but one inseparable from what he perceived as "la vraie culture," the perfect blending of West and East under the Mediterranean sun and sea. Appropriating the old Romantic dichotomy nature/culture, Camus privileges "nature" over "culture, and using it (nature) as synonymous to the new "Mediterranean humanism," "la vraie culture." This new culture, Camus affirms, does not exhibit its superiority over other cultures. On the contrary, "it liberates humanity from degrading political dominations." As Camus insisted, his Mediterranean was not Latin and therefore opposed Bertrand's exaltation of Western colonial domination. Accordingly, the Mediterranean genius contrasted with the Latin genius—emblematic of colonial ideals, and Western tyranny. As he pointed out,

Mais non. Ce n'est pas cette Méditerranée que notre "La Maison de la culture" revendique. Car ce n'est pas la vraie. Celle-là, c'est la Méditerranée abstraite et conventionnelle que figurent Rome et les Romains. Ce peuple d'imitateurs sans imagination imagina pour-tant de remplacer le génie artistique et le sens de la vie qui leur manquaient par le génie guerrier. Et cet ordre qu'on nous vante tant fut celui qu'impose la force et non celui qui respire dans l'intelligence (*Essais* 1958, 1331).

[Oh no! It is not this Mediterranean that our "Maison de la Culture" is demanding. For it is not the real one. It is the abstract and conventional Mediterranean of Rome and the Romans. This nation of imitators without imagination, however, imagined replacing the artistic spirit and the love of life that were lacking in them, with a spirit of war. And this much vaunted order was the type that is imposed by force, and not the kind that breathes intelligence.]

Implicit within Camus's discourse, then, is the statement of difference, perhaps even superiority over the more traditional colonialist view represented in Bertrand's latinity, which according to Camus, is characterized by abstraction. The intellect and politics—abstract features—are products of the "Latin genius," "incapable de s'attacher à la vie." The Mediterranean genius, on the other hand, relied on his intelligence to generate the concreteness of the world and to give culture "son vrai visage de santé et de soleil" (*Essais* 1958, 1332). The secret of this "Mediterranée où l'intelligence est soeur de la dure lumière" (ibid.) is that it liberated man from the weight of history, politics and religion, which are all abstract concepts designed by the intellect (Haddour 1989, 52). Indeed, in his inaugural speech at La Maison de la Culture (1937), Camus defined further his own terms as follows:

Servir la cause d'un régionalisme méditerranéen peut sembler, en effet, restaurer un traditionalisme vain et sans avenir, ou encore exalter la supériorité d'une culture par rapport à une autre et, par exemple, reprenant le fascisme à rebours, dresser les peuples latins contre les peuples nordiques. Il y a là un malentendu perpétuel. Le but de cette conférence est d'essayer de l'éclaircir. Toute l'erreur vient de ce qu'on confond Méditerranée et Latinité et qu'on place à Rome ce qui commença dans Athènes. Pour nous la chose est évidente, il ne peut s'agir d'une sorte de nationalisme du soleil. Nous ne saurions nous asservir à des traditions et lier notre avenir vivant à des exploits déjà morts. Une tradition est un passé qui contrefait le présent. La Méditerranée qui nous entoure est au contraire un pays vivant, plein de jeux et de sourires. D'autre part, le nationalisme s'est jugé par ses actes. Les nationalismes apparaissent toujours dans l'histoire comme des signes de décadence. Quand le vaste édifice de l'Empire romain s'écroule, quand son unité spirituelle, dont tant de régions différentes tiraient leur raison de vivre, se disloque, alors seulement, à l'heure de la décadence, apparaissent les nationalités. (*Essais* 1958, 1331)

[It may indeed seem that serving the cause of Mediterranean regionalism is tantamount to restoring empty traditionalism with no future, or celebrating the superiority of one culture over another, or, inciting the Latin against the Nordic peoples by adopting, for example, an inverted form of fascism. This is a perpetual source of misunderstandings. The aim of this lecture is to try to clarify them. The whole error lies in the confusion between Mediterranean and Latin, and in attributing to Rome what began in Athens. To us the matter is obvious: any kind of nationalism of the sun is out of the question. We could never be slaves to traditions or bind our living future to exploits already dead. A tradition is a past that distorts the present. But the Mediterranean land around us is a lively place, full of games and joy. Moreover, nationalism has condemned itself through its actions. Nationalisms always make their appearance in history as signs of decadence. When the vast edifice of the Roman empire collapsed, when its spiritual unity, from which so many different regions drew their justification, fell apart, then and only then, at a time of decadence, did nationalisms appear.[19]

Camus's presentation of the Mediterranean as an apolitical ideal, and therefore ahistorical, was rather peculiar, for the simple reason that at the time, he himself, unlike Audisio, was actively engaged in politics. His brief adherence to the Parti Communiste Français (P.C.F.), the founding of La Maison de la Culture, one of whose expressed objectives was to restore harmony in colonial conflicts, his various writings on the Algerian colonial problems in *Alger Républicain* attested to a rather active involvement in politics. The metaphor of the Mediterranean is used within a political context as a symbol of "harmony (assimilation of conflicts)"; yet it (the metaphor) transcended all racial antagonism, all colonial ideological conflicts, reconciling colonizer and colonized. Here, a brief look at the immediate political climate in which Camus established La Maison de la Culture, might help.

One landmark of the historical and political context of La Maison de la Culture (1937) was the establishment of the *Front Populaire*. It was an era of progressive/liberal ideologies. French intellectuals, wearied of the various political turmoils posed by fascist advances, gradually opted for a more socialist outlook. It was also a time of intense political commitment. Any intellectual worth the name was committed to the defense of one cause or the other, but usually under one unifying banner such as the defense of man or the promulgation of social equality, social rights, etc. It was at this time that many were lured to the Communist Party, "which at the time had donned the humanitarian's immaculate robe."[20] One of the major political factors that consolidated the new party (*Front Populaire*), and which was to galvanize a tremendous support for it, among the French intelligentsia, was the party's opposition to the rise of Fascism in Europe. Intellectuals's anti-fascist stand was manifested as early as 1932 with the formation of the anti-Fascist Amsterdam-Pleyel movement, and the subsequent formation in 1933, of the *Association des Ecrivains et Artistes Révolutionnaires* (AEAR) (Lottman 1978, 79). The latter (AEAR)'s magazine, *Commune*, significantly subtitled *La Grande Revue pour la Défense de la Culture*, was to have a tremendous impact on Algerian youth, as evidenced by the one stated objective of Camus's Maison de la Culture, namely the defense of "culture."

The politics of the *Front Populaire*, as regarding Algeria remained confusing. The "Marxist" faction within the party, grouped under the *Parti Communiste Français* (P.C.F.), was initially vehement in its denunciation of all totalitarian systems, colonialism, fascism etc. . . . The growing threat posed by Germany, Italy, and Spain would lead, however, to a sort of "nationalization" of the Party, whereby issues not affecting the metropolis directly were relegated to a secondary position. Following the Franco-Soviet pact of 1935, when the Soviet Union "dropped the Arab liberation movement in Algeria as a token of good will" (Braun 1974, 35), the P.C.F. will abandon its anti-colonial mottoes to channel its political efforts solely against Fascism gaining ground, and threatening Europe. Algerian colonial problems which were initially at the forefront, would henceforth be regarded as ancillary to domestic problems. "Le cabinet de Léon Blum [socialist Premier under Front Populaire] ne croyait [plus] à l'importance des questions algériennes et jugeait qu'il fallait concentrer les efforts sur les problèmes métropolitains" (Julien 1961, 22). Clearly, then, the struggle against Fascism submerged colonial issues. Coincidentally, Camus's own short flirtations with the Communist Party ended at the same time that the P.C.F. moved from internationalism to deal with "home" politics. In a letter to Quillot, Camus affirmed that he [Camus] joined the party in 1934 and left in 1935 because of the change in its political position toward the Algerian colonial problem.

Writing to Grenier much later, he explained that "Communism has unfairly annexed the cause [of Arabs and working population]. I understand now that if I have a duty, it is to give the best of myself to my people, I mean, to try and defend them against lies."[21] Both dates and the reason put forward are incorrect, and one wonders why. I wish to explore here Durand and McCarthy's interpretations of Camus's involvement with French communism.[22] Within the Algerian colonial framework, the position of the Communist Party, the hard core of Algerian leftists is an ambiguous one, to say the least.

An examination of its position might be beneficial here, since it helps to shed light on Camus's entry into and departure from the party. The P.C.F. initially rallied behind the socialist policy of assimilation until around 1925, when it turned anti-colonialist. (Theoretically, it always remained anti-colonial, even with the shift of emphasis from colonial matters to domestic problems.) This change in attitude, from assimilationist stance to anti-colonialist one, had an inevitable effect on membership of the Algerian section of the party, which plummeted from one thousand to two hundred and fifty. The reason is simple enough: As stated rather humorously by a critic, "If you scratch at a Communist, you find a European conqueror underneath."[23] For the average European worker, being a communist and anti-colonialist are two distinct realities. Arabs who adhered to the party complained of being treated as "poor relations." So Arab membership was rather minimal. The only outstanding indigenous leader in the 30s was Amar Ouzegane, who would join the F.L.N. in 1937. The party was reluctant to accept Arab history or the Arab language. In short then, the base of the party, as well as its voters resisted the anti-colonialist line, for the Communist party comprised largely "Algerians of European origin, who were deeply imbued with the racist prejudices of the pied-noir tradition" (Tarrow 1985, 18).

However, the mounting Nazi threat, and that of Mussolini within Europe and North Africa, would galvanize the party into greater efforts; when Camus joined the party in 1935, it was nearing the peak of its affluence (McCarthy 1982, 55). The so-called happy years of the party were short, though, because the P.C. never resolved its old dilemma: Arab members' demand for a stronger anti-colonialist line and European members' objection. The party's subsequent failure itself is symptomatic, being "the hardest test of European-Arab relations" (Tarrow 1985, 19). Communism held a tremendous appeal for the segment of Algerian society where the two communities met: the urban working class. This was one ground on which Arab and European met in a common struggle for better working conditions; it was also the ground for the greatest conflict: the existence of different wage levels, and the competition for jobs. The P.C.'s failure in reconciling the two groups simply reflects the failure of a French colonial Algeria. The party's rigidity in the face of historical changes may indeed be the cause of its failure (Tarrow 1985, 20). This rigidity however reflects Camus's own attitude vis-à-vis the Algerian nationalist movement and demand for social and political changes.

Shortly after Camus's entry into the party, the Algerian section of the P.C.F. was granted autonomy, leading to the formation of the *Parti Communiste Algérien* (P.C.A.). Surprisingly, Camus, whose role in the then P.C.F. was to recruit Arabs for the party, was not too much in favor of this new development. According to Durand, this algerianisation of the party, a "préfiguration, sur données marxistes, d'une 'Nation Algérienne,'"[24] accounts for Camus's malaise, and eventual retirement from the party. She explains that "Camus eut soin de se désolidariser très vite d'un parti, fût-il en pleine 'baraka,' qui tendait déjà (sous couvert sans doute du respect des nationalités), à l'abandon de populations incontestablement 'françaises' de coeur, sinon de race [...]" (ibid.). It is within this malaise generated by the threat of

Algerian nationalism that Camus's "internationalism" and "Mediterranean humanism" of the Maison de la Culture must be viewed.
Despite his own assertion that he left the communist party because of
the change in its position towards the indigenous colonial Arab, his
own political action in La Maison de la Culture was in harmony with
the ambiguous nature of most "liberals" at the time, incapable of
thinking in any other terms than those of French colonizers.

In La Maison de la Culture, Camus stressed on "la nécessité d'une
culture méditerranéenne, à condition qu'elle ne fût pas une mystique de
la latinité telle que l'exploitait la propagande fasciste."[25] Commenting
on Camus's vision of a Mediterranean culture, O'Brien remarks that

> Although he rejects Maurras's conception of the 'Latin West,'
> with its pro-fascist associations—at this time of Mussolini's
> invasion of Ethiopia—his own Mediterranean reposes on a
> supposed linguistic unity derived from the similarity of Romance
> languages: and this in a country of which the majority of the
> inhabitants were Arabic-speaking. (1970, 12)

Camus was one of the Algerian intellectuals to actively support the
Blum-Violette project in May 1937 that would enfranchise some
twenty thousand Moslems "without loss of their Koranic statute"
(Tarrow 1985, 23). He saw this project as a step in the right direction
towards "civilization" and "humanity," and towards "enhancing the
French image among the Arab population" (ibid.). In *Jeune
Méditerranée*, a journal run by La Maison de la Culture, Camus
insisted that "the left-wing intellectual's role is to defend the culture of
the popular masses, and that Moslem culture cannot flourish when the
people are oppressed, uneducated, and poverty-stricken" (ibid.). What
does one make of Camus's insistence upon Arab culture within the
French colonial framework, especially in the light of O'Brien's critique
of the so-called "linguistic unity derived from Romance languages"
(1970, 12)? Tarrow observes that Camus's emphasis on Moslem
culture, is "at variance with assimilationist policies, which would
continue to consider French language and culture of prime importance"
(1985, 23). Indeed, given the expansive and co-opting hegemony of
French assimilationist politics, indigenous cultures invariably faced the
prospect of succumbing completely to Western (French) culture. Arabs,
and by extension Black Africans, shorn almost entirely from their
traditional cultures by the colonial intrusion, "are embattled within a
historically racist hegemony that in theory offers equality and aspects of
its 'humanism' as models for emulation but in practice denies equality
and blocks the access to 'civilized' humanism through segregated
education, economic exclusion, and so forth" (JanMohamed,

"Humanism and Minority Literature" 1988, 34). The French segreg-ationist practices towards the indigenous Arabs were not unknown to Camus, since he himself wrote extensively on the various injustices perpetrated against the Arabs by the colonial system. Regarding the fate of Arab culture which Camus insisted upon, the question begs to be asked: what exactly does the "maintenance of Moslem culture" within the assimilationist framework entail? Camus's simultaneous insistence upon Moslem culture within the colonial structure is highly problematic.

I would say that the aim here is to downplay the importance and legitimacy of indigenous cultures. Such a move fits in perfectly with Camus's own stance which is primarily assimilationist, subsuming the other culture (Arab) into French culture, or at best retaining the indigenous culture as a subordinate one within the French hegemony. Camus persistently maintained throughout his writings on the various crises in Algeria (i.e., "Misère de la Kabylie") that the road to perfect harmonization of the two opposing groups in Algeria lay in the assimilation of the indigenous population into the cultural and political life of the French which offered the prospect of equality for all. Camus for a long time, insisted that it was possible "to put indigenous on equal terms with the pieds-noirs without it being necessary for the latter to make any unpalatable sacrifices" (Hargreaves 1986, 80). Such a belief reflected a good deal of naiveté, since within a colonial framework rapport between settler and indigenous, was highly predetermined. Camus's commitment to the ideals of assimilation may be well intentioned; but it also reveals "his underlying inability genuinely to go beyond the horizons of his French background" (ibid.). Indeed, not only does Assimilation assume that French civilization represented an ideal on which non-Europeans should model themselves, but its implementation—were it seriously carried out—implied continued French control. Typically, at the time when Camus was advocating a Mediterranean culture (a kind of fusion of races, of cultures), the "linguistic unity" he talks of and the one upon which is predicated the supposed Mediterranean culture, is a "similarity of Romance languages."

Camus's position was that of assimilating a cultural majority into a cultural minority. Evidently, he was not rallying under the French left-wing intellectuals' "(theoretically) proclaimed" anti-colonial banner. While introducing the Mediterranean as a harmonious ideological context in which to resolve the threat of Fascism and totalitarianism, Camus overlooked the colonial conflict; the latter was coalesced into a universal issue. The Mediterranean was not an apolitical context, judging from his own involvement in colonial politics. Caught, on one hand, by impending political issues, i.e., Nazi and Fascist threat which displaced the significance of colonial issues in the Marxist agendum, and on the other hand by his own continued advocacy of assimilationist program which already proved a failure, Camus, it would appear, sought refuge in a "utopia" outside history and politics. It was an attempt to relocate the Algerian problem into a Mediterranean collectivism. His writings on historical revolutions (which will be looked at later) may also be viewed in the light of his utopianism.

Camus's efforts (this cannot be overemphasized), like Bertrand, and Audisio before him, were oriented towards a reconciliation (harmonization) of opposites (colonized and colonizer). It was also generative of a colonial discourse, or a discourse of the "colonial subject" undifferenciated and depoliticized. It is rather telling that within this "Mediterranean collectivism" he increasingly distances himself from the colonial problem attendant to such a discourse. Camus explicitly denounced the Italian colonial mission in Ethiopia. He seemed, however unaware that his own identification of indigenous culture as "Mediterranean" premised upon a "unité méditerranéenne," justified and legitimized (just as Bertrand's Latin myth did) the French colonial mission. After the failure of the *Front Populaire* government to carry out its Blum-Violette program (this was massively boycotted by the settlers), *l'Ecole d'Alger* and the *Jeunes Algériens* (the indigenous *évolués*) both strong advocates for assimilation, would henceforth part company.

L'Ecole d'Alger would, however, maintain the colonial ideal of assimilating the Indigenes into the Latin West. The obvious anachronism of assimilationist politics would nevertheless lead Camus to insist more and more on the natural bonds which unite colonized and colonizer: the sun, the sea, one human condition outside politics and history. This exit from politics and history caused Camus to posit the non-disjunction of opposites; such a harmony, without impingement from politics, could only be effectively achieved within a universalist plane. By evading the colonial conflict, Camus reconstructed a "mise-en-scène," a Mediterranean universe, where the colonized Arab—and the colonizer for that matter—were located outside the colonial context, history and ideology. Despite his disapproval of crimes perpetrated by colonialism, his lyrical essays and fictional writings re-enacted, and maintained the colonial order by focusing on what were primarily Western metaphysical and moral issues—the absurdity of life, the problem of death, and revolt as a stance in the face of the absurd.

In my next section, I shall take a closer look at the "Absurd" and "Revolt," insisting yet again that both are extrapolated from political realities, and arguing as critics such as Pierre Nora have, that Camus's metaphysical alienation is but a transposition of a political (colonial) malaise.

Politics of the Absurd: From Colonial Malaise to Metaphysical Alienation

In the previous section, I have sought to analyze Camus's political position within the Algerian colonial context. I propose now to look at how this position has been encoded within what, short of better terms, can be called Camus's philosophical theories. In this area, I am much influenced by critics who have interpreted the "Absurd" for instance, as a metaphysical transposition of a historical situation. Pélégri, for instance, affirms that

[C]e qui me frappe [...] c'est l'importance dans toute son oeuvre, l'obsession de ce thème de l'exil. De *l'Etranger* à "L'Hôte," ce thème revient constamment sous sa plume, au propre et au figuré [...] Peut-être même le sentiment de l'absurde n'est, chez lui, que la transposition métaphysique de ce thème. L'homme exilé, de son pays, s'exile du ciel.[26]

[What strikes me {...} is the importance, in all his work, the obsession for this theme of exile. From *L'Étranger* to *L'Hôte*, this theme constantly recurs beneath his pen in the literal and figurative sense. {...} Perhaps the feeling of the absurd is only but a metaphysical transposition of the same theme. Man exiled from his country is also exiled from paradise.]

Both Camus's "absurd sensibility" and "révolte éclairée" have socio-political significations. I shall therefore endeavor to place these philosophical theories within the socio-political context analyzed previously.

Jean Grenier was probably the first writer to have given a philosophical dimension to the metaphor of the Mediterranean. His seminal thought would find further development in Camus's literary and philosophical discourses. Grenier's essay *Inspirations Méditerranéennes* depicts the emptiness of human existence, man's mortal condition. He attempts to resolve this condition in a sort of Mediterranean pantheism, whereby he achieves what he calls a "métaphysique qui soit à égale distance du culte de l'Absurde et du culte de l'Action" [a metaphysics that is equidistant from the cult of the Absurd and from the cult of Action].[27] Grenier argues that unity (or man's quest for unity) can only be achieved in a poetic moment. From the lyricism of the Mediterranean, he asserts, "giclera de la poésie, des jours sans commencement, des nuits sans fin, une vie lyrique, le soleil marié à l'ombre" (1961, 155).

Audisio and Camus's initiation into the Mediterranean cult can be traced back to Grenier. Camus who has constantly acknowledged his debt to the author of *Inspirations Méditerranéennes*, through various dedicaces and explicit statements, will extrapolate from this essay an "aesthetic of the absurd" In his preface to *Les Iles*, another work of Grenier's, Camus states that:

> Il nous fallait des maîtres plus subtils et qu'un homme, par exemple, né sur d'autres rivages, amoureux lui aussi de la lumière et de la splendeur des corps vînt nous dire, dans un langage inimitable, que ces apparences étaient belles, mais qu'elles devraient périr et qu'il fallait alors l'aimer désespérément. [...] La mer, la lumière, les visages, dont une sorte d'invisible barrière soudain nous séparait, s'éloignèrent de nous, sans cesser de nous fasciner. *Les Iles* venaient, en somme, de nous initier au désenchantement; nous avions découvert la culture.[28]

> [We needed more subtle teachers, and a man born on other shores, though like us enamoured of light and bodily splendors, came to tell us in peerless language that these outward appearances were beautiful, but that they were doomed to perish and should therefore be loved in despair. {...} The sea, the light, people's faces, from which a kind of invisible barrier suddenly separated us, receded, but still exercised their fascination. *Les Iles*, in short, had just initiated our disenchantment; we had discovered culture. (*Lyrical and Critical Essays* 1968, 327)

The title of Grenier's work, *Les Iles* suggests man's isolation and solitude. The theme of "voyage," illustrated by the essay reveals the transitory nature of human existence. According to Camus, "le voyage décrit par Grenier est un voyage dans l'imaginaire et l'invisible, une quête d'île en île" ("Préface" 1959, 11). The "quest" however, which is much more self-seeking (seeking oneself) than a search for the Other, does not lead to the envisaged fulfillment, but to a nothingness. The confrontation with the beauty of alien landscapes leads the traveler to a form of alienation, cultural alienation, which in turns becomes thematic of man's metaphysical anguish. Grenier's journey which ends with a meditation on the "absolute" and the "divine" hypostatises the absurd- "L'homme s'émerveille et meurt, où est le port" (1959, 11)? The Northern man (the traveler) escapes from the bleak European settings, to discover the pleasures (la mer, la lumière, le soleil) offered by the

Mediterranean. Yet, physical pleasures are all that the Mediterranean sun can offer; there is no refuge from death. So in effect, the Mediterranean landscapes with all that they have to give, "sont des sollicitations perpétuelles à la mort. Ce qui devrait nous combler creuse en nous un vide infini" (*Les Iles* 1959, 86-7). The imminence of death, producing "ce vide infini" (re)defines the spiritual life of "l'île sans avenir" as immediacy and hedonism. "L'île sans avenir" (*Le Mythe* 1942, 29) describes the spiritual life of the absurd hero. The term also suggests a desertic landscape, an embodiement of the absurd hero's spiritual exile. "Le soleil fait le vide et l'être se trouve face à face avec lui-même—sans aucun point d'appui. Partout ailleurs le ciel interpose ses nuages, ses brouillards [...] et voile à l'homme sa pourriture sous prétexte d'occupations et de préoccupations" (*Les Iles* 1959, 87). [The sun creates emptiness and man is face to face with himself—with nothing to lean on. Everywhere else the sky interposes its clouds, its fog {...} and conceals man's rottenness to himself under the guise of occupations and preoccupations.]

The sea and desert, darkness and light, form a cluster of images (a decor) through which Grenier's theme of metaphysical alienation (what Camus calls "l'absurde") is expressed and manifested. In the midst of the Kingdom, there is Exile. "La mer, la lumière" give man the sense of his humanity to be enjoyed momentarily, for the Mediterranean "light" does cover a dark reality; these two sides of the coin are transposed into two symbols, "sea" (life) and "desert" (death). The physical joy offered by the Mediterranean raises man's consciousness to a greater awareness of the human condition. Even if in that poetic moment (art) a unity is achieved, the course of life does not stop. Death is the ultimate end. The contradiction between the plenitude of physical life on the Mediterranean shore and the sense of human mortality, constitutes a point of departure for Camus. Such an ambivalence and alternation will inform his view of life. From *L'Envers et L'endroit* (1937) which reenacts his own experience of the absurd, to the lyricism of *Noces* (1938) which establishes a sustained self-consciousness of "an artist who prefers to live on the surface of life with all the contradictions of a nihilist world" (Haddour 1989, 61), Camus insists on the binary polarization, of life and death, hedonism and religion, the simplicity of North African life and the complexities of Western "abstractions."

Naturally, these opposing ideas are topographically defined. The Mediterranean, for Camus, incarnates youth, play, life; it is "l'endroit," opposed to Europe, "l'envers" of old age, of death, of Western solitude. These three enemies of man, solitude, old age, and death, are presented as conveying a feeling of discrepancy. Three old people are presented in succession. They share in common a voracious hunger for human contact, to shield their inner void and the imminence of death. "L'ironie" addresses not only the problem of loneliness and inevitability of death, but the impossibility of finding solace in Western religion, "[ce] tête-à-tête décevant avec Dieu" (*L'Envers et l'endroit* 1937, 41). One of the old people depicted is abandoned by her daughter to confront the darkness of a lonely night. The woman's piety is described as hypocritical, betraying her own fear of death. "[Elle était] livrée toute entière à ce mal dernier [Dieu], vertueuse par nécessité. [...] Que l'espoir renaisse et Dieu n'est pas de force contre les intérêts de l'homme" (ibid., 39). Old age, death (night), and fear all concur to alienate the woman from human company. Her refuge in God, apart from being insincere (motivated solely by fear) provides no escape. The North African landscape, on the other hand, provides—albeit fleetingly—moments of happiness, the fleetingness itself adding more intensity to the moments. The theme of alienation explored in this short essay is developed further in "Amour de vivre" and "La mort dans l'âme" (obvious here again, are the binary polarizations of the titles). In the presence of an alien culture, Czechoslovakia ("La mort dans l'âme"), Camus describes his own inability to interact with people. "Amour de vivre" depicting "la nuit à Palma," "la vie [qui] reflue," "des rues noires et silencieuses," takes up the same theme of estrangement. Cultural alienation which Camus experiences in foreign lands, translates a metaphysical estrangement. For both Camus and his teacher, physical settings are the lieu of discoveries. For both of them tourism or "voyage" leads to physical alienation, a collapse of all the familiarities that mask the absurd.

Camus, however, will outdistance his mentor. The discovery of the absurd, Camus persistently maintains, is but a starting point. Commenting on the absurd and on Camus's subsequent refusal of all "metaphysical hopefulness," Chavannes contends that while Camus, as well as his teacher, experiences and articulates man's anguish, death and solitude, there comes a point where Camus clearly marks a departure from his mentor.

Il [Camus] s'écarte de Jean Grenier dans la mesure où sa pensée se ferme dans un refus de Dieu et de l'espérance et dans une révolte métaphysique contre la création. L'influence de Jean Grenier ne semble donc pas être cause de la révolte et du refus qui caractérisent l'incroyance d'Albert Camus. Le maître a pu cependant communiquer à son disciple un certain scepticisme et le sentiment de la vanité et de l'absurdité d'une existence privée de Dieu. Etre ou néant? Jean Grenier n'a pas tranché; Camus optera contre Dieu et pour le néant d'une mort sans espoir.[29]

[He [Camus] distances himself from Jean Grenier to the extent that his thought centers on a denial of God and Hope, on a metaphysical rebellion against the creation. The influence of Jean Grenier does not therefore seem to be the cause of the rebellion and refusal characteristic of Albert Camus's unbelief. The mentor has, however, been able to communicate to his disciple a certain scepticism and the feeling of futility and absurdity of an existence deprived of God. Being or nothingness? Jean Grenier made no choice; Camus will take a stand against God and for the nothingness of a death without hope.]

If the descriptions of the absurdist landscapes encapsulate Grenier's nihilistic stance, Camus moves a step forward. He goes on to examine what could be a possible outcome of the absurd: suicide. One remembers the now famous opening words of *Le Mythe de Sisyphe*, "Il n'y a qu'un problème philosophique vraiment sérieux: c'est le suicide" ("There is only one serious philosophical consideration: suicide") (1943, 15). Camus's whole purpose in this essay appears to be to demonstrate that suicide can be no solution to the absurd. If the latter results from the clash between man's demand for "meaning" (dramatized in *Noces* by the old men's desire for human company) and the unreasonable silence of the universe (i.e., the callous indifference of the daughter), it cannot be resolved by destroying one of the terms of the polarity that gives rise to the problem. Our choice must be for life, and for lucidity, by which alone, one can live the absurd with "dignity and honor." There must be no cheating, at any cost, neither through suicide, nor through hoping, nor through "self-inflicted annihilation." What Camus calls revolt, or, a rebellious stance, in the face of the absurd, marks his divergence from his schoolteacher. Camus would later view the nihilistic attitudes of Grenier and the existentialists as a "deification" of the absurd, a "transcendentalism" akin to, if not, a "philosophical suicide." As in the case of physical suicide, transcendentalism, which confers a certain hopefulness on the absurd, dissipates it.

Camus's ethic of indifference, it seems, entails a kind of hedonism. Man, faced with the absurd, bets on physical pleasures which in themselves do not offer remedies. "[Les] plaisirs n'ont pas de remèdes. Ses joies sont sans espoir. Ce qu'il[l'absurde] exige, ce sont des âmes clairvoyantes, c'est-à-dire sans consolation. Il demande qu'on fasse un acte de lucidité comme on fait un acte de foi" (*Noces* 1938, 55).

In a sustained self-consciousness (rebellion) of the human condition, like Sisyphus fully aware of the futility of his task, Camus insists that life must be lived by moments with a "clairvoyant indifference." In rebellion against the Christian God, he opts for the realm of the "possible," the "now" the "ile sans avenir" where the absurd hero lives as a "miserable lord." Within this optique, one begins to understand Camus's fascination for Don Juan, who according to him, is one of the great heroes of the absurd. He goes from woman to woman, untramelled by any cathechism. "Having no hope of another life, he finds it logical to insist on satiety."[30]

Thus, the beauty of the Mediterranean landscape was a starting point for both Grenier and Camus, towards the absurd. Having discarded suicide and the issue of a possible appeal to the "beyond," Camus would further mark his diverging response to the discovery of the absurd, by introducing the theme of Rebellion. Here again, the Mediterranean plays a vital role, more or less as an imaginary setting. In *Noces*, as in *L'homme révolté*, Camus introduces the Mediterranean as a setting for rebellion "hors de l'histoire, à l'état pur, dans sa complication primitive." Through the agency of his poetic imagination he attempts to recreate reality. Approaching the Algerian colonial space as an "imaginative" setting, yields a point of view on the world. From the Algerians—a people in its "infancy," those lucid "barbarians", "worshipers of fleshly and eathly pleasures"—in short, the colonial melting-pot of different races, Camus extrapolates a worldly religion: "le grand libertinage de la nature et de la mer" (*Noces* 1938, 15). In Tipassa he says,

> je vois équivaut à je crois, et je ne m'obstine pas à nier ce que ma main peut toucher et mes lèvres caresser. [À Tipassa], nous marchons à la rencontre de l'amour et du désir. Nous ne cherchons pas de leçons, ni l'amère philosophie qu'on demande à la grandeur. Hors du soleil, des baisers et des parfums sauvages, tout nous paraît futile. (1938, 15)

> ["I see" equals "I believe," and I do not insist on denying what my hand can touch and what my lips can caress. [In Tipassa], we march forth to meet love and desire. We do not look for lessons, nor for the bitter philosophy one demands from greatness. Apart from the sun, the kisses and wild perfumes, everything seems futile to us.]

Life alone is a certainty for the Algerian youth. This certainty, they consume on a sensual living. The Algerian landscape itself is portrayed as offering them no other consolation than self-gratification and a pagan praise of immediate physical life. In recognition of the inevitability of death, they refuse to believe in the hereafter. With "Noces à Tipassa," one is reminded of Bertrand's "ville de la mort," the Roman ruins. Unlike Bertrand, however, Camus does not seek to rescusitate the ruins to make room for the resumption of Latin rule. For him, "ce marriage des ruines [death] et du printemps [life]" (ibid.), invokes a metaphysical question. Tipassa is thus used as a metaphor by both Bertrand and Camus. While Bertrand appropriates it within a historical context to justify colonial rule, Camus's own usage underlies the absurd sensibility. Amidst the ruins of Tipassa, there towers one single truth: physical pleasure is endowed with the same perishable quality as man himself.

Camus's Algeria, that of a pre-historic harmony collapsing all ethnic barriers, is also that of an "empty space," untainted by politics, presenting an ideological void. The inferred "cultural void," the celebration of sensualism, invoking a stage of infancy, naturally serves to suppress a political situation overwhelmed by colonial violence. France's political and cultural paternalism, coupled with the rise of indigenous hostility towards the settler population, as stipulated, generated among the Pieds-noirs not merely "unspoken" feelings of hatred towards the metropolis, but also a very well articulated denigration of the Arab who was mostly seen as a threat. In the context of *l'Ecole d'Alger,* however, Camus attempted to harmonize the various conflicts generated by the political situation. Unlike the *Algérianistes* who took more cognizance of the situation, even in the midst of their own myth making, a close analysis of Camus's Mediterranean reveals a perturbing political evasiveness. Thus, one is perhaps at liberty to say that his Mediterranean metaphor constructs a "utopia" for existential and political refuge.

Leconte talks of Camus's contribution to "existentialism" as that of having "adorned the absurd with an epicurian sensibility. "[Il a] greffé un fond épicurien sur le sens de l'absurde et de la mort."[31] Camus's hedonism, the celebration of the body in its contact with the sun and the sea—eclipsing all colonial violence—is a precarious one, bordering on the tragic. "On sait cette harmonie provisoire, on vit cette angoisse permanente de la tragédie possible et de la mort. . . . La peur donc, consciente ou inconsciente, produit du "tragique". . . angoisse mêlée de jouissance comme l'envers et l'endroit, le positif et le négatif. . . " (Leconte 1980, 160). [We know that this harmony is temporary; we live this permanent anguish of possible tragedy and death. . . . Fear then, conscious or unconscious, produces the "tragic" . . . Anguish mingled with pleasure like the wrong side and the right side, the positive and the negative. . .] However, this harmonious order, the shared brotherhood of the sun created in *Noces*, would soon find itself disrupted by colonial and anti-colonial violence.

Rebellion and Colonial Violence

"Les hommes meurent et ils ne sont pas heureux."[32] Amidst the beauty of the Mediterranean landscape, the "truth" of man's temporality stares one out in the face. Despite the abundance of life, the inevitable death lurks "at the corner." This discovery, following the death of his beloved sister/mistress, led the young king Caligula, to the equally disturbing realization that life was meaningless. "[Seul] le Trésor a de l'importance [...] la vie humaine n'en a pas" (*Théatre* 1962, 22), and that, of vital importance, is one's response to such a discovery. "Qui le reconnaît conquiert sa liberté" (ibid., 25). Camus's *Lettres à un ami allemand* (1944), a collection of four articles (letters) written during the war (when he was himself actively involved in the underground Resistance movement) reads as an indictment against Caligula's "logic." The German friend is most likely a fictitious one. The choice indicates probably the influence of German thinkers such as Nietzsche on him, but more certainly his own mistrust regarding German post-Nietzscheans such as Karl Juergens, Rosemberg, whose pessimism or "cult of violence" had been instrumental in the development of Nazi ideology.

As I have analyzed, Camus did share an initial nihilistic moment, for which he sought and advocated physical pleasure, as sole certainty and choice of life for the lucid mind. Caligula's position forces us to reevaluate what a "logical" response to the absurd could be. The question that needs to be asked is the following: If we start from the notion that the world is absurd, that beyond the physical beauty of the universe, there is only that infinite void ("le vide indéfini"), and that neither God nor any transcendent principle dictates our conduct, how then are we to escape Caligula's conclusion that our actions are morally indifferent, and that everything is therefore permitted? Beyond hedonism, Camus offered no answer at the time. He was still groping. His obvious distaste for Caligula's "logic" marks yet again his renunciation of the absurd as a global philosophy. As he tells the German friend:

> Vous admettiez assez l'injustice de notre condition pour vous résoudre à y ajouter, tandis qu'il m'apparaissait au contraire que l'homme devait affirmer la justice pour lutter contre l'injustice éternelle, créer un bonheur pour protester contre l'univers du malheur. Parceque vous avez fait de votre désespoir une ivresse, parceque vous vous en êtes délivrés en principe, vous avez accepté de détruire les oeuvres de l'homme et de lutter contre lui pour achever sa misère essentielle. Et moi, refusant d'admettre ce désespoir et ce monde torturé, je voulais seulement que les hommes

retrouvent leur solidarité pour entrer en lutte contre leur destin révoltant. Pour tout dire, vous avez choisi l'injustice. Vous vous êtes mis avec les dieux. Votre logique n'était qu'apparente. J'ai choisi la justice au contraire, pour rester fidèle à la terre. Je continue à croire que ce monde n'a pas de sens supérieur. Mais je sais que quelquechose en lui a du sens et c'est l'homme, parcequ'il est le seul à exiger d'en avoir.[33]

[You admit sufficiently to the injustice of our condition to bring yourself to add to it, whereas it seemed to me, on the contrary, that man ought to affirm justice in order to fight eternal injustice, create happiness in order to protest against this universe of misfortune. Because you have turned your despair into an ecstacy, because you have delivered yourself from this despair by setting it up as a principle, you have consented to destroying the work of man, and to fighting man to end his fundamental misery. And I, refusing to accept this despair and this tortured world, only wanted men to discover their solidarity in order to fight their appalling destiny. To sum up, you have chosen injustice. You have sided with the gods. Your logic was only apparent. I, on the contrary, opted for justice, in order to remain faithful to the earth. I continue to believe that this world has no meaning beyond itself. But I know that something in it has meaning, and it is Man, because he [Man] is the only one to insist on meaning.]

Camus's proclaimed "faithfulness" springs therefore from the midst of the absurd as a force opposing the absurd. "Ce quelque chose qui a du sens" in the absurd universe is identified as "man" and his desire for happiness and friendship and justice. Most of the letters consists in defining these various terms. Man, for Camus, is "that force which opposes tyrants and gods; in other words, the fighter for freedom and the creator of meaning" (Braun 1974, 76). Happiness, of which friendship is a part, is but that harmonious communion between man and nature, the nuptials, illustrated in *Noces*. Justice is the wish to remove *natural* and *social obstacles* that stand in the way of man's happiness. Herein lies the basis of Camus's unswerving ideal reasserted time and again against "all glorification of hate and violence [and] all power ideologies" (ibid.). It is against this background that his stand against nationalism, whether French, German or Algerian, has been viewed. The paradigmatic nature of the opposition France/Germany is made obvious, in the preface to the *Letters*; we are reminded that the contrast posited is not so much between France and Germany, as between all fascist threats and free men in all camps. Camus specifies that he loves his country too much to be a nationalist. Anti-nationalism is erected, so to say as a first condition—a negative condition I would say—for the emergence of a human order, a human world devoid of all nationalistic barriers. This human world would signal "the end of national egotism, . . . the end of national short-sightedness that prevents nations from seeing any light beyond their boundaries" (ibid.).

Camus's invocation of Rebellion as the possibility of overcoming despair, but which ultimately reads as his own indictment against ideologically based, contemporary violence, takes on a peculiar twist, when looked at closely, within the Algerian colonial setting. As Willhoite indicated, Camus sought persistently to interpret and comment upon events in the Franco-Algerian crises, "from the distinctive standpoint of *his understanding of true rebellion*" (1968, 165). From this standpoint, it would seem the colonized Arabs in resorting to terrorism as a revolutionary means, had overstepped the boundaries "respected by the genuine rebel." The Arab "dream of eradicating the existence of the French in Algeria; to deny the presence of a million Frenchmen, in Camus's eyes . . . exceed[s] the limits of justifiable rebellion" (Quillot, "Albert Camus's Algeria" 1962, 44). Camus's concern for the plight of Frenchmen in Algeria is understandable. The genesis of this French presence on the Algerian soil need not detain us further (cf. chapter 1).

More controversial, however, is Camus's disclaimer of the Arab rebels. What, one may ask, is that "justifiable rebellion" in a politically and economically determined situation as that of colonialism (keeping in mind Algeria's added peculiarity as a "colonie de peuplement")? One problem confronting us here is the ultimate [i.e., Camus's] definition of Rebellion. Indeed, what is Rebellion? This query may seem rather inconsistent with foregone statements. *L'Homme Révolté*, Camus's treatise on Revolt/Rebellion, inferring from the opening pages, is an attempt to understand those forms of contemporary violence and inhumanity which have an ideological basis and which proclaim in apparent contradiction of their deeds, "that human well-being is their goal." The book begins by emphasizing the virtues of revolt and ends with pleas for moderation and gradual political reforms. If indeed this strikes one as obviously inconsistent, it is mainly because of the lack of clarity concerning the nature of revolt itself. Revolt, as analyzed previously, is man's response to the absurd. In other words, it is a metaphysical concept and a philosophical attitude. In the closing pages of the book, however, revolt has come to mean refusal to accept political extremism and the Marxist interpretation of history, as well as the corollary that historical change was the ultimate reality; in which case revolt becomes something quite different—a brand of political philosophy. Similar equivocation exists regarding the absurd, since it reads both as a metaphysical experience and a social experience. This ambivalence in the case of the absurd does not present any serious consequence, since both categories of the experience are valid. Revolt, however, as a political concept becomes problematic. Revolt as a political phenomenon is no longer a response to a universal human condition, but rebellion against ideology, a response to a particular historical situation. In a way, *l'Homme révolté* can be read as an elaboration on *Lettres à un ami allemand*, repudiates Caligula's murderous logic, where nihilism, and also ideology lead to suicide and murder, or to what Brau calls, "a suicidal-murderous apocalypse of the Hitlerian kind" (1979, 115).

With the decay of belief in transcendent limitations, an urgent task for man as Camus sees it is that of finding or establishing a modern basis for ethics. In the absence of any transcendent ground, these ethics must be rooted in human experience. "Values" and "measure" are two vital notions here. The rebel by his very act invokes a value. The rebel's gesture, Camus says,

> s'appuie, [...] sur le refus catégorique d'une intruision jugée intolérable et sur la certitude confuse d'un bon droit, plus exactement l'impression, chez le révolté, qu'il est 'en bon droit de... La révolte ne va pas sans le sentiment d'avoir soi-même, en quelque façon, et quelque part, raison. [...] Il affirme, en même temps que la frontière, tout ce qu'il soupçonne et veut préserver en deçà de la frontière. Il démontre, avec entêtement, qu'il y a en lui quelque chose qui vaut la peine [...].[34]

> [relies {...} on a flat refusal of an intruision deemed intolerable, and on a dim certitude of a justified right, more specifically, the impression that he [the rebel] is right. Revolt does not occur without a feeling that somehow and somewhere one is justified {...} Along with the limit, he affirms everything he suspects and wants to preserve on this side of the limit. He demonstrates, stubbornly, that there is within him something which has value.]

By the same token, the rebel discovers in his act, that the dignity he fights for, the limits he insists must be maintained, are not his solely. They are the common ground for all men of a natural community. "Le mouvement de révolte n'est pas, dans son essence, un mouvement égoïste . . . Le révolté exige sans doute pour lui-même le respect, mais dans la mesure où il s'identifie avec une communauté naturelle" (1951, 29). [In its essence, the movement of revolt is not an egoistic movement . . . The rebel demands respect for himself, no doubt, but to the extent that he identifies with a natural community.] Thus, "in the act of revolt the rebel transcends his own [egotistic interests], and together with the defense of his own dignity, he discovers human solidarity" (Braun 1979, 117). One fundamental difficulty, which the essay never addresses, arises when Camus proceeds from a subjective experience, therefore from a subjective perception of these values to the assertion of their objective validity. Another difficulty is one related to the very basis of these values. If, as Brau asks, "metaphysical foundations of ethics have been discarded, with what right does Camus assert that certain human aspirations can be regarded as ethical to the exclusion of others" (1979, 121)? Indeed, within Camus's own framework, we are at liberty to wonder why dignity, solidarity, fair play must be considered more ethical than, say greed, or the will to power, or André Gide's "ferveur," or any such innate disposition. Faced with the issue, Gide admitted honestly that these values were not ethical but aesthetic. Would this have been Camus's answer if he had faced this question objectively?

The notion of solidarity is yet another intricate part of Camus's thought. This solidarity of all men, friends and foes alike, presupposes a certain universal human nature, "that something peculiar to man." The age old problem of human nature has been formulated with great lucidity. Malraux asks:

> Existe-t-il une donnée sur quoi puisse se fonder la notion d'homme? La notion d'homme, a-t-elle un sens? Autrement dit: Sous les croyances, les mythes, et surtout sous la multiplicité des structures mentales, peut-on isoler une donnée permanente, valable à travers les lieux, valable à travers l'histoire, sur quoi puisse se fonder la notion d'homme?[35]

> [Is there a given fact on which to base the notion of man? Does the notion of man have any meaning? In other words: given all beliefs, myths, and especially the multiplicity of mental structures, can one isolate a permanent truth valid in all places, throughout history on which we could found the notion of man?]

While Sartre, unequivocally insists that there is no *a priori* "nature" or "essence" that defines man, and therefore no pre-existing, non-human criterion through which human acts are measured, Camus upholds that human acts reveal certain innate traits common to all—such as the human demand for coherence. The latter perspective would seem to suggest a certain spirituality, the existence of transcendental values. "Rebellion," Camus would maintain, *is* one affirmation of a "nature common to all men." This nature eludes the world of power. Human nature is, moreover, that which opposes history, the "dogmatic ideologies that deny man's freedom in order to turn him into a tool" in a messianic vision of history. Human nature, says Camus, craves happiness, beauty, and friendship. Aside from these vague generalizations, Camus's concept of human nature remains not only uncertain, but also borders on sentimentality. As Braun points out,

> [t]he author of *The Rebel* sometimes seems to follow the shallow conception of human nature propagated by the anarchists, believing in the intrinsic goodness of man and in salvation by the idea of human brotherhood. Such a doctrine may be soothing and therefore attractive in "times of crises and catastrophes," appealing especially to the slave and the dominated in society, but does not offer a constructive solution to that very state of slavery. (1979, 126)

Indeed, lacking all dialectics, the concept does not envisage nor offer as such an end to the system that perpetuates slavery. Between the slave's present state and his aspirations, there seems to be a perpetual abyss.

It might be interesting to see how much of Camus's conception of human nature opposed to history and ideologies, points yet again to what Archambault[36] and Braun[37] refer to as the "Hellenic sources" of Camus's thought. According to Braun, "human nature," in classical Greek philosophy, was characterized by reason, understood as *logos* or the ability to create an intelligible world out of the chaos of appearances" (1979, 127). "Creating" or imposing order on chaos is one of Camus's underlying ideas, elaborated in "Révolte et art." However, "reason" is for Camus distinguishable from the "intellect." Reason, which often seems interchangeable with "measure," is "not the ability to deduce and argue logically about cause, effect and identity, but rather he ability to discover purpose and a principle of unity in the chain of events, and of imposing them on human affairs" Commenting also on the contradiction in Greek philosophy and the notion of universal brotherhood, Braun remarks: "it seems ironical that in a work advocating universal brotherhood and protesting against the master-slave relationship, Camus should have borrowed one of his main ideas from a civilization that admitted slavery and professed the superiority of Greeks over Barbarians" (ibid.). If the idea of self-restraint is vital to Greek thought, it is only in as far as it legitimizes their superiority over Barbarians, since the latter and slaves were deemed incapable of the "precious virtue of self-restraint, the pride of human nature" (ibid., 128). These—Barbarians and slaves—were ruled by passions, and thus unavoidably fell to a subhuman level.

Let us dare to admit it: Camus's conceptualization of rebellion is fraught with confusion (even keeping in mind that "his approach to philosophical and even political issues is more lyrical than intellectual" [Isaac 1989, 377]). A rebellion contingent upon a kind of universal brotherhood is historically problematic, for the very reason that there is a "human condition," which is not metaphysical, but politically and economically determined. Camus's position on rebellion appears severely limited; the effectiveness of such a rebellion remains questionable, especially, if one considers "world history as little else than the chaotic story of power relations" (Braun 1979, 134). Camus's insistence on Rebellion as a value, is tantamount to imposing an alien framework of abstractions upon unyielding realities.

The imposition of Camus's political philosophy upon a colonial order involves, however, a rational mutation, from the ethical to the aesthetic. Let us recall here the link Camus maintains between "Révolte" and "Art." Faced with both the threat of ideology and that of the absurd, Camus posits an aesthetic theory, whereby creativity becomes a challenge to man's mortal condition, thus opening hedonist principles to exhaust the self quantitatively. The romanesque universe, Camus insists, is not a refuge from reality but a confirmation of the absurd. This universe becomes the *locus* where the artist refuses the real but does not escape it. Within romanesque practice, Camus contends that revolt is stylization, the transfiguration of the "real." It is a form of correction that the artist imposes on the real to give it beauty. "Cette correction, que l'artiste opère par son langage et par une redistribution d'éléments puisés dans le réel, s'appelle le style et donne à l'univers recrée son unité et ses limites" (*L'homme révolté* 1951, 332). Within this optique (art as a means of giving the world its lost beauty), the apolitical representation of the Mediterranean appears as a stylized representation of colonial reality. Camus refutes history and politics as products of the intellect. Yet his own stylization of colonial reality— displacing the Algerian setting outside its colonial political and historical specificities—involves him in an intellectual exercise, for the Mediterranean images are intellectual symbols which reify and objectify experience.

Camus projects "rebellion" into an ahistorical and apolitical context; the two terms "rebel" and "revolutionary" are, however, defined only in relation to historical contexts and political institutions. Examples of rebelliousness and revolutionary movements are all drawn from the Western world. He contends that the bourgeois revolution of 1793 signals the end of rebellion and the beginning of revolutionary movements. This bourgeois revolution was made possible by the French revolution of 1789 (revolt against the Christian God embodied in an absolute monarch), and German romantic ideologies, which together generate a dynamic process manifested in the production of contemporary history and its attendant Nihilism. Contemporary Nihilism manifested in Nazi, Fascist and Communist movements is unique to Western civilization. The latter, Camus views as "producer of history" in contrast to the mystical East (the "Orient"). The problem of revolt seems to take on a precise meaning only within Western thought. "Le problème de la révolte ne semble prendre de sens précis qu'à l'intérieur de la pensée occidentale. . . . Le problème de la révolte n'a [...] de sens qu'à l'intérieur de notre société occidentale" (*L'Homme Révolté* 1951, 33). And this is because, "[l']égalité théorique [qui recouvrirait les] grandes inégalités de fait," is non-existent in "certaines sociétés primitives" ("theoretical equality [which would hide] all the great inequalities, does not exist in some primitive societies") (ibid). Unfortunately, however, Camus does not offer much explanation regarding the meaning of the supposed "theoretical equality." But perhaps one could hazard a guess. If rebellion as Camus advocates, is indeed a stance against Nihilism, it hardly constitutes an effectual weapon against that violence perpetrated by an unjust political and economic structure, i.e., colonialism. Camus, as stated, views politics and history as products of the intellect. The intellect, from his point of view, is one trap into which existentialist thinkers have fallen. By conferring a certain hopefulness upon the Absurd through abstraction, they tended to rationalize away the very experience of the Absurd. Yet Camus's own conceptualization of rebellion, purported to be a reaction against that same experience, falls within a theoretical and abstract system, which is the very theoretical premise he rejects. Through intellectualization condemned in others, he transforms a colonial order into a rational order—by a process of sublimation involving the very rationalism that he theoretically refutes.

L'Homme Révolté takes up the binary order presented in *Noces*, Europe/Mediterranean. Europe is the seat of History, Power and Revolution, while the Mediterranean is that of mystery, innocence and rebellion. The discourse evolves around this dichotomy. The "Mediterranean humanism" is opposed to History, Power, and political Nihilism. It is within this Mediterranean context—presented as an ideological void, outside the religious and political polemics of Western revolutions—that Camus anchors a "metaphysical" rebellion. The Mediterranean context, presented in *Noces* as a cultural vacuum untainted by Western religious and political mythos, ultimately establishes the context for *L'Homme révolté*, where on one hand, colonial conflict is dissimulated—stylized—and on the other hand, Western political Nihilism is transcended in an attempt to harmonize Western ideologies.

Thus, contemporary Nihilism remains in contradiction with Camus's vision of the humanist Mediterranean tradition. Rational tyranny and totalitarian ideologies are direct consequences of Nihilism. Paradoxically, though, if Camus condemns totalitarian ideologies that have been at the root of colonization, he seems oblivious to the specificities of colonial rule in the Mediterranean culture. As Haddour rightly points out, colonized Algeria illustrates what Camus calls the "excesses" of the Western world (1989, 70). But let us remember that Camus's Algeria here is a mythic one of a pre-historic context, and it must remain so for the purpose of the Mediterranean scheme. Within this mythic vision, Algeria is reconstructed as an orderly, but highly simplified world. Unto this mythologized vision of Algeria, Camus projects his anti-Christian and hedonist principles. In so doing, Camus, the artist, in an act of "revolt," driven by a need for coherence ("un besoin de cohérence"), "refait le monde à son compte, [et] tire du désordre naturel une unité satisfaisante pour l'esprit et le coeur" (L'Homme révolté 1951, 316). "Le roman," Camus insists, "fabrique du destin sur mesure" (ibid., 319). [The artist refashions the world in his own way, and draws from natural disorder a unity that is satisfying for the mind and heart. The novel fabricates a destiny that suits it perfectly.] The work of art involves the artist, by necessity, in myth-making. As a manufactured universe, Algeria fulfills that exigency for unity. In a highly sublimated vision of Algeria "[une Algérie] hors de l'histoire, à l'état pur" (ibid), Camus thus achieved a philosophical unity and coherence which eluded him in the politics and history of Europe.

Notes

1. Messali was the founder of the Etoile Nord Africaine, the earliest nationalist group to demand political independence for Algeria.

2. For more details of the Sétif massacre, see David G. Gordon, *The Passing of French Algeria* (London: Oxford University Press, 1968), 53–54. The number of Moslems killed during the clash remains a matter of dispute. What is crucial to us here, is not so much the number, as the fact that the event did occur at all, and the spirit of repression underlying it.

3. See Camus's essay "Hungary" in *Resistance, Rebellion, and Death* (New York: Alfred A.Knoff), 157–171.

4. Fred H. Willhoite, *Beyond Nihilism: Albert Camus's Contribution to Political Thought* (Baton Rouge: Louisiana University Press, 1968), 162.

5. See also, "Preface" to Frantz Fanon, *The Wretched of the Earth*, "[The] violence [of the colonized] is ours, which turns back on itself and rends them [...] Read Fanon: you will learn how, in the period of their helplessness, their mad impulse to murder is the expression of the natives' collective unconscious" (18). A word of caution is called for here: comparing Sartre's position on Algeria to that of Camus is perhaps tantamount to the proverbial comparison between apples and oranges. That woould be a simplistic and reductionist endeavor. One could even argue that although Sartre's stand seems more laudable, given his emotive—and perhaps physical—distance from the scene, and in the comfort of the Hexagone, such a position is much easier to maintain.

6. Three years later (and months after Camus's death), the statement will be taken up by Jules Roy, a friend and admirer of Camus's work. In *La Guerre d'Algérie* published in 1960 while the Algerian war of Liberation was at its peak, Roy remarks, speaking directly to his friend: "Pour moi, j'ignore, Camus, si je suis comme toi capable de placer ma mère au-dessus de la justice. Comment oserais-je parler de cela? Ta mère vit encore tandis que la mienne. . . . Il ne s'agit pas de préférer sa mère à la justice. Il s'agit d'aimer la justice autant que sa mère. Ce que je sais seulement, c'est qu'au-dessus de la justice, je placerai toujours le royaume de Dieu où les enfants légitimes n'ont pas forcément rang sur les bâtards."
("As for me, I do not know if I am capable, as you are, of placing my mother above justice. How could I? Your mother is still alive while mine. . . . It is not a question of preferring one's mother above justice. It is a question of loving justice as much as one's mother. What I know is that above justice, I would always place the kingdom of God where the legitimate children are not necessarily above the bastards." My translation.) Quoted by O'Connell 16–17. This passage, while expressing Roy's esteem and reverence for the memory of Camus, also registers a mild indictment of Camus's position inferred from the replique.

7. Philip Thody, 1961 *Albert Camus, 1913–1960* (London: Hamish Hamilton, 1961), 3.

8. *L'Ecole d'Alger* reflects a sensibility rather than a rigourous mouvement or school. This sensibility, as I shall insist, reflects the colonial malaise of the Pieds-noirs liberals, caught in cultural and political ambiguities.

9. M. Eliade, *Aspects du mythe* (Paris: Gallimard, 1963), 15, quoted by Haddour "Camus: The Other as an Outsider in a Univocal Discourse" (Ph.D. diss., The University of Sussex, 1989), 23-24.

10. Amrouche, Jean. "L'Éternel Jugurtha. Propositions sur le génie africain," *Arche* No. 13 (1946): 90.

11. Jules Roy, *Etranger à mes frères* (Paris: Stock, 1982), 97. "Pour Camus, Amrouche était un esprit faux, un serpent qui avait profité de la culture française et qui se permettait de travailler contre la France, pour l'indépendance de l'Algérie. [For Camus, Amrouche was a fake, a snake who

had taken advantage of the French culture and was working against France, for Algerian independence.]"

12. "Always taking on the face of the other, miming to perfection the other's language and customs."

13. J. Amrouche, "Contre le désespoir," *Etudes Méditerranéennes* (June 1963): 11-114, quoted by David G. Gordon, *The passing of French Algeria* 168.

14. It is rather surprising that the influence of Audisio (*Jeunesse de la Méditerranée*) and that of Jean Grenier (*Inspirations Méditerranéennes*), upon Camus, have been mostly overlooked by critics. It is my intention here to highlight these two influences.

15. Gabriel Audisio, *Sel de la mer* (Paris: Gallimard, 1936), 213.

16. Gabriel Audisio, *Jeunesse de la Méditerranée* (Paris: Gallimard, 1935), 78.

17. F. Leroy, "Méditerranée," *Revue de la Méditerranée* 40 (1950) 645, quoted by Haddour "Camus: The Other as an Outsider in a Univocal Discourse" (Ph.D. diss., The University of Sussex, 1989), 37.

18. "Tête d'Afrique ou le génie de l'Afrique du Nord," *Cahiers du Sud* 310 (1951): 438.

19. Translation is from Albert Camus, *Lyrical Essays* edited and with notes by Philip Thody, translated by Ellen Conroy Kennedy (New York: Alfred A. Knopf, 1968), 189–190.

20. Lev Braun, *Witness of Decline, Albert Camus: Moralist of the Absurd* (Associated University Presses, Inc., 1974), 34.

21. Albert Camus, *Correspondances*, 1938, quoted by Susan Tarrow *Exile from the Kingdom: A Political Rereading of Albert Camus* (The University of Alabama Press, 1985), 16.

22. I am aware of the widespread opinion that Camus was in actual fact expelled from the Communist Party. Was he really? According to Quilliot, "la question est parfaitement oiseuse. Il était de tradition au parti comuniste qu'un militant resposable qui l'abandonnait en fût aussitôt exclu: simple question de procédure" (Quilliot, "Politique et Culture Méditerranéennes," *Essais*, 1316). Camus's dismissal, if indeed such is a case, may have coincided with his own growing disinterest with the party. In which case it is worth probing the cause of this disinclination.

23. Emmanuel Sivan, *Communism and Nationalism in Algeria, 1920-1962*. Thesis presented at the Hebrew University of Jerusalem. Quoted by Patrick McCarthy in *Camus, a Critical Study*, 55.

24. Anne Durand, *Le Cas Albert Camus* (Paris: n.p., 1961), 41.

25. Jean Grenier, *Albert Camus* (Paris: Gallimard, 1968), 38.

26. Jean Pélégri, "L'Exil et le Royaume," *Simoun* 31 (1960): 47.

27. Jean Grenier, *Inspirations Méditerranéennes* (Paris: Gallimard, 1961), 12.

28. A. Camus, "Préface" to *Les Iles* (Paris: Gallimard, 1959), 10.

29. M. B. Chavannes, "Albert Camus. L'origine de son incroyance," *Cahiers religieux d'Afrique du Nord* 9 (Oct.–Dec. 1958): 310.

30. Nathan A. Scott, *Albert Camus* (New York: Hilary House Publishers, 1969), 23.

31. D. Leconte, *Les Pieds-noirs* (Paris: Seuil, 1980) 159. Quoted by Haddour 1989, 67.

32. Albert Camus, *Théâtre, Récits, Nouvelles*, edited with Introduction and Notes by Roger Quilliot (Paris: Gallimard, 1962), 16.

33. Albert Camus, *Lettres à un ami allemand* (Paris: Gallimard, 1945), 72.

34. Albert Camus, *L'Homme Révolté* (Paris: Gallimard, 1951), 25.

35. A. Malraux, *Les Noyers de l'Altenburg* (Paris: Gallimard, 1948) 130, 146, 150. Quoted by Lev Brau, 125.

36. See P. Archambault, *Camus's Hellenic Sources* (Chapel Hill: The University of North Carolina Press, 1972).

37. This portion of my reading owes much to Braun's insightful analysis of the Greek influence on Camus's thoughts. See "Revolt and values," in *Witness*, 107–34.

Chapter 3

Camus, Mammeri, Feraoun and *L'Etranger* : Landscapes of the Absurd and Colonial Landscapes

Vous pouvez dormir, monsieur le juge: il est bon après tout que le sommeil du juste suive le sommeil de la justice. Mais que m'importe à moi (et aux autres) le sommeil d'une nuit . . . , ou d'un jour? Qu'importe même le sommeil de tout un an: il n'est que la mort dont on ne s'éveille pas. (Mammeri, *Le Sommeil du juste*)

[You may sleep on, honorable judge: it is appropriate, after all, that the slumber of the just follows the slumber of justice. What does the slumber of one night. . ., or one day matter to me (and to others)? What does even the slumber of one whole year matter: it is only death from which one does not wake up.]

Introduction

Stephen D. Ross's essay, *Literature and Philosophy: An Analysis of the Philosophical Novel*, "puzzles" over how so many readers confront Camus's *L'Etranger* "without reacting *morally* to the killing of the Arab, or to the various troubling aspects of Meursault's character."[1] A retrospective reaction to the reading of *L'Etranger*, it appears, is to ponder that instantaneous—I am tempted to say "unreflected"—sympathy, one feels towards Camus's protagonist, Meursault, who after all does commit murder, a crime that should elicit at least a certain malaise from the reader.[2] The latter is in actual fact cajoled throughout the narrative to commiserate with Meursault. His/her sympathy is cleverly manipulated away from the victim of the crime, the Arab, to the victim of "injustice," Meursault, thereby "killing" the reader's moral response to a homicide. Various elements within Camus's narrative have contributed immensely to this shift in reader reaction. The presentation of Meursault is of an "indifferent" hero or anti-hero, completely detached from the norms of his bourgeois class, so that one cannot by any stretch of the imagination accuse him of sharing in its prejudices. The killing is depicted as an "absurd" occurrence, totally unmotivated, unpremeditated, seemingly to reflect the discrepancy between one's intent and one's act. The narrative focuses on the *non-sequitur* logic of a legal system that charges Meursault with murder, yet condemns him for not weeping at his mother's funeral. A more subtle element, but of great importance to us here, consists in the narrative downplay of the victim of the killing, the Arab, who becomes clearly peripheral to the central issue—especially with the second half of the novel—namely the irrationality of the judicial system. Through a narrative that relegates the Arab outside of its scope, one is able to establish the idea that society condemns in Meursault his lack of moral codes, rather than his crime. The murder thus becomes a "pre-text to the trial, one that shifts the event at the center of the novel to preface the narrative of 'l'étranger'" (Haddour 1989, 86). B. T. Fitch views this shift as a "coup de plume," a technique that dispenses the reader from a "moral" identification with the victim of the crime. "Il s'agit d'éliminer tout ce qui, jusqu'ici, a empêché le lecteur de s'identifier au héros. . . . Et il est nécessaire de permettre au lecteur de se ranger du côté de l'accusé, . . . de voir Meursault en victime et non pas en coupable."[3]

These various components of Camus's narrative, coupled with the authorial voice manifested in various pronouncements about the hero, have allowed for a certain interpretation of the novel. Camus, it appears, did confirm "in a private conversation in 1956," that Meursault is "one of the absurd men whose fuller description is to be found in *Le Mythe de Sisyphe*" (Thody 1961, 37). According to J. Conilh," *L'Etranger* describes the universe of indifference in which the life of the absurd man is played."[4] Sartre's "An Explication of the Stranger" predating and perhaps influencing these various critical positions, borrows a line from Camus's essay, *Le Mythe de Sisyphe*, to identify Meursault as the absurd hero, "who, at certain moments, confronts us in the mirror." According to Sartre, "The stranger [Camus] wants to portrait is precisely one of those terrible innocents who shock society by not accepting the rules of its game" (1962, 110–11). I believe however, that the theological malaise or even the "absurdities" of the French legal system, of which Meursault seems the victim, is concurrent with another type of malaise generated by an inequity, which is much more pertinent to the setting of the novel, namely colonial injustice of which the Arab is victim. What is called into question is the logic of the judicial system that charges Meursault for murder and finally condemns him for not showing filial grief at his mother's death. The entire case for the eventual condemnation is, however, construed by marginalizing the victim of the crime, the Arab from the scene, thus replicating the oppressiveness of a colonial system that relegates the Arab outside its judiciary scope. According to Susan Tarrow, the novel "calls into question many aspects of an oppressive colonial regime" (1985, 66). The judicial system, in pushing the murder to the periphery and conferring a central position to Meursault's lack of social conventions, does seem to "encode colonialist and racist attitudes" (ibid.). Camus's narrative which insists throughout on the protagonist's innocence, shifts the focus to articulate Meursault's own theological malaise, as well as, his helplessness in the face of the absurd trial. The failure to explore fully the political potency generated by the crime makes it difficult to entirely subscribe to the view that the novel is an authorial condemnation of colonialist structures. The dubious and opaque representation of the Arab, a more logical victim, reveals a certain flaw in the plot. The Arabs introduced in the novel are "shadows, silhouettes largely empty of human characteristics" (Holsinger 1986, 73). Camus's *L'Etranger* speaks from a colonial setting, but does not specifically address the colonial situation it exploits. The novel does, in a way, replicate the stereotypical "cluster of colonialist values," but only to point to Meursault's "non-criminal soul." The concept of justice, entirely de-politicized to imply "Justice," in its most abstract formulation, becomes a problem in the novel. Through the prism of the intellect which Camus constantly refutes (cf. chapter 2), he is able to transform a concrete reality into a universal notion of human existence. Camus's presentation of the absurd involves him in a rational exercise, what he condemns as "abstraction," to explain and subsume man's despair in a transcendent vision, an oxymoronic binary of hopeless hopefulness: man's lucidity or, that lucid indifference ("indifférence clairvoyante"). What could indeed have been an authorial condemnation of colonialist structures is presented in a diffuse context; what eventually comes to the forefront are the institutionalized violence of which Meursault stands as victim, as well as the protagonist's absurd destiny. The latter, from all appearances, follows the premises set forth in *Le Mythe de Sisyphe*. Colonial polemics pertinent to the geographical setting of the novel are thus rationalized and presented as metaphysical problems pertinent to Man. Meursault, the "absurd" hero, becomes the universal man *par excellence*; not only is he *aux prises* with a world which is absurd, he is equally a victim of an absurd legal system that charges him for a crime, yet eventually condemns him for a different reason. If Meursault does elicit our sympathy, it is because the story focuses on the very helplessness of the hero confronted with the silence of the universe— with his physical pleasures as sole certainties—and with the Institution (French legal sytem) that sentences him to death. Thus, the narrative registers a constant tension between a cosmic injustice from which the hero suffers and an equally absurd moral and legal system.

However, as I shall point out, the second part of the novel, the trial of Meursault, which brings to the fore the political problems attendant to the French colonial occupation of North Africa, undermines Camus's universalizing point of view espoused by the novel. The peripheral issue, that of the murdered Arab, unwrites the very universalist rhetoric of the novel. What is left unsaid—that which is marginalized— becomes a pointer to a pernicious political system. The first part of this chapter provides an exploration of the various factors within Camus's narrative—especially the psychological portrait of Meursault, and his peculiar mistrial which by necessity underwrite him as an absurd hero. The relegation of the Arab figure to the periphery determines Camus's presentation of the absurd. The second part of the chapter is an attempt to "deflate" the absurdist landscapes against which the Camusian hero has so far been read. I propose to effect the latter through an intertextual dialogue between Camus's text and that of two North-African writers Mouloud Mammeri and Mouloud Feraoun, whose appropriation of the themes of "l'étranger" and "le monde du procès" provides counter-readings to Camus's novel. The different fields of vision presented by these writers divulge the colonial malaise presented by Camus as a universalist problematic. I will insist here again that Camus's universalist vision is tangential to *L'Ecole d'Alger*'s proposal to assimilate the Other into a humanist empire. This move which confers upon the Indigenes, the place of "l'étranger" is a process of "desertification" or a *mise en sac* of the cultural and social panorama of the colonized. The writings of Mammeri and Feraoun—both advocates of assimilation, both sharing the ideological settings of *L'Ecole d'Alger*—reveal the contradiction inherent in the colonial laws. These, while offering the illusory promises of assimilation, worked to dispossess the colonized both materially and spiritually.

The Landscapes of the Absurd

'God is dead,' proclaims Nietzsche's madman, and we have killed him. The Christian God is no longer believable. Yet this cosmic deed remains light years away from being understood. It is a frightful, portentous event. For when the belief in God evaporates, the entire structure of Western beliefs must come tumbling down. Is this not a cataclysmic event? Does it not threaten to wrench from the West the root structure of the meaningful drama by which we live? But we do not yet know that we no longer believe. We still go through the rituals, say the right words on the right occasions, and act as if our life had cosmic significance. But our belief lacks coherence and substance, its shell is cracking, and our civilization totters on the brink of the cataclysm.[5]

This vision of the Western world, expressed by Nietzsche, echoes the "most elusive and yet profound resonances" of human experiences. "Nietzsche did not murder God, writes Camus. He found out that he was already dead in the soul of his time" and that men through various hypocritical stratagems were camouflaging from themselves this devastating truth" (Willhoite 1968, 106). The reality of God's "death" was, however, beginning to "gnaw at the vitals of the Western civilization like a cancer in the body of politic" (Sprintzen 1988, 14). Human life from then on becomes a mere mimic-ritual lacking all coherence. The emerging legacy of Nihilism is a logical one. It is the systematic belief in nothing. With the collapse of the religious tenets, morality loses its foundation; everything is permitted, but nothing makes any difference. "Every thing is permitted" means the law of force, power, and efficiency (ibid.). From Nihilism to Nazism is only a matter of time.

The 19th-century pessimism finds prophetic fulfillment on the political and intellectual scene of 20th-century Europe. "It is a scene of cynicism and despair witnessed by a generation of men born at the beginning of the First World War who had reached [adulthood] just as Hitler was seizing power and the first revolutionary trials were taking place" (Camus, *Speech of Acceptance of the Nobel Prize* 1958, x). The First World War catastrophes in human and material loss compounded by psychological trauma of survivors served to create an atmosphere of general malaise to which the French intellectual youth gave expression one way or the other. "The experience of an entire generation sentenced to death in the prime of life—like Camus himself smitten with tuberculosis—constituted the perfect absurd situation, to which they responded with an equally desperate lust for life" (Braun 1974, 33). The sense of loss and despair found articulation in prewar French literature. Both Dada and the surrealist movements which appear on the surface as "unruly youthful pranks" (ibid.) exhibit deep symptoms of discontent. The scene below is emblematic of an attendant loss of coherence:

La scène était dans la cave, et toutes les lumières éteintes [...] Il montait par une trappe des gémissements. Un farceur, caché derrière une armoire, injuriait les personnalités présentes [...] André Breton croquait des allumettes, Ribemont-Dessaignes criait à chaque instant: "il pleut sur un crâne." Aragon miaulait [...] Un jeune Dada déposait des bouquets de fleurs aux pieds d'un manequin de couturière [...] pendant que deux autres dansaient avec des glous-sements de jeunes ours, ou, dans un sac, avec un tuyau sur la tête, se dandinaient.[6]

[The scene was in a cave, and all lights were turned off {...} Moans escaped through the trap. A comedian, hidden behind a wardrobe, was hurling insults at those present {...} Andre Breton bit into match sticks, Ribemont-Dessaignes was yelling at each instant: "it is raining on a skull." Aragon was miaowing {...} A young dada was placing bouquets of flowers at the feet of a mannequin {...} while two others were dancing around chortling like young bears, or paraded in a sack with a tube on the head.]

The disjointed and the incongruous, apparent in this scene, echo the absurd sensibility which pervades all serious literature of the period. This is presented under various garbs and cloaks. Malraux's *Le Temps du Mépris* (1935) and Sartre's *Le Mur* (1939), to cite just two, portray the mood in the form of man sentenced to death awaiting execution, an apt symbol for a trapped generation. Stressed in these two works and countless others is the encounter of healthy flesh with death imposed from outside—a slow, inescapable death closing in on the victim at the height of his vigor. Another and most prevalent theme is that of the stranger. "The alienation of man from himself and his surroundings" (Braun 1974, 34), is illustrated by Sartre's *La Nausée* (1938) wherein the hero, Roquentin, finds himself hunted down by the opacity of things. The general ambiance of malaise expressed in these various works provided a ready context for Camus's works, and their subsequent interpretation.

Camus, "entering the intellectual and political life of France in the dark years preceding the Second World War," naturally inherited the prevalent disposition. Perhaps also, his own brush with death early in his life gave him an outlook that predisposed him towards the general mood of the period. The threat of death enhanced in him a passion for life mixed with despair—the double tension which characterizes the feeling of absurdity. It is thus, basically from his own experience—coupled with a more global unease—that Camus extrapolates the feeling of absurd as inherent in human condition. Absurdity as Camus explains later, stems from a discrepancy. What is absurd is neither the universe nor man, but the confrontation of the two. Man's demand for an ordered, meaningful existence, and the eternal indifference of the world, together generate our experience of the absurd.

Not surprisingly, it seems, Camus's works have widely been read teleologically to fit into the author's expositions on the absurd. This sentiment expounded more fully in *Le Mythe de Sisyphe* provides, according to Maquet, "the key to *The Stranger*" (1955, 53). The novel is said to illustrate a mood of estrangement (Lewis 1959, 203), a person's "complete lack of relatedness to other human beings."[7] This assessment regarding the hero's "unrelatedness" to others is, however, not entirely true. Meursault relates in a very natural way to a number of individuals, among whom are Céleste, Masson and mostly, Raymond, whose friendship he accepts without question, and despite "public opinion." Marie once called him "bizarre," but this was due to Meursault's unconventional views on marriage and love. In this section I shall explore the various traits of the character of Meursault that have led to the quasi-unanimous view of the personage as illustrating the absurdist hero. I would like to submit, eventually, the thesis that the presentation of Meursault as a "figure representing man's metaphysical status, as an outsider, a being who does not feel he belongs . . . to the world in which he has been placed" (Cruisckshank 1959, 166) is sustained only through a suppression of other elements of the narrative, which are tangential to the colonial setting. Of equal importance also is the fact that various elements detract from the portrait of Meursault as an absurd character.

I believe my reading will reflect the tension created by this pole of disjunction. Until the near end of his life, Meursault does not really experience that awakening of consciousness, the necessary prelude to man's confrontation with an indifferent world. Neither does he lose the habitual décor of his life, which might precipitate such a consciousness. It is interesting however that the life of the hero up to a point, seems to fit into the mold of absurd orthodoxy. He presents, to borrow Maquet's words, "this singular case of a conscious mind lulled to sleep but linked with a behavior that supposes a wide-awake state" (1955, 53). My reading of *L'Etranger* in this section will, I believe, substantiate my thesis that the presentation of Meursault so as to fit the slot of the absurd hero detracts from an important thematic of the novel, namely the overriding indictment of the judicial system and its difficulty in establishing Meursault's guilt, a situation which clearly puts into question his subsequent death sentence.

Sartre's summary of the novel mimics the laconic telegram Meursault receives at the beginning of the story, and reads as follows: "Meursault buries his mother, takes a mistress, and commits a crime" ("An Explication" 1962, 115). However, let's fill in a few details. In the opening scene of *L'Etranger*, Meursault is notified of his mother's death. The telegram reads: "Mère décédée. Enterrement demain."[8] [Mother deceased. Funeral tomorrow.[9]] Meursault's immediate reaction is interesting as it registers, first, the irreality of time ("Cela ne veut rien dire. C'est peut-être hier.") (1942, 1), and second, the inconvenience or resistance to the disruption incurred by Mother's death. Nevertheless, Meursault travels to the Home for the Aged where he had placed her three years earlier. At the funeral, we are made to understand that there is something not quite right when he refuses to view his mother's body, smokes, and accepts an offer of "Café au lait." To compound this unease, Meursault also is shown at the beach a day after the funeral, where a chance encounter with an old female acquaintance, Marie, marks the beginning of an affair. Shortly after, Meursault is also drawn into the dealings of his floor neighbor, Raymond. He then becomes the involuntary participant in a physical confrontation between a group of Arabs and Raymond. At a later stage, Meursault, seemingly blinded by the sun, pulls a trigger and kills one of the Arabs. The initial act of pulling the trigger is presented as a reflex against the excessive heat. -Il m'a semblé que le ciel s'ouvrait sur toute son étendue pour laisser pleuvoir du feu. Tout mon être s'est tendu et j'ai crispé ma main sur le revolver. La gâchette a cédé" (1942, 95) [It seemed to me as if the sky split open from one end to the other to rain down fire. My whole being tensed and I squeezed my hand around the revolver. The trigger gave. (1989, 59)]. Meursault proceeds, however, to fire four more shots into the dead body ("Alors, j'ai tiré encore quatre fois sur un corps inerte..." [ibid.] [Then I fired four more times at the motionless body]), apparently to assume responsibility for an act he had no control over initially. Underscoring also the absurdity of the protagonist's drama is his gratuitous involvement in the conflict and the equally gratuitous killing of the Arab.

The second part of the novel relates Meursault's trial and his subsequent death sentence. While waiting for his execution he is offered the consolation of a possible reconciliation with God, which he refuses, preferring to savor fully the short time he has left. Of importance is the metamorphosis within the character of the protagonist during the second half of the novel. The killing of the Arab, strategically placed at the center of the story, underscores its own importance within the narrative. It is the one event that binds together the disconnected succession of moments in Meursault's earlier life. It allows (through the trial) for an ordered reconstruction of the past, making it accessible for appraisal and judgment, and possible condemnation. Meursault's life which is presented to us in the first part as juxtaposed instants, seemingly without continuity, is reconstituted in the second part of the novel as a logical whole gathered together and organized by the working of reason and the "power of words." Part Two of the novel is the rewriting of Part One: As the French legal system (the court) reconstructs his life, in order to establish criminal motives, Meursault, as a spectator, watches his life unfold on the screen of the French legal apparatus. Within the confinement of the prison walls, Meursault is forced to evaluate for the first time his relationship with the world. *L'Etranger* can thus be seen as a novel of development in which the protagonist moves from a passive spectator of the first part of the story to a conscious awareness of his own system of values. Noyer-Weidner correctly points out the discrepancy between the two parts of the novel which Sartre's analysis ignores. In his study of the narrative styles of *L'Etranger*, Noyer-Weidner points to a first style of the narrative, which translates what Sartre terms "the obsession with silence" (1962, 115). If Sartre however fails to see in such "haunting silence" a certain inability on the part of the hero to grasp conceptually his reality, Noyer-Weidner succinctly demonstrates that the first section of the novel, up to the killing of the Arab, depicts in its raw form, "a lived reality which cannot be encapsulated in concepts"; while the second half of the novel falls within a systematic "discourse" which underscores a certain "theatricality" or falsehood of social conventions.

Much has been made of "l'âme clairvoyante de Meursault" who records his life in a diary.[10] I wish to dismiss from the onset the idea of Meursault as consciously "clairvoyant" and by implication, a consciously absurd hero. The absurd hero emerges only towards the end of his life when he opens up to "that tender indifference of the world." Until then, his life followed a pattern of quasi-total indifference to social norms.

In reading *L'Etranger*, one tends to overlook the two distinct personalities assumed by Camus's protagonist. The Meursault of the first part of the novel and the Meursault we see in the second part are two different characters. The protagonist in the early part of the novel is very much akin to the "barbarians" described in Camus's *Noces*. "Like the Cagayous, he lives on the surface of life" (Haddour 1989, 80). Camus, it seems, has created in his personage, the ordinary man *par excellence*, with no pretension or ambition, interested simply in a physical existence. The first part of the novel thus portrays the hero, indifferent to social conventions, restrictions and taboos. The only pleasures he acknowledges are purely sensual, derived from such simple things as the color of the bay, the embrace of the cool air as a relief from the burning sun, or the sweep of the sea waves over his body. One peculiarity of these pleasures is that they are entirely rooted in the present. As one reader puts it,

> Meursault lives entirely for what he is feeling *now*; he does not remember what he felt yesterday, nor does he anticipate what he will feel tomorrow. His life is a succession of unrelated instants, valuable in themselves, but losing all value when they are over. Not looking backwards, he cannot know remorse. Not looking forward, he cannot know hope. These words are to him empty generalities. (Masters 1974, 23)

Meursault appears then as a stranger to a society that places great and equal value upon its past, present, and future, firmly convinced that the three are inevitably linked. Against the conformist bourgeois society whose existence depends upon everyone's concession to its codes and rituals, Meursault who, according to his creator, "does not play the game," is a threat, and as such must be destroyed. Years after the publication of *L'Etranger*, Camus (in a preface to an English-language edition of the book) affirmed that:

> The hero of the book is condemned because he doesn't play the game. In this sense he is a stranger to the society in which he lives; he drifts in the margin, in the suburb of private, solitary, sensual life [...] If you ask yourself in what way Meursault doesn't play the game, the answer is simple: he refuses to lie.[11]

To say that Meursault refuses to play the game presupposes a certain awareness which, in my estimation, is lacking in the hero. Meursault, as I have stated, lives in a kind of rousseauiste pre-civilized realm, entirely detached from such notions as norms, rules, and even "truth," so that whatever perception of things and people he has at the time is itself, detached from any ethical presupposition. Meursault, totally given to a life of the physical senses, seems devoid of that intellectual sophistication necessary to link, or effect any causality between, past present and future. Susan Tarrow sees this as "an intellectual confusion . . . stem[ming] from the limits of his education" (1985, 68). Far from being a moralist, he is simply at home with the physical setting of Algiers. Contrary to Sartre's reading, Meursault's consciousness of the absurd emerges with the killing of the Arab. Meursault becomes then, an "intelligent," articulate being. He "develops from ["total indifference and apathy" and], from an acquiescent figure . . . to a combatant who claims the right to be different" (ibid., 66).

What triggers this awakening is the absurdity of the system which denies his hedonistic mode of life, his right to enjoy his human "nature." This leads to the tension, clearly an antagonistic confrontation between two philosophies: his hedonism and the Catholic moral tenets upon which are predicated French societal norms. It could be inferred that for the judges who condemn him, Meursault is primarily an anti-Christ, having rejected both the Christian eschatology and the Christian God, for which both the priest and the judicial system stand as representatives. Meursault's description of the priest in prison, the evangelist of the Lord as a dead corpse, is significant. As Tarrow notes, "the prison chaplain embodies exactly what Meursault rejects: a nonphysical relationship with the world and with human beings, a passive submission to the injustices of God and society, and a dogmatic faith in a better life in the future" (1985, 89). The novel does put into question the divine authority invested in the laws of the Old Testament—the very laws which shape societal moral codes. We may thus say that in a way, it "constitutes an attack on the accepted norms of bourgeois society" (ibid., 66), for which Meursault presents an anomaly. His confrontation with the Institution of law implicates him by necessity in a confrontation with the divine law. The latter confrontation is given materiality through the trial. Inevitably then, the death sentence finds its equation within God's condemnation of man to death. To Camus, both "death sentences" amount to one and same absurdity. From the moment the two "injustices" coalesce, it seems that Meursault's guilt itself becomes that of Man, the universal.

Meursault is no more guilty than his judges. The latter, assuming a quasi-divine authority, may deny Meursault his mode of life, and may condemn him to death. However, the "privileges" of the judges are relativised by the absurd, since these privileges will be eventually denied by death. Such an inevitable end undermines the very position of the judges themselves. The institution condemns Meursault for not weeping at his mother's death, seeing in this failure his refusal to abide by the conventions of social existence. Meursault, who at the beginning perhaps intuitively perceives the futility of mourning the dead, comes at the close of the novel to a full consciousness that his own intuition had been right all along. With it comes the awareness of the plight of the judges themselves. The social conventions which they so tenaciously defend will not protect them from the inevitable death penalty awaiting man.

> Du fond de mon avenir, pendant toute cette vie absurde que j'avais menée, un souffle obscur remontait vers moi à travers des années qui n'étaient pas encore venues et ce souffle égalisait sur mon passage tout ce qu'on me proposait alors dans les années pas plus réelles que je vivais. Que m'importaient la mort des autres, l'amour d'une mère, que m'importaient son Dieu, les vies qu'on choisit, les destins qu'on élit, puisqu'un seul destin devait m'élire moi-même et avec moi des milliards de privilégiés qui, comme lui, se disaient mes

frères. Comprenait-il donc? Tout le monde était privilégié. Il n'y avait que des privilégiés. Les autres aussi, on les condamnerait un jour. Lui aussi, on le condamnerait. Qu'importait si, accusé de meurtre, il était exécuté pour n'avoir pas pleuré à l'enterrement de sa mère? (1942, 127)

[Throughout the whole absurd life I'd lived, a dark wind had been rising toward me from somewhere deep in my future, across years that were still to come, and as it passed, this wind leveled whatever was offered to me at the time, in years no more real than the ones I was living. What did other people's deaths or a mother's love matter to me; or what did his God or the lives people choose or the fate they think they elect matter to me when we are all elected by the same fate, me and billions of privileged people like him who also called themselves my brothers? Couldn't he see, couldn't he see that? Everybody was privileged. There were only privileged people. The others would all be condemned one day. And he would be condemned too. What would it matter if he were accused of murder and then executed because he didn't cry at his mother's funeral? (1989, 121)]

Meursault's outburst and introspection prior to his death, points to the "leveling" of all destinies in an absurd world. *L'Etranger* thus illustrates not only the absurd destiny of Meursault alone, but that of humanity in general. It articulates also the tension between a nihilistic vision and ethical demands. Meursault is presented as a man with an "achromatic vision," whereby he views the whole conventional moral apparatus as a kind of "senseless rigmarole with no basis in reality" (Olafson 1967, 17).

Meursault stands, indeed, outside the whole moral words, in a peculiar state described as "innocence." The trial becomes all the more incongruous in the light of the hero's acclaimed innocence, since he apparently does not recognize the moral framework within which he is being tried. The novel, thus, dramatizes, on one hand, what Camus calls Meursault's "innocence," and on the other hand, society's guilt in its critical misjudgment of the case. Both positions point yet again, to the difficutlies of establishing the basis for guilt in a world that affords no transcendental sanction for human judgments of right or wrong. It is however difficult to imagine how what is clearly a nihilistic attitude towards all values, can generate a positive ethic of human fraternity. Also, Meursault's predicament purported to be universal, is presented here selectively, the universality restricted to the Western male, represented here by Meursault. The selectiveness of Camus's cast forms the basis of what I alluded to earlier as a certain *manipulativeness* of reader-response, and reinforces the "theatricality" of

Camus's presentation that conceals another reality, what Pierre Nora has summed up as a sublimation of concrete reality. I shall read the theme of the "absurd" that pervades the narrative as a "colonial farce" predicated upon a peculiar *mise en scène* that excludes the colonized, here the Arab both before and after the killing, from the discursive field. The marginal-ization of the Arab as a personage prior to the crime, and the presentation of the murder as peripheral in the second part of the novel become thus a narrative device which determine Camus's presentation of the hero's "innocence."

The "Absurd" as Narrative Displacement

In summing up Meursault's case, the prosecution relies solely on those actions which bring out the protagonist's emotional state following the death of his mother. What emerges in the court's scenario are his dubious morality, compounded by his extramarital relationship which falls outside the moral norms of the society, and his self-gratification or indulgence manifested in such pleasures as swimming and going to the movies. It is Meursault's questionable morality which is transformed into a charge of criminality. To prove his criminal soul, secondary witnesses are brought in during the trial ranging from the warden of the Home for the Aged where his mother resided until her death, to Céleste, the owner of the restaurant where Meursault habitually lunches. The "evidence," more impressionistic than real, is recapitulated by Meursault, who like an audience, watches a "grand mime" (here, that of his own life) in a theater of the absurd. Meursault watches as a different version of his life is enacted in the court, a "plausible scenario" of his life recreated. The evidence presented, which consisted mostly of a cup of "café au lait" and "cigarettes," interestingly reveals not only his humanity, but also his criminal soul. It appears as though the judges condemn in Meursault their own human needs emblematically presented in him. One could argue of course, that it is not the act of smoking or drinking a cup of coffee that is being condemned here, but rather the inappropriateness of the circumstances. From a lack of decorum to criminal charges there is, however, a wide gap.

The marginalization of Meursault's real crime renders the trial nothing but absurd. In *Le Mythe de Sisyphe*, Camus states: "'C'est absurde,' veut dire: 'c'est impossible,' mais aussi: 'c'est contradictoire.' Si je vois un homme attaquer à l'arme blanche un groupe de mitrailleuses, je jugerai que son acte est absurde" (1943, 120). In the absurd then, we have a sense of something not right, of an incongruity. So also, the case of a whole legal system pitted against a man whose sole crime is a lack of decorum is equally absurd. For, what is truly Meursault's life? On the surface, it seems rather normal: a working man, although lacking "ambition"; like all French Algerians, he loves to swim on the beaches of the Mediterranean, he dates, goes to the movies, he drinks "café au lait" (which he loves) at his mother's funeral thereby exhibiting a lack of decorum. Meursault, as Girard sees him, lives "the prudent and peaceful life of a little bureaucrat anywhere and of a French petit bourgeois in the bargain."[12] Such a moderate way of life, he says, "should constitute a good insurance against nervous breakdowns, mental exhaustion, heart failure, and *a fortiori*, the guillotine" (ibid.). Obviously then, none of the activities indulged in, or attitudes exhibited by the hero calls for a confrontation with the legal system, let alone the guillotine. His failure to show grief at his mother's death may elicit, at most, disapproval and criticism from neighbors and friends. From criticism to the scaffold, there is a distance; a distance that only a murder can bridge. The murder confers a materiality on Meursault's criminal soul. "Oui, s'est-il [le Procureur] écrié avec force, j'accuse cet homme d'avoir enterré une mère avec un coeur de criminel" (1942, 148). Meursault's "faulty" relationship with his mother renders him a threat to society: "lorsque le vide du coeur tel qu'on le découvre chez cet homme devient *un gouffre où la société peut succomber*" (ibid., emphasis added).

Meursault's neglect of his mother and his apparent indifference at her death are emblems chosen by the French court (itself a representative of the French colonial administration). For indeed, one is at liberty to ask why this colonial arm of justice is so interested in the defendant's relationship with his mother, as to make it a prima-facie evidence in the trial. The protagonist's mother, judging from the son's assertion that "maman ni moi n'attendions plus rien l'un de l'autre . . . et que nous nous étions habitués à nos nouvelles vies" (1942, 135), is equally detached from her son. Textually, she is not presented so as to evoke any sympathy; and the court obviously does not have any particular interest in her *per se*. The peculiar attention that the court lavishes on her and her son's negligence stems from the state of motherhood that she represents. It is a state that constitutes, before the colonial establishment, something vital to its very existence, and which Meursault's way of life puts in jeopardy. David Ellison, who analyses succinctly the link between Colonial France and the state of Motherhood, argues that not only does Meursault constitute a threat to the system with his disregard for social institutions (i.e., marriage), but also, he does so by his refusal of continuity and causality. For his "absurd" way of living, each present moment for itself, "rubs against the grain of the representatives of State and Church."[13] Motherhood, of all social roles, represents or ensures continuity and/or at least a link between past, present, and future. Meursault's "flawed" rapport with his biological mother is thus emblematic of his equally "diseased" rapport with *la mère patrie* (Motherland). The crime for which Meursault is accused—the moral murder of his mother—becomes to the court a symbol of his mode of existence, the nature of which puts into question all the tenets upon which the *patrie* is built. So in effect, what is being jealously and passionately defended in court is not so much the hero's mother (she herself is a pretext), but the mother country itself (France), and all that it stands for. The sequential juxtaposition of Meursault's trial and the next on the agenda, the murder of a father becomes significant. The hero's abdication from the norms of his class, his revolt against the paternal values are akin to parricide, symbolically perceived as such by the Institution which condemns him.

However, the presentation of the murder as a peripheral case does fit into the narrative logic of the story. For the Arab himself has been presented all through the early part of the novel as an "out-cast" on the margins of humanity, and lacking individual identity; he is an extension of the landscape. The subsequent failure by the court to acknowledge him as human is rendered possible through the depiction of the Arab, not as a sentient being, but as completely subsumed by the landscape. One remembers Meursault's encounter with the Arab. Even though the murder is described as a case of self-defense, the question begs to be asked, "a defense against what?" Meursault apparently reacts against the Arab's knife, but only in so far as this knife is rendered potentially dangerous by the glinting of the sun upon it. If Meursault shoots in self defense, it is a defense against (or rather constructed against) an impersonal agent: the Arab subsumed into a landscape, the sun. Significant also is Meursault's initial reaction to the killing. His first awareness was not that of having killed a human being, but of having disrupted the equilibrium of the day, the silence of the beach: "J'ai compris que j'avais détruit l'équilibre du jour, le silence exceptionnel d'une plage où j'avais été heureux" (*L'Étranger* 1942, 95). Thus, his subsequent four shots fired into the already fallen body of the Arab, were perceived as four knocks on the door of misery: "comme quatre coups brefs que je frappais sur la porte du malheur" (ibid.). It is only by denying the Arab all integrity as a cogent individual that death and homicide can subsequently be treated as irrelevant. This presentation allows for the focus on Meursault's absurd sensibility.

For the sake of our argument, let us for one moment suppose that the victim of the murder had been one of the dominant minority group, i.e., a Frenchman. Such a redistribution would undermine Meursault's innocence, owing to the exigency of effectively condemning him for murder. P. J. Amash in his short article, "The Choice of an Arab in *L'Etranger*," comes to a similar conclusion. An emphasis on the murder, he says,

> would, to a great extent weaken and even destroy the theme of the novel which Camus summarized in this paradoxical sentence, 'Dans notre société tout homme qui ne pleure pas à l'enterrement de sa mère risque d'être condamné à mort.' Camus could not choose a Frenchman to be the victim, for then Meursault would have been tried, mainly, for killing a fellow Frenchman.[14]

The political and cultural context plays a role here in *L'Etranger* only in as far as each allows for the presentation of the Arab as part of "the neutral emotional and moral sphere of interests" (Haddour 1989, 89) in relation to the Frenchman. In colonial Algeria, the victimization of the Arab does not arouse much interest—a fact which is textually taken into account in the novel. Thus the murder of the Arab is never taken as a criminal act in itself but only to the extent that it enables Meursault's more outrageous crime—his insensibility to social conventions—to be brought to light. At a very superficial level, Meursault's condemnation is fitting, since it illustrates the perfect dispensation of justice. O'Brien observes that "such a novelistic representation of French justice in a colonial setting underscores certain laxity" (1970, 20). The court here, he argues, is presented as if it were a court in a European town dealing with a homogeneous group. Indeed, it is doubtful that French "justice" in Algeria at the time would condemn an European to death for shooting an Arab, especially an armed Arab, who had previously slashed the hands of an European (Raymond). O'Brien concludes that "in condemning Meursault to death for killing an Arab, Camus denies the existence of a partial colonial justice, and thereby involves [himself] in the presentation of a myth: the myth of French Algeria" (1970, 23). Ibrahim also regards the condemnation of Meursault for the murder of the Arab as "unrealistic." He (Ibrahim) however sees this peculiar judicial sentence as a symbolic condemnation of an unjust and guilty regime. One problem with both O'Brien and Ibrahim's arguments is that they overlook an important fact in the case: Meursault is not condemned for killing an Arab. Yet O'Brien's statement, as pertinent as it is, becomes flawed when viewed within the narrative context of the novel. The arguments against Camus's unrealistic portrayal of the colonial court can only be pursued and sustained if we admit that the hero is effectively sentenced to death for killing a human being. As his creator himself admits, his hero "is executed because he did not cry at his mother's funeral, for in our society any man who does not weep at his mother's funeral risks being condemned to death."

Réné Girard argues that Camus's own interpretation of the protagonist's plight reposes on a serious fallacy. Only by transforming Meursault's crime into a blameless act, an "innocent murder," can it be claimed that Meursault was condemned rather for his social defects. However, a necessary condition for Meursault's peculiar trial is that the victim be one that does not arouse sympathy in court, nor in the reader. Far from being a fallacy as Girard suggests, the choice of an Arab, apart from offering a realistic political context, also suits "the aesthetic and political necessities" (Tarrow 1985, 74) of the narration that requires a down-play on the importance of the victim; for it is only through an "effacement of the victim in the eyes of the court, . . . that the full absurdity of the judicial system, rather than the crime itself, can be emphasized" (ibid.). So then the choice of a colonized man in a colonial setting becomes expedient (Amash 1967, 7) since a European victim could not be so easily dismissed from the mind of the jury. Our hypothetical murder (killing another European) would more overtly pose a challenge to society's belief in the sacredness of human life. As Haddour points out, "there would be no room [consequently] for the operation of the absurd since Meursault would be judged on the basis of his action [the destruction of human life] rather than a state of mind, his indifference to the moral codes of society" (1989, 90).

It appears then that the marginalization of the Arab within the narrative is geared toward Camus's exposition of his philosophical ideas. What is thereby exploited is injustice but in an inverted way, a travesty of injustice. The theme of justice evidently permeates the entire novel; it is however exploited to illustrate the injustice of institutionalized violence against which Meursault is an emblematic victim. What is interesting is that this formulation puts the writer in a peculiar position of having to present colonial injustice as unprob- lematic. It could be, and has been, argued, that Camus is in effect offering a realistic portrayal of colonial justice. The inherent racism of the colonial system is evidenced by the fact that the crime, a homicide, fails to pass as sufficient ground for incrimination. The murder of the Arab can stand as crime only if it is reinforced by other unrelated details which confirm Meursault's "spiritual insensibility." One could infer then that had Meursault not had the misfortune of lacking moral decorum, had his crime been limited to killing an Arab, there would have been no case against him. In exploiting the absurdity of the trial, the *non-sequitur* logic of the legal system, the narrative inverts the terms of injustice seemingly to exonerate, and to bring out Meursault's innocence.

Also, Camus's depiction of the Arab as part of the natural milieu denoting a certain "barbarie" pertains to the domain of colonial images remininiscent of those presented in such texts as Flaubert's *Salammbo*, or Isak Dinesen's *Out of Africa*. Comparing Conrad and Camus's representation of Africa, Monad Fayad asserts that both authors "chose to place themselves within the European imaginary, and particularly the imperialist imaginary [which] they also chose to undermine."[15] This choice involves a novelistic bracketing of the native populations in *Heart of Darkness* and in *L'Étranger*, reducing them to insignificance. A lot has been said about Camus's unnamed Arabs and the native phantoms of Conrad's narrative seen through Meursault's and Marlow's eyes.

> J'ai vu un groupe d'Arabes adossés à la devanture du bureau de tabac, Ils nous regardaient en silence, mais à leur manière, ni plus ni moins que si nous étions des pierres ou des arbres morts. (*L'Étranger* 1942, 79)
> [I saw a group of Arabs leaning against the front of the tobacconist's shop. They were staring at us in silence, but in that way of theirs, as if we were nothing but stones or dead trees. (1989, 48)]

> He stared at me with his metallic eyes that shone without expression in his brown horse-face, then he raised his hand. Still impassive, he seized me by the lower lip, which twisted slowly until he tore my flesh . . . then he turned away to go to the others standing against the wall. (*Heart of Darkness* 1995, 39)

Camus's text, which postdates that of Conrad by at least fifty years, echoes the latter in establishing the vital distinction of "us" and "them" that is characteristic of a locked discourse. Christopher Miller and Edward Saïd have used the terms "Africanist discourse" and "Orientalist discourse," respectively, to underscore the recurrent narrative construction of Africa as "the unconscious/repressed/dark side of Europe" (Fayad 1990, 300). Through their narratives governed by Meursault's and Marlow's points of view, the inanimate prevails over the animate, the animal over the human (the frozen stance of the Arabs, their lack of individuality, the "metallic" stare of the Congo natives) all reinforcing the objectivizing and dehumanizing gaze of the protagonists.

Orientalist discourse, Erickson remarks, "is based on exteriority and necessitates objectification in Camus's depiction of the Arab" (1988, 73). During one of Meursault's subsequent encounters with the Arab at the beach, the tableau presented is that of an "idyllic vision of visually colorful characters" (1988, 77) against a background of flute music and water sound. The beach can be seen here both symbolically and literally as the domain of the European, where the Arab is a trespasser. Elaborating further, Erickson states:

> Objectification here is not the function of the critically objective mind, but of a subjective intelligence which both subsumes and reifies the 'other.' In accordance with this position of exteriority, the Arab is presented as a stranger in his own homeland. (ibid.)

The process of objectification will be carried to the extreme in the killing of the Arab, since death is the ultimate agent of dehumanization. The Indigene as an outsider, belongs to a culture alien to the concerns of the privileged class. The isolated figure of the Arab, alienated from the representational and discursive fields of the colonizer, provides a convenient tool for Camus to illustrate the injustice of the legal institution that Meursault confronts. The society portrayed by Camus in universal terms must, however, be seen in its specificities. Only then does it emerge as highly contextualized and dominated by colonial violence. What we are confronted with is a historical reality: that of a colonialist society. The European approaches the "alien," the Arab, with a certain trepidation mingled with fear and anxiety, for the latter in his alienness poses a threat to the "stability of colonial hegemony." The existential problematics formulated in *L'Etranger* must be read as a transposition of the colonial malaise of the pied-noir society on the brink of its own demise, faced with an antagonistic dominated culture.

L'Etranger (written in 1940 and published in 1942) underscores the precariousness of the white man's position in French Algeria. In that time frame of cultural seclusion dominated by the myth of conquest and justified by the French burden of a civilizing mission, the Indigene, the recipient of its benefits, is paradoxically a threat; as a result, the colonial project is concomitant with a feeling of insecurity. The French Algerian community isolated in barbarie "conserve le sentiment que tout reste à faire et que tout risque d'être défait" (Nora 1961, 172). The resulting antagonism has been viewed as a manifestation of the natives' medieval obscurantism and religious fanaticism. In his essay, "À la Recherche de l'Esprit Méditerranéen," Louis Bertrand points to the frustrations facing the Latin civilizing mission in North Africa: "la civilisation n'a jamais été et ne sera qu'un ilot perdu dans un océan de barbarie. [civilization has been and will always be, only an island lost in a sea of barbarism.]" And furthermore, "un des grands obstacles à [la] pénétration [civilisatrice] latine, sinon le plus grand, c'est le fanatisme, ce sont les préjugés religieux [one of the great obstacles, if not the greatest, to (the) penetration of (civilizing) Latin is fanaticism and religious prejudices.]" (1931, 165–6).

The colonial encounter in North Africa involves two sets of religious prejudices, a fact overlooked by Bertrand's statement. However, Bertrand's assertion summarizes the cultural move of the European whose cultural existence depends on the effacement, or at least a down-grading of the cultural values of the Other. It is worth recalling the underlying impulse of the settler's insistence upon a supposed superiority. This superiority must be seen within the context of an ideological distinction which a group employs to justify domination and exclusion. The barbarisation of the Other is simply the process whereby "we attribute to that which is different what is in reality the result of cultural nearsightedness" (Marx-Scouras 1986, 6). Such a process not only serves to legitimize the "spiritual adventure" called civilization, but it also helps to domesticate identity and meaning "by relegating that which is heterogeneous and unfamiliar beyond those borders patrolled by notions of origin, unity, homogeneity and legitimacy relevant to the dominant group" (ibid.). With *Algérianistes* such as Bernard, the unremitting effort to repel the Other correlates the unconscious realization of the illusiveness of the venture.

Let us remember that the colonial experience in North Africa faced two major obstructions that were felt to a lesser extent in the Subsaharan part of the continent, namely religious and sexual barriers. These two secluded domains constituted a formidable weapon for the indigenous culture and a threat to the colonizer. The latter's effort to overcome religious antagonism and penetrate the domestic life of the colonized remained unyielding, thus contributing to the insecurity of the settler in colonial space. The Arab's culture of the *serail* aided greatly in isolating and insulating the indigenous culture. The subsequent reification of the Arab woman within Western myth and orientalist discourse was an attempt to vulgarize that which was kept hidden. The image of the "oriental" woman as a "prostitute," or a mere object of desire was significantly related to the European endeavor. So also, the absence of indigenous women from the colonial arena created a certain inequality in which the colonizer felt rather vulnerable. It also rendered the conflict much more violent. Raymond's relationship with the Mauresque woman in *L'Etranger* can be interpreted in the light of such an antagonism. Raymond is a European pimp having control over an indigenous prostitute. He is both a lover and a master. Let us keep in mind that it was this conflict which triggered the entire drama of the novel.

Of great significance also, was the Arab male's (brother of the woman, and friends) attack on the Europeans. It was a protest against the violation made to their honor, and one that set in motion subsequent incidents leading to the murder on the beach. Also significant was the fact that the Arabs were shown as "trespassers" on the beach. I believe that the narrative components here do have symbolic values. Raymond's relationship with the mauresque, which replicates the master/slave dialectics, is a colonial male's intrusion into the protected space of the harem. It is an act of violation aimed at defiling that which has been held "sacred." By putting the indigenous woman to work as prostitute for his financial benefits, Raymond not only devalues the "sacred" world of the Arab woman, he also reenacts symbolically the colonial appropriation and exploitation. The beach here can be seen as a symbolical ground, representing that domain of the indigenous culture which had been violated, appropriated, and from which the Arab had been dispossessed. The Arabs' antagonistic moves dramatize the Indigenes' hostility to the colonial intrusion.

Pierre Nora reads into Raymond's act and into the murder of the Arab manifestations of colonial paternalism and colonial hatred. The homicide, according to him, expresses simply the European's sub-conscious desire to eradicate the Arab from the colonial space, despite conscious awareness that his own privileged existence depended on the presence of that which he wished to weed-out. "Each individual crime perpetrated against the Arab in the slummiest area of Algeria," Nora maintains, "is done in the name of the collective group."[16] Inferred from this is that the murder of the Arab in *L'Etranger* is but a fictionalization of this sub-conscious wish. The novel would seem to illustrate both the French Algerian paternalist and racialist aggression generated by his own insecurity.

L'Etranger reveals not an "absurd sensibility" but a historical one because it reflects a concrete reality, an intricacy of sentiments within a colonial structure. Camus's novel on the absurd, Nora concurs, "apparait sur le plan psychologique comme l'expression vraisemblab-lement sublimée d'une situation réelle, décantée jusqu'à l'épure" [seems plausibly, on the psychological level, like the sublimated of a real situation, distilled to purity] (1961, 190-91). Viewed in its historical context, the novel typifies "le roman noir" (Gourdon 1974, 118) in colonial literature. It is a reflection upon the political situation of the 1940s and the antagonistic relationship between colonizer and colonized. The condemnation of Meursault, far from dramatizing a Kafka-like trial, foreshadows the historical conflict attendant to the French occupation of Algeria, and the colonizer's historical culpability. *L'Etranger* delineates symbolically the French Algerian's feelings of insecurity, the fear that the French colonial structure could come undone, and his increasingly contested domin-ation. "[*L'Étranger*] transfigure ce rapport [Français-Arabes] sur le plan de la symbolique inconsciente, le seul [roman] où les Arabes figurent dans la constellation psychologique des Français" [[*L'Étranger*], the only novel in which Arabs appear in the psychological constellation of French people, transfigures this French-Arab relationship on the level of the unconscious symbolic] (Nora 1961, 192).

Meursault's initial appearance on the scene shows him as frozen in a historical moment. His phenomenological perception of life, his stance as a "voyeur"[17] disrupts the "equilibrium" of social existence. But his encounter with the Arabs brings to life colonial antagonism lurking under the Mediterranean depicted in the early part of the novel. The hero's confrontation with the Arabs which correlates his confrontation with the burning Mediterranean sun, triggers the dynamism of a racial intercourse. It is worth keeping in mind that the situation exploited here, namely colonial injustice, was extrapolated from Camus's own experience as a journalist with *Alger Républicain*, and his involvement in colonial politics. As a reporter, he had had to deal with numerous cases of social injustices against the indigenous population.

One particular case is worth recalling here. The [mis]trial of El Okbi, an indigenous leader of the Ulemas (the religious-based movement that opposed the assimilationist drive of the French, and insisted on a separation of the Colonial government and the Islamic Institution), illustrates what Julien calls the "futile parody" (1961, 18) inherent in colonial structures. The Ulema leader became more of a scape goat, a way of suppressing the Ulemas' vehement opposition to the assimilationist laws which were always proposed, but never promulgated. The trial, which Camus, as a journalist, must have followed quite closely (cf. *Fragments d'un combat*), is interesting in two respects. First, its manipulativeness reveals the theatricality of colonial justice. Second, it also shows the colonizer's effort to suspend the course of history by protecting the colonial domain against both the assimilationist demands of the native *Jeunes Algériens* and the nationalist movements of the period. Neither augured well for the colonial apparatus.

With *L'Étranger*, Camus unwittingly unwrites the harmonious setting of *Noces*. Despite the attempt here to transpose Meursault's relationship with his mother (*mère*) into a existential dilemma, the setting of the novel ultimately reflects a colonial conflict; the latter is, however, sublimated into the realm of fiction set in a mediterranean "mer/e." In his reading of the murder, Ibrahim insists that Meursault's act betrays an unconscious aggressivity, typical of the pied-noir: "en tuant l'Arabe, Meursault, et partant Camus, se défoule d'un complexe du petit-blanc ... réalise de manière subconsciente, le rêve du pied-noir qui aime l'Algérie mais ne peut concevoir cette Algérie que débarrassée des Algériens."[18] [By killing the Arab, Meursault, and by extension, Camus, works off a complex of the little white man ... unconsciously fulfilling the dream of the *pied-noir* who loves Algeria but can only conceive of this Algeria as a place rid of Algerians.]

The title of Rénée Quinn's study, "Le thème racial dans *L'Etranger*" (1969), speaks for itself. Quinn also interprets the novel within a specific political context, that of racial prejudices. These last two critical positions echo the reading of Henri Kréa who also contends that "quand Meursault, 'l'étranger,' tire sur l'Arabe, il tue magiquement une entité raciale ... Cet acte, qu'il croit causé 'par le soleil,' est la réalisation subconsciente du rêve obscur et puéril du petit Blanc que Camus ne cesse jamais d'être" (1961, 16).

Many critics have shunned a racist reading of Meursault. Braun, for instance, points out that "Racism is far too strong and inadequate" a term for Camus's protagonist. He explains further that

Racism is a pseudo-scientific concept, a theory of blood determinism invented by Gobineau and others, later taken up self-righteously by American Southerners, then used savagely by the Nazis. *Simple people do not think so far.* (1974:214; emphasis added)

I would venture to say that Braun's explanation represents an acute form of denial, and at best, a "muddled argument," to borrow his own words. It is worth pointing out that one does not require a knowledge of Gobineau, nor any level of intellectual sophistication to exhibit a racist attitude, which means that "simple people," are not by essence exempted from such an attitude or outlook. It would, however, be absurd to abscribe the term "racism" to Meursault, for the mere reason that he himself stands on the periphery of social conventions and by extention, racial prejudices. Meursault, let us remember, is eventually condemned for subverting the status quo.

Kurkarni, in his critique of O'Brien (*Albert Camus of Europe and Africa*), and Saïd ("Camus and the Imperial Experience") condemns their attemp to place Camus's work in the "colonial discourse of Algeria." He views O'Brien's and Saïd's readings as implicating Meursault in the ethos of colonial violence. Kurkani argues, somehow unconvincingly, that Meursault's creator had a much more "complex relationship with Algeria," and thus, could not be adequately summed up in the character of Meursault (1997, 1528).

The importance of these various critical positions to my own reading lies in the fact that they refer the novel to its political and cultural context. One may argue that the danger inherent in such an interpretation (including my own) is that it overlooks the philosophical problem articulated in the novel, and that such readings displace the authorial point of view or "intention," namely the exposition of the absurd, expressed in *L'Etranger* as a certain "indifference" of the world, and a reciprocal stance of "indifference" to the world, to the social and moral norms, the latter presented as "implacable mechanisms" that crush Meursault to death. But, as has been insisted upon, Camus's discourse is one of displacement that seeks to transfer the political conflict of the 1930s and 1940s—clearly a colonial drama, into an existential one. It is a move that undermines the writer's own political activities; or perhaps reflects, rather, his political position. While in his various political essays on the Algerian issue, he advocates social reforms for ameliorating the conditions of the Arabs, his fiction presents colonial injustices as unproblematic.

Camus's novel, *L'Etranger*, does in effect exploit a concrete political context, that of colonial injustice. The latter is, however, pushed to the periphery, as the narrative sets forth the protagonist as a hero of "the absurd" and a victim of an inconsequential legal system. Meursault's sole crime in this absurd illustration of justice, it appears, is "his abdication from the mores of the privileged class," a stance which threatens the very tenet of French colonial society. The colonial institution condemns Meursault to be executed "sur une place publique *au nom du peuple français*" (1942, 112; emphasis added). The framework for Meursault's condemnation overlooks ethnic barriers here. In sentencing Meursault "au nom du peuple français," other ethnic identities collapse, seemingly implicated in the "peuple français." What Camus insists on as the central problem of *L'Etranger*, namely Meursault's innocence and the problem of the absurd, is articulated only through a textual violation of the concept of fundamental justice denied by the colonial structure. The ability to diffuse a political reality into an aesthetic of the absurd, is a move that one can also detect in the writer's essays on the Algerian crises.

Camus, despite his awareness of various problems attendant to colonial rule in the 1950s, never addresses colonialism itself as a source of conflicts. Such ellipsis is also seen in Camus's short story, "l'Hôte," where an Arab is arraigned before justice for killing another Arab. The reason given for the killing—"stolen grain"—points to the economic crises of the native population. Camus's essay, *Misère de la Kabylie* was written as a protest against the sub-human economic situation of the Indigenes. *Crise en Algérie* was also a response to the

Sétif massacre (cf. chapter 2). These two essays, moving in their lyricism, fail however to explore the deep roots of the crises. Myopically, Camus attributes famine and conflict to economic and demographic problems.

[A]vant de passer à d'autres aspects de la malheureuse Kabylie, je voudrais faire justice de certains arguments que nous connaissons bien en Algérie et qui s'appuient sur la "mentalité"kabyle pour trouver des excuses à la situation actuelle. Car je ne connais rien de plus méprisable que ces arguments. Il est méprisable de dire que ce peuple s'adapte à tout. M. Albert Lebrun lui-même, si on lui donnait 200 francs par mois pour sa subsistance, s'adapterait à la vie sous les ponts, à la saleté et à la croûte de pain trouvée dans une poubelle. Dans l'attachement d'un homme à sa vie, il y a quelque chose de plus fort que toutes les misères du monde. Il est méprisable de dire que ce peuple n'a pas les mêmes besoins que nous. S'il n'en avait pas eu, il y a beau temps que nous les lui aurions crées. Il est curieux de voir comment les qualités d'un peuple peuvent servir à justifier l'abaissement où on le tient et comment la sobriété proverbiale du paysan kabyle peut légitimer la faim qui le ronge. Non, ce n'est pas ainsi que nous les verrons. Car les idées toutes faites et les préjugés deviennent odieux quand on les applique à un monde où les hommes meurent de froid et où les enfants sont réduits à la nourriture des bêtes sans en avoir l'instinct qui les empêcherait de périr. La vérité, c'est que nous côtoyons tous les jours un peuple qui vit avec trois siècles de retard, et nous sommes les seuls à être insensibles à ce prodigieux décalage. (*Essais* 1965, 913–14)

[[B]efore moving on to other aspects of the Kabyle's miserable condition, I would like to respond to some of the arguments which we know very well in Algeria, arguments that rely on the "Kabyle's mentality" in order to find alibis for their present predicament. For I know of no arguments as contemptible as these. It is despicable to say that these people adapt to everything. Mr. Albert Lebrun himself, if he were given 200 francs a month for subsistence, would adapt to life under bridges, to filth, and to bread crumbs from the garbage can. In man's attachment to life, there is something far stronger than all the miseries of the world. It is despicable to say that these people do not have the same needs as we do. Even if they had not had the same needs, we would have since created them. It is curious to see how the qualities of a people could serve to justify the humiliation to which they are subjected, and how the Kabyle peasant's proverbial moderation can be made to legitimate the hunger that is eating at him. No, this is not the way we see them. For the ready-made ideas and prejudices become odious when applied to a world where men die of cold and where children are reduced to the food of animals without having the

latter's instinct that would prevent them from perishing. The truth
is that we live daily with a people three centuries behind, and we
are the only ones insensitive to this extraordinary gap.]

The above passage clearly raises a very important issue: the
dehumanizing living conditions of the natives. Camus clearly points to
poverty, backwardness, and exploitation as cyclical and self perpetuating. What is also denounced is the racist claim that "ce peuple
s'adapte à tout [même à la misère]." True, within Camus's universalizing perspective, no distinction between Albert Lebrun (President of
the Republique, 1933–1940) and the native Kabyle exist. But such an
equalizing stance ignores the fundamental inequalities inscribed in
colonialism. Camus addresses here a specific problem, specific to the
people subjected to colonial rule. It is that unfair distribution inherent
in a capitalist system, compounded here by dominant colonialism.
Within Camus's universalizing discourse, however, the political preg-
nancy of the racist attitude "qui s'appuie sur la 'mentalité' kabyle pour
trouver des excuses à la situation actuelle" (*Essais* 1965, 914) is
diffused.

Interestingly, while Camus denounces his country fellows' racist
inclination, he himself seems to find a certain virtue in the Indigenes'
ability to adapt to their economic wretchedness: "Il est curieux de voir
comment *les qualités d'un peuple* [my emphasis] peuvent servir à
justifier [son] abaissement" (ibid.). Admirably, he seeks to deconstruct
the colonialist arguments which rely on stereotypes concerning the
mentality of the natives, their innate inferiority and ready adaptability
to physical hardship. Yet Camus's *L'Etranger* replicates the same
"dehumanized" traits of the Arab in order to bring out Meursault's
innocence and spiritual alienation. It is only against the background of
this conventional depiction of the natives that the murder of the Arab
becomes unproblematic, and therefore convenient for the illustration and
exposition of the absurd in *L'Etranger*.

From the Universe of *L'Etranger* to Colonial Malaise

Thus as analyzed, Camus, in order to expound the myth of the
absurd, fuses the physical world and the particularities of colonial life
into a generalized vision of the world of indifference, and the absurdity
of the French legal system. For Camus, the absurd implicates a
universal "truth," the unquestionable reality incarnated in bodily
pleasures. For Meursault, the rock, the wind, and the sea under the

Algerian sun are sole certainties; thus, seemingly underscoring an authorial point of view. If Meursault has been presented as liberated from the falseness of the bourgeois society—implicated in the Institution that condemns him—he seems by the same token also exempted from the colonial guilt of the establishment that convicts him.

I have read in this mis/presentation a fair deal of staging necessary for the transposition of colonial injustice into a universal theme. As a *mise en scène*, however, it violates the rule of vraisemblance. The very French judicial system used as prop for the helplessness of the hero reveals the reality concealed beneath the mythical vision of a harmonious landscape against which the sole plight of man, is his metaphysical anguish. What emerges from the falsehood of the trial, is not Meursault's innocence, but the guilt of the entire colonial framework. A confrontation with the legal institution, itself an emblem of the colonial structure, has been a central theme of much artistic and literary endeavors of various indigenous writers. Mouloud Mammeri and Mouloud Feraoun, who share in the ideological premises of *L'Ecole d'Alger* in the early stage of their literary production, have put on the fictional stage heroes in grip with government institutions. Their representation naturally enacts a different language and a different field of vision. They exploit the theme of estrangement within a domain of cultural signification, not to delineate the metaphysical torment of their hero, but to replicate the Arab/Berber's alienation, his political and existential absence from the colonizer's cultural universe. Colonialist dynamics suppressed in *L'Etranger* surfaces in the writings of these authors as the language of colonization, oppressive and alienating. From their field of vision, a vision nourished from the same political and cultural fountain, as that of Camus, the figure of "l'étranger" speaks a different "truth"—that of the colonized.

Emmanuel Roblès's *Les Hauteurs de la ville* (1945), inspired perhaps by Camus's *L'Etranger* (1942), adds further insight into Camus's representation of the colonial universe of *L'Etranger*, offering yet another perspective. Whereas *L'Etranger* denies the Arab individuality, *Les Hauteurs de la ville* presents the Arab as a rebel, with a voice. It is an Arab capable of claiming "justice." If however, Roblès's hero confronts a political enemy, it is not the French colonialist. The Arab and the French are presented as a unified front against a common enemy: the Nazi. Haddour observes that both "Roblès [and] Camus ignore the arbitrariness of the colonial system which verges on Fascism" (1989, 60). The presence of the German enemy serves to camouflage a more pertinent opponent, the French. For one concurrent theme underlying the narrative but never explicitly stated is that

Smaïl's position as an *Indigene* is that of a prisoner in colonial political space. Roblès, like Camus, belongs to the pied-noir culture. The works of both writers advocate a certain "godless sainthood." Joyaux correctly states that *L'Etranger*'s entry into the North African literary arena has tremendous impact not only on indigenous writers, but on other pied-noir writers as well; and that Roblès in *Les Hauteurs de la ville*, uses the same clusters of images as in *L'Etranger* to express "the absurd" (1960, 15).

Les Hauteurs de la ville narrates the story of a Kabyle youth, Smaïl. The latter, like Meursault, has committed a murder for which he is condemned to die. Almaro, the victim is a German agent. Smaïl, echoing Meursault, comes to the realization that his trial and condemnation precede the actual crime. "Des juges respectables me condamneraient solennellement à mort et cela me paraissait un peu vain puisqu'avant même de tuer Almaro, j'étais déjà condamné" (1945, 207). If the question of homicide is not diffused in Roblès's narrative as it is in Camus's *L'Etranger*, it is nevertheless used here to emphasize the hero's "metaphysical rebellion" which hinges on deicide. Both Smaïl and Meursault reject divine authority as irrelevant. "Dieu a crée toute vie et toute vie n'appartient qu''a Dieu! Aucun de nous, s'il veut être sauvé, ne peut transgresser ce commandement . . . Mais vous ne croyez pas en Dieu, non plus, Monsieur Lakhdar. . . ." (1945, 209). Lakhdar Smaïl's faithlessness is substantiated by his criminal act, equivalent to a denial that "toute vie n'appartient qu'à Dieu." Smaïl's crime when it occurs, is presented as a liberating act, and also an act of rebellion. His crime, however, far from being gratuitous and unpremeditated as in the case of Meursault, is endowed here with political signification. Smaïl comes to a confrontation with Almaro for the first time, when he (Smaïl) is caught sabotaging the Nazi propaganda. "J'étais occupé à mettre en morceaux, à coup de canif, une affiche fraîchement collée" (ibid., 15). Asked for his motives he declares, "Je ne veux pas que les ouvriers d'ici travaillent pour les Allemands" (ibid., 91)!

The background of the novel clearly then reflects the political context of the time: Nazism and its propaganda in North Africa. By a twist of historical irony, France takes the position of the "colonized" within her own colony, Algeria. Smaïl's motives for wishing to destroy Almaro are selfless. It is in the name of a collectivity, "les ouvriers d'ici," in recognition of human solidarity with others. "Je commençais cependant à découvrir que je ne voulais pas tuer Almaro seulement parce qu'il me méprisait, moi, mais parce qu'il méprisait des milliers d'hommes dont je me sentais solidaire. Arracher le mal...Oui" (1945, 146). [I was however beginning to discover that I did not only want to kill Almaro because he despised me myself, but because he despised thousands of men with whom I feld in solidarity. Uproot evil... Yes.] Roblès's hero identifies, then, with an oppressed humanity. Meursault, as we remember him,exhibits no conscious identification with any group. Smaïl in solidarity with other victims of Almaro, "avait voulu détruire de sang-froid, un infirme rouage de la mécanique de guerre nazie" ("had wanted impassively to destroy one wek cog in the wheel of the Nazi war machine") (ibid.).

In *L'Etranger,* the act of killing dehumanizes and objectifies the Arab. The dead Arab is also a symbolic representation of an objectified and dehumanized being, itself emblematic or pointer to ethnocide. In Roblès's novel, homicide as a process of destruction has as its object an entire institution, the Nazi. The narrative point of view of the Indigenes (Smaïl), while serving to cast the story against its political background, presents some disturbing aspects, as we shall presently illustrate.

Smaïl's story, we are told, is the fictionalization of a historical event. "[Dans]*Les Hauteurs de la ville* . . . Il s'agit d'Ahmed Smail, condamné à mort sous le régime de Vichy, et qu'un don de poète promettait aux belles créations littéraires."[19] [In *Les Hauteurs de la ville* . . . the subject is Ahmed Smail who is condemned to death under the Vichy regime, and whom a poet's gift was promising to beautiful artistic creations.] Thus, the political context of Roblès's story was one of intense Muslim anti-colonial consciousness. It was the time that ex-assimilationists (indigenous elites) drafted a "manifesto" demanding political autonomy. It was the era of nationalist activities that would ultimately lead to the crisis of May 1945. *Les Hauteurs de la ville* written during this turbulent period of Algerian political life, surprisingly, however, suppresses the anti-colonial voice of the political crises of 1945. Roblès's narrative puts forward an Arab solidarity with France in North Africa in the face of the Nazi threat, thus ignoring colonial hatred. The hero is not only a spokesman for Arab laborers, but also for the French; eventually what is addressed is the problem of metropolitan France under the German occupation. *Les Hauteurs de la ville* overlooks one of the two layers of political reality, German occupation and French occupation, both tangential to two oppressive ideological systems. By repressing the French colonial issue, the narrative eradicates the anti-colonial consciousness which manifested itself in the various upheavals of the 1940s and 1950s. Roblès's hero is introduced as clearly assimilated unto French political environment, and defending solely its political causes.

As though to further obfuscate the colonial drama, Roblès introduces his personage as god-like figure, "a master of his own destiny." *Mastery,* however, does imply an existential and political freedom, which is lacking in the life of Smaïl. The latter is objectively a colonized subject who suffers from an alienating and a racist system. These are, however, presented as simple undercurrents, which never come to the forefront.

During the Algerian war, Roblès effects a radical re-writing of the novel, apparently to account for the colonial crises. He modifies the early opaque political background of his narrative, giving voice, this time, to the Algerian political crisis. In the revised version (1960 edition), the latent structure of racist feelings become specific issues. Smaïl's liaison with Monique, a French girl, for instance, is subjected to the disapproving gaze of the European society. "Je me souviens . . . qu'une vieille dame européenne nous avait croisés et que je ne m'étais pas soucié de son regard réprobateur. Pensez! une Française avec un Arabe! [I remember . . . that an old European woman saw us, and that I did not worry about her disapproving look. Imagine! A French woman and an Arab man!]"[20] This narrative addition significantly unwrites the early harmonious union of French and Indigenes in the face of Nazism. It divulges the essentially antagonistic nature of colonialism. Indeed, in the new narrative, Smaïl emerges, not as perfectly absorbed into the French society, but rather as a typical "bicot" incapable of being assimilated into the French cultural kingdom. Smail's French friend, Fournier who murders a Nazi agent, unwittingly opens Smail's eyes to his estrangement from the French ideals of civilization. Fournier who is ready to kill again for his country France, if need be, tells Smaïl:

> Je place mon pays très haut [...] A mes yeux, la France ce n'est pas uniquement un vaste hexagone de terres aimables et de masses d'individus auxquels je suis lié pour le meilleur et pour le pire. C'est aussi une civilisation [...] dans laquelle je me sens à l'aise, où je peux m'épanouir librement, trouver toutes mes dimensions. Je n'aurais pas tué sans la certitude que la sauvegarde de ces valeurs exigeait ce sacrifice [...] On tue comme on meurt pour sa patrie. (1960, 146)

> [I place my country very high. {...}. To me, France is not only a vast hexagon of pleasant lands and masses of individuals to whom I am attached for better or for worse. It is also a civilization {...} in which I feel at ease, where I can develop freely, fulfill my potential. I would not have killed without the certainty that the safeguard of these values called for such a sacrifice {...} One kills as one dies for one's country.]

To which Smaïl replies: "Peut-être suis-je imperméable à cette civilis-ation que tu [Fournier] vantes. je ne parviens pas, comme toi, à m'y épanouir"(ibid.). The idea of the Indigenes' impermeability to the colonizer's civilization would form the core of both Feraoun and Mammeri's writings (I shall return to this presently).

Faced with the pressures of decolonization and the polemical writings of the 1950s, Roblès, who asserts the need to rationalize history, attempts to explicate "l'évènement en cours en le désignant (par une artifice d'écriture) comme prévisible dès les lendemains de la guerre mondiale" (Gourdon 1974, 243). If Roblès truly unwrites his initial position to account for the aftermath effect of the World War Two on the Algerian political scene, he does so, solely by sharpening his hero's awareness of the injustices prevalent in the colonial structure. Albeit treated as specific issues, they still remain secondary to the main fight of Smaïl, which is Almaro, the German agent. In other words, the political universe of the novel would remain unchanged. The revised version retains to some extent the myth of the French-Arab unity. If the novel draws any parallel between the German and the French systems, it is to posit the superiority of the French civilization and the threat to its accomplishments incarnated in people like Almaro. "C'est qu'en effet on la [civilisation française] défigure assez ici" (1960, 146). Inferred from this is the German threat to the civilizing mission of the French, thus rendering French threat to indigenous culture a subsidiary one at best. It ultimately reflects the author's stance vis-a-vis the colonial problem. Roblès, like Camus believed firmly in the future of Algeria only as linked with that of France. As Gourdon points out such an aspiration informs the writings of both:

> [Ils] impose[nt] [aux] esprits la nécessité de "ces réformes de structure" dont le courant libéral pensait qu'elles assureraient l'avenir d'une Algérie associée à la France. Si le principe même de leur nécessité est clairement posé dans le roman, le contenu qui est assigné est moins clair [...] C'était l'époque des pourparlers de Melun, mais *Les Hauteurs de la ville* est encore loin de l'idée d'une "Algérie Algérienne." (1974, 243)

> [[They] impose on people's minds the necessity of "these structural reforms" which the liberal movement thought would secure the future of an Algeria tied to France. If the very principle of their necessity is clearly laid down in the novel, the content assigned to them is less clear. {...} It was the period of the Melun negotiations, but *Les Hauteurs de la ville* was still far from the idea of an "Algerian Algeria."]

I already stressed both the anachronism and the utopianism of Camus's stance in advocating for structural reforms within a continuing

French rule, a position echoed by Roblès. Also of further importance is their narrative evasiveness of colonial politics. By introducing the Nazi figure as a common and sole enemy of a harmonious collectivity— French-Indigenes—Roblès clearly displaces the space of conflict. The existential dilemma of the *Jeunes Algériens* and the mass of Indigenes, which is obfuscated in the writings of both Camus and Roblès to make room for more universal problematics, would, however, surface in the works of various indigenous writers. The estrangement of the colonized from the cultural universe of the colonizer would become the central issue of their fiction. Both the political and cultural aspirations and the exclusion of the native— leading to his alienation within the colonial space—find articulation in these works.

Mouloud Mammeri's *La Colline oubliée* (1952) provides an interesting link with Camus and Roblès for various reasons. One obvious reason is that the story is cast against a background of colonial politics. Interestingly, if the novel offers us an indigenous point of view, it is that of an acculturated youth, looking at his tradition through the prism of French culture. *La Colline oubliée* narrates the love story of a Kabyle married couple, Mokrane and Aazi. The marriage, although a happy one, remains barren. Aazi (the wife), according to traditional law, must be repudiated. The hero's father understands that he and his son belong to two different worlds, and as such cannot interfere with his son's life. Mokrane is, however, drafted into the army and goes off to fight for France. The father, taking advantage of this departure, ends the marriage. The novel articulates two major thematic concerns: the first is the rebellion of the hero against "a backward and barbaric tradition," a popular theme of Louis Bertrand's colonialist rhetoric, and the second is the native's participation in the World War Two. *La Colline oubliée*, an overt attack on the Indigenes' backwardness, duplicates a colonialist rhetoric, by presenting the Kabyle customary marriage as "une coutume barbare."[21] the very term used by the colonizer to denigrate the indigenous cultural heritage, and to posit the superiority of Western cultural values.

Mammeri's westernized characters, in borrowing the colonialist discourse of the masters, sustain what Memmi calls the negative complex of the colonized. Colonization, as Memmi points out, creates a contested image for the dominated. The latter in turn, by and large, "appropriates the very language of the colonizer with its colonial stereotypes and negative representations of the cultural life of the indigenes" (*Colonizer* 1965, 158). Mammeri's characters caricature their society, seeing it through the prism of a colonialist discursive apparatus; hence for them, "Il n'y a que les dégénérés, les produits anémiés d'une civilisation fatiguée qui doutent et qui souffrent [There are only the degenerate, anemic products of a worn out civilization, who doubt and suffer.]" (1952, 41).

Such "backward" (worn out) civilization clearly constitutes a hindrance to the jeune élites's progress and entry into the French cultural city. However, if the various characters introduced recognize dimly that "action" (leading to progress) is necessary for reviving the agonizing indigenous culture, they paradoxically turn their back to it, fully anticipating their inclusion into Western culture. *La Colline oubliée* emerged within a specific historical moment marked by the failure of the French assimilationist project; yet the novel espouses *L'Ecole d'Alger* assimilationist stance since it is presumed that the necessary revitalizing action must come from the West. The novel, an ethnographic narrative, is predicated upon a binary opposition, the French "idées éclairées" (French enlightened ideas) (1952, 24), and those "méthodes barbares de nos aïeux" (barbarous customs of our ancestors) (ibid., 153). Equivocally though, if Mammeri describes accurately the "backwardness" of his native society, the poverty of his own people, as well as the corruption of cultural institutions, he fails to effect a link between colonialism and the "mummified" state of the colonized's cultural life. Instead, the hero, Mokrane remarks: "L'histoire dit qu'en 1445 des hordes de turcs barbares et cupides, les yeux brulants de convoitise, se sont rués sur Bysance, la ville sainte, où depuis plus de mille ans, des docteurs infiniment subtils discutaient toute la vie l'essence ineffable de la divinité [History tells us that in 1445 hordes of barbaric and greedy Turks, eyes shining with lust, pounced on Byzantium, the holy city, where for more than a thousand years, very subtle doctors discussed, all their life, the ineffable essence of divinity.]" (ibid., 154).

Mammeri's novel does not impute the decadence of the indigenous culture to French colonial mission, but to those "hordes de turcs barbares et cupides." Through the use of the word "Bysance" (Byzantinum) the narrative rejoins Louis Bertrand's thesis of North Africa as a Latin empire, and the colonial mission as a re edification of Latin history in North Africa. The authorial identification with a Latin Occident sustains the political ideals of both the *Algérianiste* school and *L'Ecole d'Alger*. The main characters of the novel, clearly uncomfortable within the parameters of their tradition, articulate the ideals of the *Jeunes Algériens*.

[L]'esprit de l'époque était à l'émancipation des autochtones par la culture française. L'idéal caressé par les éléments instruits était de pouvoir mener une vie "à la Française," non simplement dans ses as-
\pects matériels et quotidiens, mais aussi dans son aspect moral et

idéologique. [Mais] leur formation française ne correspondait pas [...] nécessairement à celle des assimilés véritables, des francisés. Mais la francisation était la tentation constante de la plupart d'entre eux, et comme l'aspiration profonde de leur être. (Merad 1976, 48–49)

[The spirit of the period was for the emancipation of the natives through French culture. The ideal cherished by the intellectuals was to be able to lead their lives in a "French" way, not only in its material and daily aspects, but also in its moral and ideological ramifications. [But] their French education did not necessarily correspond to that of the truly assimilated, the Frenchified. However, this "Frenchification" was a constant seductive lure for most of them, and the profound yearning of their being.]

The failure of the French system to fully assimilate the Indigenes, the latter's discomfort within the boundaries of traditional life, point to a "social and historical catalepsy" (Memmi, *Colonizer* 1965, 131). The *jeune évolué*, prototype of Mammeri's hero, more often than not, lives in a "mummified" society, as an outsider.

One factor linking Mammeri, Roblès and Camus together is ultimately the diffused background of their representation of colonial life, which is a bit problematic when viewed within their actual context. Mammeri's *Le Sommeil du juste* (1955) manifests a more pronounced political consciousness. The protagonist, Arezki, like Roblès's hero, Smaïl, is a westernized youth seeking justice within the colonial structure. The early part of the story introduces the young Arezki committed to the ideals of the French mission. His participation in World War Two, however, brings about a political volte-face. Denise Brahimi sums up the effect of the war on the protagonist:

Cette participation a plusieurs effets: d'abord ouverture sur un monde beaucoup plus vaste que celui, limité et clos, de la Kabylie. C'est la rupture avec l'appartenance régionaliste, qui peut parfois retarder la prise de conscience nationale. Ensuite, découverte des impostures et des leurres que comporte la relation des Algériens musulmans avec la France [...] Le héros Arezki prend conscience à la fin de la guerre qu'il n'est et ne peut être autre chose qu'un colonisé. Ce constat lui est d'autant plus cruel qu'étant un intellectuel, il a cru aux idées humanistes, universalistes et égalitaires prônées par la France à travers sa littérature. Le roman exprime à cet égard une immense désillusion. [22]

[This participation had several effects: first of all, an exposure to a world much larger than the limited and confined space of Kabylie. It is a break from a sense of regionalist belonging, which could sometimes delay the awakening of national consciousness. Then, the discovery of the impostures and lies which characterize the Algerian Moslem's relationship with France. {...} The protagonist Arezki, at the end of the war, comes to the realization that he is nothing but a colonized. This discovery is all the more cruel because as an intellectual, he had believed in the humanist, universalist and egalitarian ideals extolled by France through her literature. The novel expresses thus an immense disillusionment.]

This one historical event (W.W.II), as with the Indigenes on the whole, has served to sharpen the hero's awareness of his position within the colonial hierarchy. The colonial institution for which he fights during the war is the very establishment that deprives him of his freedom as an autonomous being. His subsequent agitations for "political rights" meet with the inevitable: his quest is deemed a criminal act and he is sentenced to ten years imprisonment. A now lucid Arezki views his life in retrospect. The trial, as he sees it, is absurd because, according to him, the judicial system had already condemned him before his trial. "Condemnation before trial" is another leitmotif bringing together Meursault (*L'Etranger*), Smaïl (*Les Hauteurs de la ville*), and Arezki (*Le Sommeil du juste*). With Roblès and Mammeri, the theme is more specific to their colonial context, for the simple reason that both hypothesize principally the condition of the colonized; in other words, their heroes are colonial subjects suffering from an unbalanced system. Their narratives do not transcend the specific reality from which the drama of their characters emerges. The analogy that "Arezki is a Meursault-like figure" (Haddour 1989, 147) can be misleading, because Meursault is not a colonial subject. Both *L'Etranger* and *Le Sommeil du juste* parody the travesty of justice, but the authorial objectives are different. What Camus insists on illustrating is his hero's innocence and the "absurd" trial that condemns him. Viewed within its political and cultural context, it is not strange that Meursault's act of homicide represents for colonial justice not a criminal case in itself but a pointer to the criminal soul of the accused. *Le Sommeil du juste,* however, illustrates the marginalization of the colonized under the colonial jurisprudence. If Arezki, or even Smaïl (*Les Hauteurs de la ville*) are guilty before their trial, they both perceive it as being linked with their existential reality as colonized.

Allais-je expliquer que d'être né Arezki des Ait-Wandlous, fils de mon père (cheveux bruns, nez droit, lèvres minces, pommettes saillantes, yeux noirs et menton rond) le 1er avril 1919 (comme si c'était une naissance pour rire), m'avait d'avance condamné à ne reconnaître de liberté que celle des autres.[23]

[Was I going to explain that being born Arezki des Ait-Wandlous, son of my father (brown hair, straight nose, thin lips, high cheekbones, black eyes, round chin) the 1st of April 1919 (as if my birth was a joke), I was condemned in advance to know of no freedom other than the freedom of others.]

Inferred from this passage is also the arbitrariness of justice, not necessarily within a colonial context. What is posited here is the arbitrariness of the position of both colonized and the colonizer, since it is only by virtue of a hazard (*jeu de hasard*), by virtue of his birth that Arezki finds himself in the role of the victim. Arezki feels that

Ce crime qui va tout nous valoir de mourir ou d'être condamnés, je sais que je ne l'ai pas commis [...] La longue observance des lois a masqué à mon juge le visage de la vérité. Ainsi installé dans la certitude sans accroc et l'étourdissement de la tâche quotidiennement achevée mais jamais assumée, il ne sait pas que c'est *par accident* que nous sommes lui du bon côté de la barre et moi de l'autre. Il ne voit pas combien est fragile entre nous la ligne qui sépare la faute du justicier. S'il cessait un instant d'être bercé par *la fausse sécurité du code*, si le bref instant d'un lapsus il remplaçait pour une fois par sa conscience d'homme les termes de la loi qui lui en tiennent lieu à bon compte, il reculerait effrayé de découvrir que la société qu'il défend pourrait ne pas devoir son pardon qu'à ma mansuétude. (1956, 253; emphasis added)

[This crime for which we were to die or be condemned, I know I did not commit it {...} The long observance of the laws has masked for my judge the face of the truth. The undisturbed certainty and daze thus established, he does not know that it is by mere accident that we are here, he on the right side of the bar, and I on the other. He does not know how fragile the line is that separates the dispenser of justice from the crime. Were he to leave, even for a brief moment, *the false security code*, if within a brief moment of time he were to replace the terms of the law with a human conscience, he would recoil with horror as he discovers that the society, which he defends, depends a great deal on my leniency.]

The roles of "judge" and "criminal," as Arezki sees it, are arbitrary. Although a result of a historical accident, the positions of the colonizer and the colonized are equally arbitrary. If the judge is able to assume his role as judge, it is due to Arezki's "mansuétude," his submission to the *status quo*; hence the line separating the judge's "righteousness" from the accused's "criminality" is but a fragile one. His eventual sentence to ten years imprisonment brings home to the hero that he has always been a condemned man. The sentence only transfers him from the metaphorical prison of colonized Algeria to another, the prison cell. By equating himself to the judge, Arezki does give another dimension to his demand, which is not political. His demand inscribes itself within the human quest for liberation, the very ideals of justice and freedom which both Arezki and the judge fought for in the World War Two. The colonial establishment has taught Arezki to fight for the ideals of "justice" and "freedom" in the context of the war. Underscoring its own absurdity is the structure that condemns Arezki for the very ideals it had inculcated in him. Mammeri's novel clearly reflects upon "le sommeil de la justice" (sleep of justice) in colonial Algeria in the 1950s. But the philosophical thrust of the story, the hero's universalizing stance, diffuses the specific colonial context of the novel, transposing it into a more opaque context where the problem of the judge's unawakened consciousness and the question of death are addressed. Such a diffused context undermines Arezki's political rebelliousness. Unlike Smaïl (*Les Hauteurs de la ville*) who kills in the name of the oppressed, he (Arezki) is merely in pursuit of his individual justice which, incidentally, "a buté sur le mur de la loi coloniale (stumbled against the walls of colonial law)" (1956, 251). Arezki's confrontation with the colonial jurisprudence and his personal frustration form the core of the novel. The hero's quest for social justice within the colonial framework reflects the dilemma of the acculturated writer Mammeri. The latter does not advocate a political divorce from France, but reparation and justice. The actual context of the novel, let us remember, is the Algerian war predicated upon the Indigenes' demand for a total break from France.

Consciously or unconsciously, therefore, the writings of Camus, Roblès and Mammeri reveal the liberal and humanist position of these writers regarding the colonial situation. Mouloud Feraoun's writings provide a critique of the opaqueness of the liberal ideological position which these writers embraced. His two fictional works *La Terre et le sang* (1952) and *Les Chemins qui montent* (1957) give further voice to what they present as undercurrents or suppress altogether in their narratives or sociological analysis of the colonial situation, namely manicheanism predicated upon a principle of exclusion.

Amer, the hero of *La Terre et le Sang,* is a helpless witness to the murder of his uncle. Both are emigrant workers in metropolitan France. The novel, while posing the problem of North African emigrants in France, delineates further the alienation of the Indigenes within the cultural universe of the colonizer. In an alien land (France) where the ethnic codes of honor are suspended, Amer experiences his own "impuissance à venger [la mort de son oncle] (his powerlessness in avenging [the death of his uncle)" (1952, 64). Unable to testify against his uncle's murderer, the case is classified by the French police as "un accident de travail" (ibid., 67).

> Si Amer avait parlé, [...] de quel poids eût été son témoignage, à côté de celui d'André? On savait bien comment les choses se passaient, dès qu'il s'agissait "d'Arabes." Il suffisait de voir la manière d'enquêter. Tout le monde était pressé d'en finir. André [le meurtrier] n'avait qu'un témoin. Le pauvre Rabah [l'oncle] avait pour lui l'équipe entière. Mais on n'insista pas. André fut mis hors de cause. (1952, 66)

> [If Amer had spoken up, {...} what weight would his witness have had, beside that of André? We all knew how things went, when it had to do with the "Arabs." One only had to see how investigations were carried out. Everyone was in a hurry to be done with it. André [the killer] had only one witness. Poor Rabah [the uncle] had the entire team on his side. But no one probed too deeply. André was acquitted.]

As in *L'Etranger* and in *Le Sommeil du juste*, the victim here fails to obtain justice because of his exclusion from the colonial jurisprudence and ultimately his exclusion from the colonizer's democratic principles. Such an exclusion is concomitant to the racist intention which characterizes colonial intercourse. The paradigm of French legal sytem within a colonial structure which these writers dramatize, albeit from different fields of vision, illustrates further the manicheanism of the colonial world described by Fanon as a world divided into compartments, cut in two, and inhabited by two different species:

> The originality of the colonial context is that economic reality, inequality, and the immense difference of ways of life never come to mask the human realities. When you examine at close quarters the colonial context, it is evident that what parcels out the world is to begin with the fact of belonging to or not belonging to a given race, a given species. In the colonies the economic substructure is also a superstructure. The cause is the consequence. (*The Wretched of the Earth* 1963, 39–40)

Thus, far from being complementary, the spaces occupied by the colonizer and the colonized are opposing, delineated by a language of violence and arbitrariness. Camus's *L'Etranger*, Mammeri's *Le Sommeil du juste*, and Feraoun's *La Terre et le sang* point to the manichean relationship as limiting on the colonized's space. By virtue of their "extraneousness," the nameless Arab in *L'Etranger*, Arezki in *Le Sommeil du juste* and Amer in *La Terre et le sang*, are outsiders, or out-laws that assume the colonial laws of exclusion. *L'Etranger*, despite its evasiveness articulates the colonial manicheanism. Camus's protagonist, as Haddour points out, "stands at the threshold of [colonial space] articulating [both] colonial violence and injustice, attempting to represent it" (1989, 155); it, however, transfigures this miscarriage of justice in the colonial arena to dramatize a universal problematic. *L'Etranger* foreshadows "le sommeil de la justice" the very thematic of Mammeri's novel, but from a universalist posture. Such a field of vision which overlooks the racist attitude of the French legal system has been noted to encode an authorial attitude. ("Le thème racial dans L'Etranger.") Feraoun's work, by presenting a different image of a colonial society, explodes the myth of Camus's mis-representation, revealing that which is suppressed in Meursault's trial.

Camus's narrative embodies a racist structure of feelings pertinent to the setting of the novel. As stipulated, the peculiar presentation of the Arab in *L'Etranger* encodes both a physical and a cultural denial of the Other; this is reinforced within the narrative by the use of, or the reference to the Arab in the form of a collective singular "l'Arabe." By lumping the Arabs together under the anonymous and collective "Il" (he) or "ils" (they), what O'Brien refers to as "the colonial 'they': the pronoun which needs no antecedent" (1970, 23), the narrative denies the Arab his subjectivity as well as his legal individuality, thereby illustrating literally and symbolically "le meurtre objectif" (Fanon, *Pour la révolution africaine* 1969, 35) of the Arab. Feraoun's themat-isation of "les chemins qui glissent doucement vers le gouffre" (*Les chemins qui montent* 1957:204) reenacts the dehumanization or the objective murder of the young Algerian hero, Amirouche, whose life ends in the abyss of suicide. "Cet homme objet, sans moyen d'exister, sans raison d'être, est brisé au plus profond de sa substance. Le désir de vivre, de continuer, se fait de plus en plus indécis, de plus en plus phantomatique" (ibid., 37).

As in a vicious circle, this dehumanization is both a cause and a consequence. It is both a direct result of colonialism and a justification for the historical crimes of colonization. This, as indicated earlier, is one succinct point raised by Camus in his *Misère de la Kabilie*. As Camus accurately pointed out, the colonized's poverty and back-wardness (a direct consequence of colonial exploitation—Camus how-ever fails to make this link) are also used as justification for further exploitation and despoliation, and for the maintenance of the colonial *status quo*. Within such tautological reasoning, it follows naturally that the colonizer is absolved of all colonial guilt. The colonized's outlawness, his relegation to the periphery of the "universal" laws of morality and legality, outside the very moral and "humanitarian" principles governing the contemporary world, serve paradoxically, to reinforce the innocence of the colonizer; the victimization of the Indigenes is thus legally legitimized. Feraoun's hero, Amer, like the Arab of Camus's novel, could not present his case (the murder of his uncle), before the French justice because of the predetermined guilt he assumes with the condition of the colonized. Feraoun's *Les Chemins qui montent*, a sequel to *La Terre et le Sang* dramatizes further the "inherited" guilt of the colonized; this is presented in terms of "original sin" eternalized in colonial wedlock. Not only does Amirouche (son of Amer in *La Terre et le sang*) live "sous le soleil de la misère," unable to enjoy the democratic privileges of the Western world upon which is predicated the colonial myth, but he is also unable to gratify his sense of Being, having been denied humanity. His plight acquires thus a double dimension: it is both a political and a metaphysical injustice, the former reinforcing the latter.

> Non vraiment, ce n'est pas de mon sort que je ne suis pas content mais plutôt de mon origine, car enfin j'aurais pu ne pas naître dans ce pays maudit. Si j'étais né en France [...] je crois qu'à vingt-cinq ans je n'aurais rien trouvé à redire. Je serais un homme au milieu de millions d'hommes, peut-être malheureux, peut-être heureux, un homme, quoi, comme tant d'autres. J'en veux à mère d'avoir fait de moi un Kabyle et qui a conscience de l'être [...] Si j'avais à choisir, certes non, je ne serais pas Kabyle à cette heure. (1957, 154)

> [No really, it is not my lot that I am dissatisfied with, but rather my roots, for really, I could have been born anywhere other than this accursed country. If I had been born in France {...}, I think at age twenty five I would have had nothing to complain about. I would have been a man among a million men, perhaps miserable, perhaps happy, but a man like many others. I hold it against my mother for having made me a Kabyle who is conscious of being one {...}. If I had had to choose, certainly not, I would not be a Kabyle at this moment.]

For Amirouche, to be born a Kabyle is to be doomed from birth to colonial enslavement. His racial origin condemns him to live in a prison of colonial iniquities. By virtue of his birth also, his civil rights are limited. Likewise, the hero is aware of a sense of culpability attendant to his position. He carries the guilt for a "crime" he never committed, the stigma of colonialism that forces him to assume the injustices of colonial practice. Feraoun's novel clearly illustrates what the Algerian writer, Jean Amrouche, calls "le mépris et l'humiliation [qui] frappent . . . l'indigène dans sa postérité, comme l'effet d'un péché originel." And as he explains further,

[L]'état colonial fait de l'indigène colonisé un étranger, un déraciné dans son propre pays. Il est réduit au rôle d'assisté, de mendiant perpétuel nourri en marge des activités économiques normales, des reliefs que lui dispensent charitablement ses maîtres. Il sent peser sur lui, jusqu'à l'étouffer et à lui rendre l'air irrespirable, toutes les conséquences de la conquête et de la spoliation coloniales qu'on prétend transfigurer en épopée civilisatrice. (Amrouche 1963, 101)

[[T]he colonial state makes of the colonized native a stranger, uprooted in his own country. He is reduced to a state of dependency, a perpetual beggar nourished from the margins of normal economic activities, from hand-outs that his masters give out on charity. He feels, weighing down on him, to the point of suffocation, all the consequences of the colonial conquest and plundering which are passed off as a civilizing epic.]

Amirouche of *Les Chemins qui montent*, a child of a mixed marriage, symbolizes the double *déracinement* of the accultured indigene, a direct result of his cultural *métissage*. The novel articulates the fundamental problem of the individual and his national identity, which for Amirouche, "le bâtard authentique" (1957, 207) is concretized by his tragic inability to have a legitimate name, "a label" and to function within any cultural system (Amrouche 1963, 116).

Interesting here is the notion of the "bastard" which is at the very basis of maghrebine Francophone literary production. Danielle Marx-Scouras, in her article "The Poetics of Maghrebine Illegitimacy," argues that "the Maghrebine writer has received the 'benefit' of a language and civilization of which he is not the legitimate heir" (1986, 3).[24] Fritz P. Kirsch terms the literary endeavor of the Maghrebine "le fruit d'un viol" (the product of rape) (1986, 85). Addressing also the issue of North-African's illegitimacy, the literary critic, Charles Bonn writes earlier that "Le roman maghrébin de langue française est né sous le regard et 'dans' le regard de l'Autre. . . ." (1974, 77). From these various critical perspectives, it becomes clear that, in mastering the language of the master of the day, the protagonist-author of the first Maghrebine novels of the fifties and early sixties will experience the French language as a weapon, but mostly as "an exile." The state of bastardy aptly describes the position of the westernized Arab/Berber whose identity crumbles under the scrutinizing gaze of both traditions. Interestingly, as in the case of the young évolues like Mokrane (*La*

Colline Oubliée) who consciously turn their back to their "degenerate" tradition, the Western culture which they seek to embrace, fails to legitimize their status, since assimilation and colonialism are incompatible. The resulting condition of "non-belonging," or cultural limbo will be sustained as "a negative state, as an identity crisis" to be surmounted through an act of reconciliation with one's past, or a further breaking away (Marx-Scouras 1986, 4). Amirouche, like his father alienated in France (*La Terre et le sang*), returns to his native village, not to reconcile with his traditional roots but to commit suicide. Amirouche's failure, his cultural and metaphysical alienation deconstructs the supposed symbiosis of cultures upheld by *L'Ecole d'Alger*. Amirouche is a product, literally and symbolically, of the proposed marriage of cultures. The tension, emerging from the hero's alienation from two cultural universes, clearly illustrates the failure of assimilation. The metaphors of "marriage" and "bastard" are both significant here, for they interpret a cause and an effect, i.e., the colonial process (the alleged marriage) which led to the cultural seclusion of the colonized (bastard), and the perpetuation of his misery within "a mummified society" (Haddour 1989, 157). Amirouche is attracted to Dehbia a young Kabyle girl, but refuses to marry in order not to perpetuate the poverty inherent in the lot of a Kabyle. For from his field of vision, the colonized, imprisoned within the colonial society, with the burden of supporting a family, is essentially a Sisyphean figure, unable to break the infernal dialectics of colonial misery.

> Je m'installais dans un cercle d'où aucune dialectique ne pouvait me sortir. Quand on me disait que le cercle était vicieux, je répondais qu'il était parfait, bien fermé, mais *que toute la question pour nous était d'y faire une brèche afin d'en sortir.* Je pense toujours de même, nous sommes prisonniers de nos coutumes, nous sommes emmurés dans l'ignorance, et des malins en profitent. (1957, 202; emphasis added)

> [I settled myself in a circle from which no dialectic could extricate me. When they told me that the circle was vicious, I replied that it was perfect, well closed, but that the *whole challenge for me was to make a break in order to get out.* I always think the same way: we are prisoners of our customs, we are entrapped in ignorance, and the smart ones are taking advantage of us.]

By refusing marriage, Amirouche hopes to operate a break ("une brèche") within the vicious circle of colonial existence: "Ce n'est pas possible, nous ne recommencerons pas. Je veux dire que nous ne nous marierons pas, nous n'aurons pas d'enfants, nous ne voudrons pas cette existence, parce nous avons le droit de repousser un injuste châtiment et que l'existence à Ighil-Nezman est un châtiment immérité" (1957, 135). Amirouche's sisyphean lucidity does not, however, lead to the Camusian lucid rebellion ("révolte éclairée)." Rather, his clairvoyance, his refusal of the system ends in the hero's "leap" into suicide, which in effect delivers him from the duty of facing his living death, the dehumanized existence of the colonized. On a symbolic level, the suicide is that of the semi-French Algerian elites. The suicide of Feraoun's hero who is imbued with *L'Ecole d'Alger*'s humanitarianist and liberalist rhetoric, is the ultimate expression of political despair in the face of the Algerian crisis. Feraoun's "outsider" introduces himself from a perspective, different from Camus's "outsider." Not only does his suicide symbolize his own effacement, and that of others from the colonizer's world, but it also correlates this alienation with his revolt and by extension that of the colonized as a collective group, against the symbols of racism inherent in colonial intercourse.

The ontological question which Amirouche raises, "Pourquoi ce sont présisément les Kabyles qui sont Kabyles et pas les autres? [Why is it that it is precisely the Kabyles who are Kabyles?]" (1957, 155). upsets the "paradigms of victimizer and victimized, colonizer and colonized, subject and object" (Haddour 1989, 158). The question, precipitating as it does, the colonial malaise into an ontological issue, anticipates an ideological suicide, in other words, the annihilation of a being (the colonized) as well as the image with which the latter identifies (the colonizer). The act of suicide as stated, points to the frustrated rebellion of the colonized against the contradictions of assimilation, and to the failure of colonial liberalism represented by *L'Ecole d'Alger*. Feraoun, a former adherent of the assimilationist stand of *L'Ecole d'Alger* relinquishes his former belief in the French democratic principles and assimilationist ideals. *Les Chemins qui montent* stands as his critique of the Camusian sociological appraisal of the Algerian malaise. Writing to Roblès, Feraoun states: "J'ai bien envie d'écrire à Camus pour réfuter un point de 'doctrine' qui me choque en tant que Kabyle. Cela me travaille depuis une semaine. Si ce n'est pas moi, c'est toi qui encaisseras ma prose, ou bien alors cela passera dans mon roman" (*Lettres à ses amis* 1969, 99). [I really want to write to Camus in order to refute a doctrinal point which shocks me as Kabyle. It has preoccupied me for a week. It is you, if not I, who will receive my prose, or failing that, it will go into my novel.] Feraoun refutes the Camusian stance expressed in *La Misère de la Kabylie*.

Feraoun's novel thus engages Camus in a political debate, putting into question the latter's evaluation of the Kabyle's economic distress as dissociated from its political cause. For Feraoun the destitution of the indigene has its root in one historical situation—colonialism.

Ce n'est pas le fanatisme qui les sauvera de la misère et l'esclavage. Voilà encore de mes grands mots de communiste raté! Mais au fond, c'est bien vrai. Ici, c'est l'esclavage et la misère. L'une est largement proclamée, connue et admise. Quant à l'autre, bien sûr, il y en a qui ne s'en rendent pas compte. Comment leur expliquer, et pourquoi? Je reviens de Paris, moi, Amirouche. J'y retournerai sans doute. A moins que [...] Là-bas, oui, nous voyons clairement ce que nous sommes. Là-bas, one ne nous parque pas, nous sommes admis partout, c'est sûr. Mais partout nous sommes des Norafs. Là-bas, il y a les riches et les pauvres, il y a les bandits et les clochards, mais nous ne rentrons dans aucune catégorie. (*Les Chemins* 1957, 125)

[It is not fanaticism that will save them from misery and slavery. Here again are my big words of a failed communist! But deep down, it is really true. Here, slavery and misery thrive. The latter is well proclaimed, known and acknowledged. But the former, of course, there are those who do not realize it. How does one explain it to them, and why? I've come back from Paris, I, Amrouche. I'll go back, no doubt. Unless {...} There, yes, we see clearly what we are. There, we are not confined; we are admitted everywhere, for sure. But everywhere we are Norafs. There, there are the rich and the poor, crooks and tramps, but we do not fit into any category.]

Colonialism, by its very nature counteracts the assimilationist project that Camus fully endorses. The latter overlooks the fact that the "Bicots" and the "Norafs"[25] (terms used in France to designate North Africans) cannot enter any social stratum of the metropolitan society: "Nous ne rentrons dans aucune catégorie" (*Les Chemins* 1957, 125). Camus, faced with the Indigenes' misery ("la misère Kabyle") proposes the introduction by France of major reforms to improve the social conditions of the indigenous population. Apart from offering higher remuneration to the overexploited colonized, these reforms must include better education for the native leading to his assimilation into the metropolitan culture. Camus, like Feraoun, addresses the problem of the north African emigrant in France. Both Camus and Feraoun follow the Kabylian itinerary of misery, "des chemins des misères ... qui se dressent devant les kabyles" (*Les Chemins qui montent* 1957, 206). Whereas Camus believes that France needs to abolish those restrictive barriers "des barrières [mises] à l'émigration" (1965, 906), Feraoun's novel points out the obvious fact that the problems confronting the Kabyle emigrant are not solely economic; neither are they entirely, problems of emigration. They are social barriers, ultimately, racial barriers. Emigration merely demonstrates an extreme manifestation of the excluded condition of the colonized.

> Les gens qui viennent chez nous ne sont pas à plaindre: ils occupent les meilleures places, toutes les places, et finissent toujours par s'enrichir. Chez nous, il ne reste rien pour nous. Alors, à notre tour nous allons chez eux. Mais ce n'est ni pour occuper des places ni pour nous enrichir, simplement pour arracher un morceau de pain: le gagner, le mendier ou le voler. Voilà ce que nous faisons. C'est cela le marché des dupes. Notre pays n'est pas plus pauvre qu'un autre, mais à qui est-il notre pays? Pas à ceux qui y crèvent de faim, tout de même. (*Les Chemins qui montent* 1957, 209)

> [The people who come into our country do not deserve any sympathy: they occupy the best positions, all the positions, and always end up enriching themselves. There is nothing left for us at home. So we also go to their country. But not to occupy positions or to get rich, but simply to snatch a piece of bread: earn it, beg for it, or steal it. This is what we do. We have been taken in. Our country is no poorer than any other, but who does our country belong to? Certainly not to those who are dying of hunger.]

The dismantling of existing social structures through the effort of the French colonial mission, and the resulting uprooting of the colonized from his possessions force the latter to emigrate. Feraoun's hero however, points to the futility of abolishing the emigration barriers as Camus suggests. Either in France or in Algeria, the Algerian is an alien. In France he is a guest whom his French host treats with disdain (Haddour 1989, 160). If he is compelled by economic necessity to seek employment in France, he does so by selling his labor cheaply, to extort a daily living.

> Il y a un siècle que les Français viennent chez nous. Il y a un demi-siècle que nous allons chez eux. *Un échange fraternel* dont je suis un bâtard authentique! C'est ce que j'ai toujours expliqué aux camarades fervents lecteurs de *La Fraternité des races*. (*Les Chemins qui montent* 1957, 207)

> [The French have been coming to our country for a century now. We have been going to theirs for half a century. A brotherly exchange of which I am the authentic bastard! It's what I've always explained to those avid readers of *La Fraternité des races*.]

This, manifestly, is a reminder to liberals like Camus, that in a system which depends on the overexploitation of one race by the other, the notion of "fraternité des races" becomes incongruous, underscoring a certain myopism or hypocrisy; for "fraternité" supposes an equality, which the system is simply in no way of granting (Sartre, "Preface" *The Wretched of the Earth* 1963, 8).

Les Chemins qui montent introduces the Kabyle immigrant as a "panderer," "une espèce de chancre," justifying the colonizer's resentment of the Noraf's presence in metropolitan France.

> Un chancre obstiné qui va se fixer dans les bonnes villes de France. Voilà ce que nous sommes [...] Les Nord-Africains découragent toutes les bonnes volontés. [Les gens] s'en détournent, la mort dans l'âme, le dégoût dans le coeur, le venin dans la bouche [...] On finit par se demander pourquoi les bonnes villes de France continuent d'accueillir une graine si malfaisante. Pourquoi ils ne resteraient pas chez eux au lieu devenir infester les pays bien policés. (1957, 198)

> [An obstinate canker that is going to plant itself in the best cities of France. That is what we are {...} North Africans discourage all good intentions. [People] turn away from them in hopelessness, in disgust, and in bitterness. {...} One finally wonders why the good cities of France continue to welcome such an evil seed. Why would they not stay in their country instead of coming to infest the well civilized countries.]

The "Noraf" as a "chancre" that dissipates the French cities underscores the novel's textual reference to Camus's *La Peste* (1947). In *L'Homme Révolté* (1951), Camus disapproves of Nazi and Communist ideologies, which he considers as "le chancre contemporain." *La Peste*, written earlier, exploits also the bubonic plague as an effective metaphor to condemn the grossness and the repulsiveness of Nazism. Physiologically both "chancre" and "la peste" manifest themselves as tumerous growth. "Chancre" has however the added connotation of a venereal disease, "syphilis" which society approaches with shame. It implies immorality, vice, etc. By borrowing the image of this evil disease from Camus to describe and justify the French "dégoût" with the North African immigrant, Feraoun establishes an implicit dialogue with Camus's novel *La Peste*. Significantly, Feraoun is one of the first critics to pinpoint the absence of Indigenes from the "Frenchified" city of Oran ravaged by the plague. In a letter to Camus (1951) he states:

> J'ai lu *La Peste* et j'ai eu l'impression d'avoir compris votre livre comme je n'en avais jamais compris d'autres. J'avais regretté que parmi tous ces personnages il n'eut aucun indigène et qu'Oran ne fût à vos yeux qu'une banale préfecture française. Oh! ce n'est pas un reproche. J'ai pensé simplement que, s'il n' y avait pas ce fossé entre nous, vous nous auriez mieux connus, vous vous seriez senti

capable de parler de nous avec la même générosité dont bénéficient tous les autres. (*Lettres à ses amis* 1969, 203)

[I have read *The Plague* and I thought I understood your book as I have understood none other. I regretted that among all the characters, there was not a single native and that Oran was for you only a banal French prefecture. Oh! it is not a reproach. I only thought that if there had not been this gap between us, you would have known us better, you would have been able to talk about us with the same generosity from which others benefit.]

For Feraoun, the gap that separates Camus from the native Algerian is ideological, compounded by Camus's failure to appreciate the problems of the natives and the distance that separates him from the colonial realities of the colonized. Much as Feraoun admires in Camus the writer—an obvious source of inspiration to many of the Algerian writers of "the generation of 54," as they came to be known—he deems Camus's stance as illustrative of a lack of understanding as well as a detachment from the realities of colonial life. Feraoun also objects to Camus's assertion of his "Algerianity." He argues that Algeria is for the Algerians who were currently fighting for her independence. Any other position is but a subterfuge, and a lie. "Pourquoi tourner autour de [l]'évidence?" (ibid.). Camus obviously is not simply defending his birthright as a native French Algerian, but also asserting the priority of his ethnic group, under the guise of assimilationist propaganda. As Feraoun was to point out in his *Journal* (1962), the politics of integration (assimilation) which Camus continued to uphold, was not simply obsolete at this point within the process of decolonisation, it had never been a solution to the French-Algerian drama.

Est-ce bien que vous pouvez nous "intégrer?" [...] Pourquoi prétendre faire de nous ce que vous ne voulez pas que nous soyons? Je pourrais dire la même chose à Camus et Roblès. J'ai pour l'un une grande admiration et pour l'autre une affection fraternelle mais ils ont tort de parler puisqu'ils ne sauraient aller au fond de leur pensée. Il vaut cent fois mieux qu'ils se taisent. Car ce pays s'appelle bien l'Algérie et ses habitants des Algériens. Pourquoi tourner autour de cette évidence? Etes-vous Algériens, mes amis? Votre place est à côté de ceux qui luttent. Dites aux Français que le pays n'est pas à eux, qu'ils s'en sont emparés par la force et entendent y demeurer par la force. Tout le reste est mensonge, mauvaise foi. Tout autre langage est criminel parce que, depuis des mois, se commettent des crimes au nom des mêmes mensonges; depuis des mois meurent des innocents qui ont accepté ces mensonges. [...] Et ces innocents sont surtout des indigènes. (*Journal* 1962, 76)

[Are you truly capable of "integrating" us? {...} Why pretend to make of us what you do not wish us to be? I could say the same to Camus and Robles. I have for the latter a great admiration, and for the former a brotherly affection, but it is wrong for them to speak since they cannot probe into the depths of their thoughts. It is hundred times better for them to keep quiet. For this country is truly called Algeria and its inhabitants Algerians. Why fly in the face of the facts? Are you really Algerians, my friends? Then your place is at the side of those who are fighting. Tell the French that this country does not belong to them, that they took possession of it by force, and intend to remain there by force. Everything else is a lie, and bad faith. Every other language is criminal because for months, crimes have been committed in the name of the same lies; for months innocent people who have accepted these lies have died. {...} And these innocent people are mostly the natives.]

What the various writers—Camus, Roblès, Mammeri and Feraoun— have pointed out, consciously or unconsciously, is that their writings by engaging themselves one way or the other in political and social issues, give voice to the political malaise of an entire generation of pied-noir leftists, and the accultured indigenes on the fringe of two cultural worlds vis-à-vis which they see themselves as bastards. Meursault of *L'Etranger* has been viewed variously as a metaphysical outsider in an absurd universe. Some have seen him as a cultural misfit in the land of his birth, thus mirroring the position of the Arab. Meursault and the Arab, it would seem, are both marginal beings. The argument that both are victims of the same social situation, is however not sustainable. The Arab is marginalized by, and a victim of the colonial establishment. Meursault's "victimization" if there is, stems from his inability to "fit into the slot specified for him" (Tarrow 1985, 76). He is condemned, as already indicated, by his own lack of conventionality, his inability to adhere to "the rules of the game." Mammeri's writings, and to a greater extent, Feraroun's, by confronting the colonial problem less obliquely engenders a collapse of *L'Etranger*'s univocal structure, wherein the "absurd" becomes a problematic effacing the colonial malaise. Camus's ambiguous position during the Algerian crisis correlates his narrativisation of the colonial drama. It is not so much a lack of humanistic values or intentions, as a social blindness. But more pertinently, his fiction mirrors the "profound differences in the collective experiences of colonizer and the colonized."[26]

Camus's *La Peste,* the focus of my next chapter, not only points again to the barriers that insulate the writer from colonial realities, but also illustrates further the political ambiguities inherent in the ideological position of the author, caught in nationalist dilemma. The novel, published two years after the 1945 rebellion (Sétif), fails to speak on the behalf of colonized Algeria, but instead purports to illustrate more important "truths and values" which paradoxically can only be articulated against a political background: German occupation as an oppressive system, thus positing a certain "hierarchy of injustice."

> Nous ne pouvons pas croire que l'attitude de Camus n'ait servi la cause d'un régionalisme méditerranéen qui a exalté la supériorité d'une culture par rapport à une autre, *reprenant le fascisme à rebours*, d'autant plus que ses préjugés à l'encontre de peuples non-latins sont flagrants. (Emphasis added)[27]

> [We cannot not believe that Camus's attitude has served the cause of Meditteranean regionalism, *a reverse fascism* that has exalted the superiority of one culture over another, because his prejudices against non-latin people are so flagrant.]

Camus's narrative of a rather "intellectualized problem," the rats, reifying German imperialism, neutralizes the political issue attendant on the topographical setting of the novel (*fascisme à rebours*). In the dual-voicedness of the narrative structure, Camus retains the Algerian setting as a transparent context for the plague, an allegory of German fascism, thus avoiding the inconsistencies which a consideration of French imperialism might divulge.

Notes

1. Stephen D. Ross, *Literature and Philosophy. An Analysis of the Philosophical Novel* (New York: Appleton-Century Crofts, 1969), 187.

2. I recall my own first reading of *L'Étranger* as a ten-year old. I remember my tears of chagrin at the end of the story. To a ten-year old just emerging from the fantasy world of fairy tales, Meursault's death sentence was rather shattering. The killing of the Arab didn't register much on my mind. My tears were brought on by the discovery I made then that heroes of stories do die some times, and that "Beauty" and the "Beast" don't always live happily ever after.

3. B. T. Fitch, *Narrateur et narration dans L'Étranger d'Albert Camus* (Paris:Minard, 1968), 44.

4. J. Conilh, "Albert Camus. L'Exil et le Royaume," *Esprit* (avril-mai 1958), 530.

5. David Sprintzen, *Camus: a Critical Examination* (n.p.: Temple Univ-ersity Press, 1988), 14.

6. Maurice Nadeau, *Histoire du Surréalisme* (Paris: Seuil, 1945) 41–49. Quoted by Lev Braun, 33.

7. Ernst Kahler, *The Tower and the Abyss* (New York, 1957) 203. Qtd. in Ignace Feuerlight, "Camus's L'Etranger Reconsidered," *Publications of the Modern Language Association*, LXXVIII. 2 (1963), 606.

8. Albert Camus, *L'Etranger* (Paris: Gallimard, 1942), 1. All citations refer to this edition.

9. Albert Camus, *The Stranger*, trans. Matthew Ward (New York: Vintage Books, 1989), 3. All translations which are not my own, are taken from this edition.

10. K. Gadourek, *Les innocents et les coupables* (The Netherlands: Mouton, 1963), 67.

11. Quoted by O'Brien, *Albert Camus of Europe and Africa* (New York: The Viking Press, 1970), 19–20.

12. Réné Girard, "Camus's Stranger Retried," *Albert Camus*, edited by Harold Bloom (n.p.: Chelsea House Publishers, 1978), 7.

13. David Ellison, *Understanding Camus* (University of South Carolina Press, 1990), 49.

14. Paul J. Amash, "The Choice of an Arab in L'Etranger," *Romance Notes* 9:1 (1967): 7.

15. Monad Fayad, "The Problem of the Subject in Africanist Discourse: Conrad's 'Heart of Darkness' and Camus's 'The Renegade'." *Comparative Literature Studies* 27:4 (1990), 300.

16. Pierre Nora, *Les Français d'Algérie* (n.p.: Réné Julliard, 1961), 54.

17. Roland Barthes asserts that what society perceives as threat in Meursault is not the "criminal" but the "voyeur," not his crime, but his complacent look which has society as its object of scrutiny. "L'Etranger, roman solaire," *Les Critiques de notre temps et Camus* (Paris: Garnier, 1970), 62.

18. A-T. Ibrahim, "Albert Camus vu par un Algérien," *De la Décolonisation à la Révolution culturelle*, edited by A-T. Ibrahim (Alger: SNED, 1981), 180.

19. Mouloud Feraoun, *L'Anniversaire* (Paris: Seuil, 1972), 63.

20. Emmanuel Roblès, *Les Hauteurs de la ville* (Paris: Seuil, 1960), 95.

21. Mouloud Mammeri, *La Colline oubliée* (Paris: Librairie Plon, 1952), 16.

22. Denise Brahimi, "Littérature algérienne et conscience nationale avant l'indépendance," *Notre Librairie* 85 (1986): 26.

23. Mouloud Mammeri, *Le Sommeil du Juste* (Paris: Librairie Plon, 1956), 250.

24. See also Abdelkébir Khatibi who quotes Jean Amrouche as saying: "le colonisé a reçu le bienfait de la langue et de la civilisation dont il n'est

pas l'héritier légitime. Et par conséquent il est une sorte de bâtard [The colonized has received the benefits of a language and civilization of which he is not a legitimate heir. Therefore, he is, somewhat, a bastard.]" *Le Roman maghrébin* (Rabat: SMER, 1979), 39.

25. "Noraf" is an amalgamation, and abbreviation of the words "Nord-Africain."

26. Donald C. Holsinger, "Exiles in their Native Land: Algerian Novelists of French Expression," *The Maghreb Review* 11, nos 2–4 (1986):73.

27. A. Zoubir, "Camus et le Cagayous," *Algérie Actualité* 6–12 January 1983, 29.

Chapter 4

Albert Camus, Mohammed Dib and the Plagues of Colonialism: A Political Re-Reading of *La Peste*

Il est aussi raisonnable de représenter une espèce d'emprisonnement par une autre que de représenter n'importe quelle chose qui existe réellement par quelque chose qui n'existe pas. Albert Camus.[1]

[It is as reasonable to represent one form of imprisonment with another as it is to represent anything which really exists with something which does not exist.]

Introduction

The plague—Bubonic, pneumonic, or otherwise—is described as a "horridly mysterious and impenetrable essence whose pathological might is made even more unsettling by its invisibility."[2] And because of its very mysterious nature, it has the capacity of generating an array of symbols. Susan Sontag in her essay, *Illness as Metaphor,* explains:

> Any important disease whose causality is murky, and for which treatment is ineffectual, tends to be awash in significance. First, the subject of deepest dread (corruption, decay, pollution, anomie, weakness) are identified with the disease. The disease itself becomes a metaphor. Then, in the name of the disease (that is, using it as a metaphor), that horror is imposed on other things. The disease becomes adjectival.[3]

Indeed, given the plague's enigmatic nature, its "murky causality" and yet disproportionate devastation, it is not surprising that "symbols have been projected onto the face of this unseen predator in order to explain or justify its catastrophic biological, social, economic, and political consequences" (Stephanson 1987, 224–5). To cite a couple of examples, the Bubonic Plague of 1346–49, known as the Black Death, claimed between one-quarter and one-half of Europe's population. The Great Plague of London (1665) left in its trail countless dead. The magnitude of the chaos and devastation naturally prompts the question: what does "the plague" stand for? Is there any significance beyond the devastations brought in its wake? By its very nature, it is perhaps first and foremost a threat to human imagination. As Stephanson accurately sums up,

> what we cannot bear is confronting an invisible presence that has no immediate identity and hence no imaginative coordinates. For how does one grasp the reality of thousands of deaths in one place at one time? Precisely because it is unknown, and because its presence can be inferred only by its effects, the plague also has the capacity to compel an array of imaginative responses and to engage the mind in symbol-making. (ibid., 226)

Thus literature, as an expression of human imaginative projection, has reflected the tendency to endow the plague with symbolic value. *The Iliad*, Sophocles's *Oedipus*, to name but two, have interpreted the plague as the punishment of a sinful people by an angry god. Max Byrd, scoffing at such "didactic interpretation," remarks that the "allegory a modern reader may search for in the plague might be political, or economic, or sociological—[all] potential[s] for man's estrangement" (39).[4] Critics confronted with plague narratives, such as Defoe's *A Journal of the Plague Year* (1722) and Camus's *La Peste* (1947) have focused on the symbolic significance of the pestilence. Such a significance resides mostly in the pestilence as reflecting societal ills. Antonin Artaud's article, "The Theater and the Plague," is worth mentioning here. Artaud insists on a link between plague and theater, for they are both "catalyst and mirror" of life. "The plague," he argues, "takes images that are dormant, a latent disorder, and suddenly extends them into the most extreme gestures; the theater also takes gestures and pushes them as far as they will go. . . . The theater [like the plague] restores us all our dormant conflicts and all their powers, and gives these powers names we hail as symbols."[5] Artaud's analogy with theater is interesting in so far as it points not only to the metaphorical significance of plague narratives, but also to the interpretive bent given to such narratives: the plague as a symbol has invariably elicited a spectrum of responses with philosophical, religious or political cast.

Similarly, interpretations of Camus's *La Peste* have run the gamut, from "cosmic alienation" to "the abstract logic of the Marxist-Hegelian theory of history" via "the Nazi Occupation of France" (Braun 1974, 54). Echoing this remark, Sterling affirms that "nearly forty years after [it's] publication, there is a broad critical consensus on the significance of [Camus's] central metaphor."[6] In more specific terms, Jacqueline Lévi-Valensi asserted much earlier that "c'est notre condition mortelle de l'homme qui est figurée dans *La Pest. . . .* Oran n'est rien d'autre qu'une image de notre terre et de notre monde absurde, et Rieux . . . et ses amis sont des incarnations des attitudes humaines devant le mal inhérent à notre condition."[7] Verthuy and Waelti-Walters have pointed to the disturbing nature of the critical assumptions on Camus's novel. Apart from focusing on "phenomena of masculine interest," the over-all criticism of *La Peste* presents a certain close circuit whereby "critics respond to each other rather than to the text, . . . thus presenting a similar concentration on a relatively restricted number of topics."[8] What I find disturbing, however, is not so much the network of criticism on Camus's work (to which I shall also be responding)— admittedly, this is rather restrictive—but the narrative of *La Peste* itself as an allegory of war or as a symbolic description of an absurdist/post-absurdist world; for while these [allegories] are germane to the novel, they reveal a number of lacunae. For instance the novel sets forth Dr. Rieux, the main character (aside from the plague itself) as the model of humanist, cognizant of his limitations, while struggling to bring some semblance of relief to man's existential woes. This chapter will endeavor to read into *La Peste* some of the problematics involved in its critical argument which is constructed implicitly to show off Rieux's philosophy of "revolt" and lucidity as an exemplary model or ideal. Such a presentation, while illustrating a specific philosophical movement reveals itself as inadequate, an ivory tower that isolates the central character Rieux together with his team of combatants, and the very preoccupations they articulate—justice, love, evil—from the cultural context of the novel.

The Algerian setting of Camus's novel has been duly noted by critics. However, as pointed out by Verthuy and Warlti-Walters, very few, if any, "have bothered to dwell on the paradoxical absence of any North-African reality in a novel that begins with a long and detailed description of its Oranais setting" (1987, 406). Haddour argues that the narrative of *La Peste* "transmogrifies the Algerian colonial context into another political context, and . . . substitutes one visage of tyranny (typhus) for another (plague)" (1989, 179). In effect, could it be said that the Algerian landscape is here a diffused context within which universal themes are tried out, at the expense of the colonial social reality, whereby the indigenous culture is reduced to "an adjunct of a mere topographical location, and where the indigenous Arab assumes neither role nor subjectivity?" (Erickson 1988, 89). Certainly such a narrativisation would be a phenomenon of historical and philosophical importance to a critical analysis of Camus. The expunged problematic reality of Camus's novelistic setting provides the thematic core of Mohammed Dib's trilogy, *La Grande Maison* (1952), *L'Incendie* (1954), *Le Métier à tisser* (1957).[9] In recasting the theme of the "plague" against the Algerian colonial background, Dib reveals the disease and its manifestations as illustrating a process of "clochardisation" attendant to colonial economic and political structures. Dib's writings establish a different ideological context in which to unearth and interpret what is suppressed in *La Peste*'s politically selective vision. Dib's writings present the inhabitants of Camus's desert as vagrants.

The first part of this chapter focuses on the thematic structure of *La Peste* in which the Algerian setting becomes a desert, and also a fertile narrative ground for the classical Camusian representation of man as victim of the absurd, the latter emblematically presented as the German Occupation. The second part recasts Camus's setting in order to focus on the colonial processes generative of the plague of typhus and famine in colonized Algeria. I wish to establish the thesis that the narrative of *La Peste* articulates a clearly defined historical situation, not necessarily involving France and Nazi ideology, but France confronted with her ideals of liberty and equality and her Algerian reality.

The Plague and Its Metaphors

Camus's epigraph taken from Defoe's *Robinson Crusoe* would seem to suggest that, as readers, we are called upon to engage in an act of interpretation, a certain act of decoding, to arrive at a hidden meaning. ". . . représenter une espèce d'emprisonnement par une autre. . . ." The plague thus stands for something else, allowing for a multiplicity of interpretations. Tarrow points to three levels of reading *La Peste*: " A straightforward narrative, . . . an allegory of the Occupation, and . . . a symbolic representation of the problem of evil" (1985, 121).

La Peste which defines itself as a chronicle of events, lends itself to a simple reading, a "straightforward narrative." Chronicles, as Laurence Porter remarks, "purport to record events passively as they happen from day to day."[10] The city of Oran is hit by a bubonic plague. Death becomes the major reality in Oran, "[cette] cité sans pittoresque, sans végétation et sans âme" (1947, 13). Underneath the theme of death runs that of a collective struggle, a progression from the pervading solitude of *L'Etranger*. All energies are concentrated on fighting the plague. In addition to the fear of death, the inhabitants know intense isolation, exile and imprisonment as the city is isolated from the rest of the country to prevent contagion. Doubrovsky sums accurately the evolution of Camus's thought from *L'Etranger* to *La Peste*. "Within the limits of the 'absurd' experience, suffering is individual. Starting from the movement of revolt, we are aware of suffering as a collective experience, as every man's adventure. 'I revolt, therefore we are.'"[11] Dr. Rieux, the narrator and the leader of the combating group, illustrates thus the post-absurdist hero. The latter's position is paradoxically privileged, having neither moral nor philosophical basis. More disturbing is their awareness of the relative futility of their endeavor. Neither Rieux's medical knowledge, nor the scientific intervention of Castel's serum, nor Paneloux's prayer prove to be of the slightest efficacy. The disease continued its course of merciless ravage. One is reminded of Camus's assertion in *Noces* that, in the face of the deadly mathematics that govern our condition, "l'esprit n'est rien, ni le coeur même" (54). Rieux's attitude to the plague reveals one of Camus's arresting "truths." Revolt exists side by side with consent. In Rieux's simultaneous "yes" and "no," Camus defines a "dialectic of confrontation" and anguish, yet without despair or transcendence.

The association of the plague with the Occupation has frequently been taken for granted by critics. Camus himself indicated that the intended meaning of his allegory was influenced by the peculiar circumstances surrounding the composition of *La Peste*. In 1942 Camus was in France recuperating from tuberculosis when the Allied troops invaded North Africa. His separation from his family finds echo in the story of Rambert and the thousands of Oranais cut off from their loved ones during the siege of the plague. In 1943, he joins the Resistance, as a writer for the clandestine journal, *Combat*. He writes the same year: "*La Peste* donnera l'image de ceux qui dans cette guerre ont eu la part de la réflexion du silence—et celle de la souffrance" (*Carnets II* 72). Correlatively then, the plague as evil has come to symbolize the Nazi. Writing for *Soir-Républicain* (11 October 1939), Camus affirmed:

In my opinion, this Hitlerian doctrine, and any that might resemble it, should be flatly rejected and condemned, because it is based on a false vision of reality and on inhuman premises and goals. Both in itself and in the regime it inflicts on the German people, it seems to me one of the most abominable forms of evil in political thought and political life.[12]

J. Cruickshank, however, objects to the simplistic association of the allegory with the Occupation, asserting that, "there is a disturbing moral ambiguity present in such products of human agency as war, oppression and injustice [which] is entirely absent in *La Peste*. By his allegory, Camus thus places the origin of suffering in a phenomenon existing outside the scope of human responsibility. . . . The plague . . . covers human wretchedness but ignores human wickedness" (1959, 72). As Tarrow, commenting on Cruickshank's statement, concurs, the latter is "partly right: the plague symbol fails to take into account human responsibility in the origins of human wretchedness" (1985, 126). I believe, however, that Camus's presentation stems from his own amputation of the biblical story of the plague.[13] Indeed, the plague as a manifestation of God's wrath seems, here, to exonerate man from responsibility. But this is only a partial story, for the plague as the Bible records it came as punishment for disobedience, thus attributing a certain responsibility to its victims.[14] By suppressing the second half of the story, Camus is able to give expression to a more absurdist resonance, here the allegory of man faced with the plague of oppression.

Camus's work on *La Peste* coincides with his active participation in politics (Tarrow 1985, 120). Thus the political and historical situation that confronts both him and Rieux, is in effect, a plague. Camus's reiterated suspicion regarding historical pretensions is well known. Unlike the Marxists, "preconceived historical goals lacked a discernible meaning for Camus" (Porter 1982, 591). The writer held to his view that no fulfillment could be achieved through history. *La Peste* consequently attempts to deromanticize history by creating monotony and futility. Opposed to the Hegelian view of history, Camus adamantly rejects the involved cost. Human lives and happiness, he asserts, are too great a price to pay for any political change. Hegelian philosophy he perceives as misleading since "it implies the sacrifice of the individual to historical progress" (Thody 1961, 103). Camus's criticism of Marx's messianic vision, his indictment of the "grand narratives" that animate the Western world, implicit in *La Peste*, will emerge forcefully in *L'Homme Révolté* (1951). During the polemics generated by his essay, he writes to *Les Temps Modernes* (1952) reiterating his position and insisting that worship of the historical process by Nazis and Communists only bred murderers (1965, 317). Camus's preoccupation with the political scene is apparent. *La Peste* can be said to transpose the author's political experience into a work of fiction. Such an aestheticisation, Tarrow observes, reveals "many of the problems underlying Camus's [political] commitment" (1985, 121).

Quilliot, summarizing what could be called an "authorial intention" here, points also to the symbolic nature of Camus's narrative:

> *La Peste* veut d'abord être l'histoire symbolique de ces jours de ténèbres que furent les années d'occupation, aussi bien pour les habitants de la zone occupée, [...] que pour les soldats exilés en Prusse Orientale, en Poméranie ou ailleurs et pour les déportés des camps de la mort, chaque jour plus nombreux. Mais *La Peste* est aussi une tentative de réponse à la question que posaient déjà *L'Etranger* et *le Mythe de Sisyphe*: comment se comporter dans un monde absurde, dominé par la volonté de puissance de quelques médiocres Caligula? Comment faire face à cette marée de souffrances qui déferle sur l'Europe comme sur l'Asie? Pourtant le mal n'est pas seulement extérieur: il menace l'homme de partout et Camus à qui la maladie livre un nouvel assaut, est mieux placé que quiconque pour le savoir. (*Théâtre, Récits, Nouvelles* 1962, 1928)

> [*The Plague* is first of all the symbolic story of those gloomy days of the Occupation; as much for those living in the occupied zone, {..} as for those soldiers exiled in Prussia, in Pomeranie or elsewhere, and for those deported in daily increasing numbers to death camps, everyday more numerous. But *The Plague* is also an attempt to answer the question which was already raised in *The Stranger* and *The Myth of Sisyphus*: how does one behave in an absurd world dominated by the will to power of mediocre Caligulas? How does one confront this tide of suffering breaking out in Europe and Asia? The evil is, however, not only from without: it threatens man from everywhere, and, more than anyone else, Camus, who is under the attack of a new wave of illness, is better placed to know.]

La Peste it seems, articulates the plight of man faced with all that is politically evil. Few Camus scholars have, however, interpreted *La Peste* as a parable of the 1945 political crisis in Algeria. In an article, "Albert Camus's Algeria," Quilliot states that "The rats [which] continued to die..., invading the gutters and the mouths of sewers are victims of colonialism and its oppression" (1962, 44). Indeed, the reiteration that the plague stands ultimately for any form of totalitarianism would suggest that such a reading is possible. *La Peste* as a possible transposition of the cultural setting of the novel reveals various representational inadequacies and inconsistencies, as we shall observe presently.

The Plagues of Political Evil:
French and German Nationalisms

A broad critical consensus on *La Peste* is, therefore, that it offers us "the widest possibilities as metaphors for what is felt to be socially or morally wrong" (Stephanson 1987, 226). One such possibility for Camus is that it stands for the French resistance to the imprisoning ideology of German fascism. The ability to represent one form of "imprisonment" with another becomes thus a powerful creative tool for Camus, and also a liberating one. He is thus able to manipulate the symbol of the plague-ridden rats to condemn Nazism without delving into the various other political problematics of the novel, the conflicting spheres of interests and the proliferation of diverse political struggles that permeate the North African space. Haddour correctly asserts that

> *La Peste* covertly dramatizes the political dilemma of World War II under the banner of a univocalised universalism and avoids a dramatization of sides in opposition. Nonetheless, the moral repulsiveness associated with the symbol of the plague, and the political pregnancy of the allegory works implicitly to condemn only one side. (1989, 120)

La Peste, written two years after the 1945 insurrection in Algeria, failed to give voice to the Algerian political crisis. The latter is seemingly subsumed into a spectrum of Western conflicts which found their expression in World War II. Camus's universalism betrays itself as highly nationalistic. At the risk of reducing Camus's *La Chute* to an autobiography, one might say that Clamence (the main character) conveys quite succinctly, the author's dilemma when faced with the Algerian political problem. "Les partis opposés me paraissaient avoir également raison et je m'abstins" (*Théâtre, Récits, Nouvelles* 1962, 1537).

In Camus's well noted editorial of *Combat*, following the fall of Hitler, he writes:

> Paris fait feu de toutes ses balles dans la nuit d'août. Dans cet immense décor de pierres et d'eaux, tout autour de ce fleuve aux flots lourds d'histoire, les barricades de la liberté, une fois de plus, se sont dressées. *Une fois de plus, la justice doit s'acheter avec le sang des hommes.*
> Le temps témoignera que les hommes de France ne voulaient pas tuer, et qu'ils sont entrés les mains pures dans une guerre qu'ils n'avaient pas choisie. [...] Paris se bat aujourd'hui pour que la

France puisse parler demain. Le Peuple est en armes ce soir parce qu'il espère une justice pour demain. [...] Le Paris qui se bat ce soir veut commander demain. Non pour le pouvoir, mais pour la justice, non pour la politique, mais pour la morale, non pour la domination de leur pays, mais pour sa grandeur. (1958, 255–6; emphasis added)

[Paris opens fire in the night of August. In this immense decor of stones and waters, all around this river whose waves are heavy with history, the barricades of liberty have once again been raised. Once again, justice must be bought at the cost of men's blood.

Time will bear testimony that the men of France did not want to kill, and that they entered with pure hands into a war that they did not choose. {...} Paris is fighting today in order for France to be capable of speaking tomorrow. The people are in arms this evening because they hope tomorrow will bring justice. {...} The Paris which is fighting this evening wants to be in command tomorrow. Not for power, but for justice, not for politics, but for morals, not for the domination of their country, but for France's grandeur.]

Interesting, here is the emphasis on France's "grandeur" as the ultimate justification for the French resistance. Camus's discourse replicates the assumptions underlying the French project of a civilizing mission generative of France's supposed role of promoting freedom and justice in the world. This role, as Camus sees it, is not political, but humanist. Nonetheless, the France which confronted the Nazi threat with such noble ideals as freedom and justice presents a Fascist face in colonial Algeria. The two major insurrections in Algeria (1945, 1954), leading eventually to the all-out war of independence, underscore the justness of Camus's statement that justice must be bought at a costly price. "la justice doit s'acheter avec le sang des hommes" (Justice must be bought at the price of men's blood) (ibid.).

Dubbing the last day of the liberation as "la nuit de la vérité, [the night of truth]" (ibid., 256), Camus amply acknowledges the validity of the French resistance to the German threat. He seems, however, oblivious to the fact that the "truth" of the Algerian nationalist insurgency shares the very premises of the French resistance movement. Thus, "la nuit de la vérité" becomes a selectively contextualized prerogative. *La Peste* re-enacts the European drama within a foreign setting. The "truth" proposed within this setting smacks of a fundamental confusion and a univocality, for it is singlemindedly mediated by expunging from the text all non-European political interests, thereby avoiding the burning and contemporary issue of colonialism. If the conclusion of *La Peste* dramatizes "La Nuit de la vérité," the political context of the novel is permeated by an "immense décor de pierre et d'eaux, tout autour de ce fleuve aux flots lourds d'histoire, [où] les barricades de la liberté, une fois de plus, se sont dressées" (1958, 255).

The plague could indeed be an allegory of the isolation of free France, exiled to North Africa and separated from Europe under Nazi domination (Haddour 1989). Such an allegory is simply a variable within the multi-dimensional symbolism of the novel. Of interest to us is really the highly political context of the novel, despite the attempt at maintaining a neutrality. Also interesting, and re-enforcing the political context of the novel, is the polarization of two major interests.

Camus's *Lettres à un ami allemand*, I believe, interprets the ideology underlying the narrative of *La Peste*. This set of four letters written to a fictional German friend (cf. chapter 2) leaves no doubt in our mind as to Camus's position in the World War II dilemma. Well articulated is his anti-Nazi position. One does not really expect it to be otherwise. The letters thus posit a clear distinction between two national identities, German and French. Within this dialogical context Camus engages in an interaction with the "other," while *La Peste* transposes the humanness of the other into a plague. The interlocution established through the exchange (of letters) presupposes that the German friend is not, however, silent. The nationalistic and dogmatic aspirations of the latter are made clear. Despite Camus's own reiterated claim that he loves his country too much to be nationalistic, on the emotional and political level the war crisis confronts him with the necessity to take sides. That he, understandably, would take the side of the French implicates him in a nationalistic dilemma, which he sought to present in universal terms. In an attempt to downplay his nationalistic feelings, Camus insists that "si parfois nous semblions préférer la justice à notre pays, c'est que nous voulions seulement aimer notre pays dans la justice, comme nous voulions l'aimer dans la vérité et dans l'espoir" (*Lettres à un ami allemand* 1945, 228). Camus's *Lettres* finds a certain parallel in "Lettre à un Militant Algérien" addressed to Azziz Kessous in October 1955. Here Camus's concept of justice fails to transcend its nationalist limitations. This failure manifests itself also in his famous replique to the harassment of an Algerian student, "Je crois à la justice, mais je défendrai ma mère avant la justice."

Camus's condemnation of Nazism, as I have stated, is entirely laudable. It does not constitute a bone of contention here. Condemnation is however possible only within a polarization, here that of two nationalisms. Thus, the concept of "justice" is specific, and defined in relation to a clearly delineated political context; it is not universally defined. What I wish to bring out is that, obviously, Camus's position combating the injustices of Nazism, as presented in the highly politicized allegory of the plague in *La Peste*, is not neutral. His stance is highly polemical, as well as political, clearly directed at what constitutes a threat, what presents itself as a menacing otherness. Even an exemplary figure as Rieux operates within a clearly polarized context. Yet, the novel contrives to keep a certain impartiality, while presenting only one side of the conflict as human. The simulacrum of neutrality is, however, a device used to transpose the problem into a universal domain by presenting it as a collective homicide. But within the pseudo-universality, Camus posits Western ideals, specifically, French national ideals of equality, liberty. He thus promotes France into a position of superiority above all the other national entities and other concerns and interests.

The presentation of Camus's univocal views of justice fails to account for the injustice prevalent in the Algerian colonial structure. His dismissal of the Algerian nationalist demands as decadent and subversive, contradicts his own nationalist structure of feelings concealed under the cloak of universalism. Within the polarization of ideologies, Nazism is reified into a transmitter of disease—the rats. Ideology, as "a product of human cogitation" inserts itself necessarily within a specific cultural context. Camus, or Rieux, attempts to speak for man in universal terms from a French colonial context; this context is ossified by the narrative. Consequently, Rieux can only speak for the victims of the plague, supposedly France, and not against the perpetrators of tyranny, the human propounders of Nazi ideology and imperialism (Haddour 1989, 124).

> Etant appelé à témoigner, à l'occasion d'une sorte de crime, il [Rieux] a gardé une certaine réserve, comme il convient à un témoin de bonne volonté. Mais en même temps, selon la loi d'un coeur honnête, il a pris délibérément le parti de la victime et a voulu rejoindre *les hommes, ses concitoyens, dans les seules certitudes qu'ils aient en commun, et qui sont l'amour, la souffrance et l'exil.* (*La Peste* 1947, 23; emphasis added)

> [Having been called to testify on the occasion of a sort of crime, he [Rieux] kept a certain reserve as it was becoming of a witness of good will. But at the same time, in line with the code of an honest heart, he deliberately took the side of the victim and had wanted to join *the men, his fellow citizens, in the only certainties they have in common, which are love, suffering and exile.*]

Rieux, taking the side of men "les hommes, ses concitoyens, dans les seules certitudes qu'ils aient en commun" (ibid.), seems to interrogate justice in an undifferentiated context of universal humanism, where the two parties, France and Germany, apparently coalesce. Re-articulated within the context of *Lettres à un ami allemand*, one cannot miss the strong polarity of "us" and "them." In the light of the letters, Nazi imperialism to Camus is nothing but "treason" and degradation of humanity. Such a defined context engenders a relativism which in turn undermines the universalism sought for, and thus invalidates Camus's definition of justice and freedom. The so-called adherence to the law of the heart's honesty, "la loi d'un coeur honnête" found a testing ground during the 1954 Algerian colonial crisis. Camus chose to take the side of the victimizer, thus disrupting the paradigm of victim-victimizer. Camus thus contravenes the law of the heart, in his disregard of colonial structure, as breeding victims.

The assumption that an eternal (unprejudiced) justice exists is itself brought into question right from the beginning of the novel. *La Peste* points briefly to the misery of the indigenous Arab population. The journalist Rambert is sent to Oran to investigate the mode of existence of the Arab.

> Il enquêtait pour un grand journal de Paris sur les conditions de vie des Arabes et voulait des renseignements sur leur état sanitaire. Rieux lui dit que cet état n'était pas bon. Mais il voulait savoir, avant d'aller plus loin, si le journaliste pouvait dire la vérité.[...] porter condamnation totale. (1947, 18)

> [He was conducting investigations about the living conditions of the Arabs for an important newspaper in Paris, and wanted information on their sanitary conditions. Rieux told him that those conditions were not good. But he [Rieux] wished to know, before saying any more, if the journalist could tell the truth, {...} and bear the mark of total condemnation.]

Rambert's mission recalls curiously a similar mission undertaken by Camus, and resulting in the publication of *Misère de la Kabylie*. The brief reference to the plight of the Arabs in *La Peste* upsets the definition of eternal justice as linked with France. Events following the liberation of France, i.e. the Setif massacre of May 1945, revealed France, not as living up to her ideals of justice and equality, but as a "bourreau." *Crise en Algérie* came as a response to France's suppression of the 1945 uprising (cf. chapter 2). But as in *Misère de la Kabylie*, the essay interprets a political crisis as a natural disaster, famine. While in actual fact the uprisings simply signaled a political consciousness, a development of a nationalist structure of feeling which challenged colonial oppression. The immediate cause of the demonstrations was France's failure or refusal to acknowledge the contribution of Algerians in the war of liberation from Nazi Germany. Colonized Algeria rightly considered that she also deserved the same freedom and equality which France had fought for with her own blood and that of Indigenes Algerians. The demand and its attendant unrest however received a different response, the most notable being harsh reprisals against the native population and the enforcement of a severe rule of mass oppression—what Camus would call in condemning Nazi Germany, a price paid "en humiliations et en silences, en amertumes, en prisons, en matins d'exécutions, en abandons, en séparations, en faims quotid-iennes, en enfants décharnés, et plus que tout en pénitences forcées" (*Lettres* 1945, 92). Camus, as Haddour maintains, "admits in his discussion of a victimized France suffering from (plague-like) famine, a point which he does not countenance in his disquisitions on the misery of the natives" (1989, 125).

However, contrary to Haddour's hasty conclusion, Camus is not blind "to the oppression and injustice of the French colonial system" (ibid.). In Camus's avant-propos to the collection of his various essays on Algeria, he affirms that

> Tels quels, ces textes résument la position d'un homme qui, placé très jeune devant la misère algérienne, a multiplié vainement les avertissements et qui, conscient depuis longtemps des respon-sabilités de son pays, ne peut approuver une politique de conservation ou d'oppression en Algérie. (*Essais* 1965, 891)

> [As they are, these texts summarize the position of a man who, confronted at a very young age with the misery of the Algerians, has repeatedly, and in vain, issued warnings, and who, conscious for very long of the responsibilities of his country, cannot approve a policy of conservation or oppression in Algeria.]

Camus's thorough understanding of the Algerian political situation makes his summary dismissal of the political dimensions of the 1945 crisis all the more baffling. *La Peste* as an aesthetic of revolt, posits a certain hierarchy of concerns, in viewing the Algerian problem as minor in relation to other, more "important truths and values" which demand articulation. Rambert, like Camus, failed to delve into the political basis of the misery of the indigenous people, because they cannot assume the responsibility of the colonial machinery, in which they are implicated, and in which they assume the position of the guilty party. So the all-out condemnation of the Nazi oppression gives way to a tepid call for reforms in *Crise en Algérie*. Neither Rambert, nor Camus is able to follow up on his investigations. Their reports are undermined by their inability to condemn totally. "Condamnation totale? . . . non, il faut bien le dire. Mais je suppose que cette condamnation serait sans fondement" (*La Peste* 1947, 18–19). Rieux's question, "Pouvez-vous porter condamnation totale?" presupposes his own awareness of the situation of the colonized indigenous population. However, by subsequently expunging from his narrative all traces of French imperialism, Rieux is able to invest his interest in a rather intel-lectualized problem, the rats. A similarity between French imperialism and the Nazi imperialist ideology is however not readily dismissed, and "by a twist of historical irony," France under German occupation finds herself in the same position as that of colonized Algeria. The implicit hierarchisation of values and truths that various critics have pointed to, whereas certain causes become subservient to others, demonstrates that "Camus's conceptualization of justice is highly politicized and selective" (Haddour 1989, 126). The problem of justice or injustice is presented in *La Peste* as a universal issue. In a letter to Roland Barthes in 1955, Camus wrote:

> Comparé à *L'Etranger*, *La Peste* marque sans discussion possible, le passage d'une attitude de révolte solitaire à la reconnaissance d'une communauté dont il faut partager les luttes. S'il y a évolution de *L'Etranger* à *La Peste*, elle s'est faite dans le sens de la solidarité et de la participation. (*Théâtre, Récits, Nouvelles* 1962, 1965–66)

> [Compared to *The Stranger*, *The Plague* marks, without any possible doubt, a transition from an attitude of solitary rebellion to the recognition of a community whose struggles one must share. If there is a progression from *The Stranger* to *The Plague*, it is in the direction of solidarity and participation.]

Many critics have taken Camus's words at "face value," and failed to see what Erickson calls "the biting irony in the nearly total exclusion of the Arab from this community" (1988, 79). Such an exclusive depiction, Erickson maintains, is potent in effect and implications. For why, he asks, "in a novel valorizing, in the author's own words, the notion of community, is the Arab so assiduously excluded—to the extent that we do not observe him even as a shadowy background figure as in *L'Etranger*?" (ibid.) The answer perhaps could be found in the project of the novel which Camus explains in the same letter addressed to Barthes:

> *La Peste*, dont j'ai voulu qu'elle se lise sur plusieurs portées, a cependant comme contenu évident la lutte de la résistance européenne contre le nazisme. La preuve en est que cet ennemi n'est

pas nommé, tout le monde l'a reconnu, et dans tous les pays d'Europe. (*Théâtre, Récits, Nouvelles* 1962, 1965)

[*The Plague*, which I wanted read at several levels, has, however, as its obvious theme, the struggle of the European resistance against Nazism. The proof is that the enemy is not mentioned; everyone, in every part of Europe, recognized him.]

The German Occupation of France as the socio-political backdrop of the allegory of the novel, it seems, calls for the narrative repudiation of the real political setting of the novel. As O'Brien explains, "the suppression of the Arabs was necessitated by the fact that with their presence such an allegory was impossible, for the French themselves as occupiers of Algeria were to the Arabs what the Germans were to the French" (1970, 55).[15]

Thus the absence of the Arabs in the novel, an absence made all the more conspicuous by Rambert's attempted investigation, underscores the intolerability of the indigenous factor in an allegory "condemning oppression while using a colonial setting and simultaneously denying colonial reality" (Erickson 1988, 79). The question has also been posed as to why Camus chose Oran. Indeed, why the insistence on a colonial setting in a novel that evades a prominent problematic of colonialism? The reason(s), Erickson insists again, "would appear to lie in the psyche of an author whose unconscious undercuts the very thesis sustained by his conscious articulation of an allegory of oppression" ibid.).

I do not, however, wish to follow the thread of such a speculation which is, of course, open to debate. It is worth remembering the author's insistence on the manifaceted symbolism of his novel ("J'ai voulu qu'elle [*La Peste*] se lise sur plusieurs portées" [*Théâtre Récits Nouvelles* 1962, 1965]). Gaillard points to the aesthetic value of the selection. He argues that Camus's acclaimed intention, ("nous présenter la 'communauté' essentielle des hommes devant l'épidémie, devant l'oppression, devant le mal"), justifies such a choice. "La ville [Oran] plus petite, ramassée sur elle-même et comme enfermée (au milieu des Arabes précisément), neutre, presque sans arbres, lui a paru, *esthétiquement*, le lieu idéal pour y faire vivre, ensemble, *les prisonniers* de tous les fléaux (The city [of Oran] which is smaller, gathered upon itself and as if closed in neutral, almost without trees, seemed ideal to him, *aesthetically*, as the place to bring alive, together, the *prisoners* of all plagues)".[16]

The pretext to universality here ("[c'est] la condition mortelle de l'homme qui est figurée dans *La Peste*") is questionable, for the universalism is envisioned in a selected group of characters (Rieux,

Tarrou, Grand), "universally" French, in a dramatization of Western religious and political problems. At best, the Algerian landscape becomes the locus of the drama in which the native populace is denied participation, unless we could talk of participation in absentia.

One could naturally argue that the Arab is removed from the setting in order to better dramatize his absence. But, the selectiveness of the cast (and such is my claim), holds a discursive sway, bearing repercussively on Camus's universalist position. In the first place, the definition of eternal justice for which Rieux and his team fight, acquires a nationalist reverberation wherein the ideals of a sovereign France takes precedence. Secondly, *La Peste* is cast against a specific political arena. And the sublimation of the Algerian problem in this context places Camus in a rather pernicious situation, a paradox of both committedness and aloofness, in other words, an emotional non-dispassionate identification and an aesthetic distance. The commitment exhibited in the denunciation of Nazi ideology unwrites itself in the indifference towards the constellation of political tension in Algeria. When all is said and done, Camus's ideal of universal justice acquires a nationalistic cast, and in the political extremity of colonial Algeria during the 50s, it becomes itself Fascist.

A similar dichotomy (distance and involvement) informs the narrative of *La Chute*. The latter, more of a confession than anything else, criticizes Europe—its colonialism, mercantilism, etc., without dealing with any specific manifestations of these Western "plagues." The tone of confession, suggesting a certain inner dialogue discards the univocality of *La Peste* for a dual voicedness. *La Chute* subsumes Algerian politics into the context of World War II. Despite the transposition, the récit does articulate a greater awareness of the problematics of French colonialism which align it to German fascism. *La Chute* expresses the author's *déchirement* and vulnerability, all reinforced by the form of confession adopted. Confession, however, points to the awareness, or presence of guilt. It is nevertheless, a guilt expressed as a universal phenomenon. Such a formulation on guilt relives the case of Meursault, a man no more guilty than the judges who condemn him to die. Meursault's nonchalance and indifference are, however, lacking in the protagonist of *La Chute*, Jean-Baptiste Clamence. The latter expresses admirably the inner conflict between one's principles and the reality one confronts. The pervading awareness in Clamence of the theatricality, the duplicity of his role of "juge-pénitent" points to the unbridgeable gap between his aspirations and his acts. Camus's admirable design to combat all forms of Fascism, specifically the evils of Nazi regime "avec le sang des hommes" if need be, crumples when the colonized natives literally take up Camus's high idealism in order to combat the evils of French colonialism. *La Chute*'s auto-reflexivity articulates the gradual awareness of such ironies.

Rambert's mandate to investigate the conditions of the natives points to the 1945 famine. While the event, as indicated previously, led to Camus's *Crise en Algérie*, he however hypothesized that the resulting uprisings—despite the underlying economic distress—are without a real inner necessity. As stated also, Camus was not unaware that the inner causes of the economic plight of the indigenous population were political. Paradoxically, and more so in the face of such a knowledge, Camus maintained that the demands for justice of Algerian nationalists were unreal, the romantic aspirations of amateur youth rebels. The main inherent danger, as Camus summarized the situation, was that such demands were Soviet masterminded, and a part of a Communist plot to undermine European liberties (1965, 1013). It would be surmised that ultimately, the threat of Algerian nationalism mirrors that of German Nazism. Algerian nationalism, the theme of many of his political essays, combines with Nazism, the plague of *La Peste*, as formidable threatening forces against French hegemony. The Algerian nationalist insurrections as Dib's writings divulge, "[sont] née[s] précisément de 'ces conditions de vie [des Arabes]' sur lesquelles Rambert n'a pas terminé son enquête" (Gaillard 1972, 33).

The Plague in Colonial Algeria

La Peste's gravest flaw, O'Brien observes, is the "ill disguised suppression of a profoundly relevant truth about the city of the plague" (1970, 58). Such a concealment as he accurately remarks, however, confers a tragic note on the work (ibid.). Another source of the tragic is the warning note upon which the story ends. "Le bacille de la peste ne meurt ni ne disparaît jamais, . . . il peut rester pendant des dizaines d'années endormi dans les meubles et le linge, il attend patiemment dans les chambres, les caves, les malles, les mouchoirs et les paperasses . . ." (1947, 279). The prophetic ending of the novel finds fulfillment on the Algerian political scene few years after the pub-lication of *La Peste*, and on the fictional stage of Dib's writing. Applying Camus's metaphor to the Algerian insurrection, O'Brien remarks that "the rats came [back] to die in the cities of Algeria. . . . The 'eruption of the boils and pus'. . . had before been working inwardly in the society" (1970, 59).

As with the infestation of the city of Oran by rats, Tlemcem finds itself invaded by alien-like creatures. The town literally disgorges them in the thousands. Their provenance is unknown. We are told however that they are "des meurt-de-faim." "[Cette] armée grouillante affluait à travers rues et venelles. Elle soulevait le sol, aurait-on pensé, pour déboucher de profondeurs inconnues" (*Le Métier* 1957, 17). In vain the colonial government seeks the reason for this sudden and strange appearance: "Pourquoi s'empilent-ils ici?. . . . L'adjoint de la commission [spéciale établie par le gouvernement de Vichy] décréta qu'il les ferait reconduire . . . oui, il en débarrasserait la ville . . . Il était indispensable qu'on extirpât cette vermine" (ibid., 80–81). From the crowd gathered around the government official, came a voice, "Ce n'est pas de la vermine, ces créatures. La vermine qui s'est jetée sur ce pays a rendu nos frères ainsi" (ibid.). Interestingly, the anonymous voice disappears never to be heard again. It has however served to insert a fissure in the official's rhetoric. From this double articulation on the appearance of the rat-like figures on the streets of the town of Tlemcem, emerge two distinct positions of enunciation, which offers us a dissenting paradigm to the problematics of the rats posited in *La Peste*, as symbolizing the problem of evil in a selectively contextualized dialectic of French and German nationalisms.

The department of Oran presented in *La Peste* is a place of moral as well as physical suffering with Rieux incarnating all that is lucid in man, and the awareness of the little hope there is of restoration to health. The selection of a disease without remedy negates the very function of the doctor, Rieux and that of a hospital, Oran; for the latter is a site of death and despair, and Doctor Rieux is keenly aware of his limitations if not the hopelessness of his efforts as a medical officer.

Mohammed Dib's trilogy, *La Grande Maison, L'incendie,* and *Le Métier à tisser,* borrows the political context of *La Peste,* which is that of World War II and a town of Oran, Tlemcem, to illustrate another kind of plague: colonialism in Algeria. In *La Grande Maison* the life of a young boy Omar unfolds in a big house inhabited by numerous families confronted with the perennial problem of hunger. The word "faim" appears countless times, conferring on the theme of hunger a place of centrality. The name "Dar Sbitar" (a transliterated form of a "hospital home") given to the house, suggests sickness and death. It is the place where the drama of colonial dynamics is played out. Dib's writings provide a literary replique on the absence of the indigenous population from the Oran of *La Peste*. Dib thus presents another facet of plague, famine and typhus which ravaged Algeria during French colonial domination.

Dib's short story, *Au Café,* which postdates the trilogy by several years, is also set in colonial Algeria. It presents the plight of an indigenous woman Fatima afflicted with tuberculosis. The story enables the author to point to the laws of segregation that preside over the dispensation of medical privileges. The French doctor "traduisait à [Fatima]. 'Voilà, on ne peut plus te garder à l'hôpital . . . C'est difficile . . . On a trop de malades, on ne sait pas où les mettre. Et puis toi, c'est qu'on n'a pas de salle pour les contagieux.'"[17] Fatima is thus sent from the hospital, that very symbol, as well as the locus of French civilization and the fight of the French (represented by Rieux) to purge (heal) her (the Indigenes) of all evil (disease). Fatima's dismissal is not simply "a passive condemnation to death" but also her exclusion from the colonizer's space of "health" and her cantonment into a space of the colonized imaged as infection. Fatima is recommended to supplement her diet with fruit and meat, an ineffectual recommendation since Fatima cannot even afford bread! For Fatima, "un monde se refermait devant elle, où elle n'avait pénétré que par surprise, comme on se tromperait de porte, un monde défendu" (1984, 58). The importance of this short story is that it puts into question the Camusian depiction of Oran as a kind of universal hospital fighting a universal evil. For as stated in the previous section, his discourse is permeated with politics and ideological biases. *La Peste* symbolically articulates the exclusion of the native population from health benefits. The novel, as Haddour argues, "devalues the efforts of the health authorities to fight against disease." The hospital thus fails in its moral function, that of restoring health, and becomes "the very symbol of segregation and colonial apartheid" (1989, 166).

Dib's trilogy has as its focus two interrelated themes, namely the economic depressions of the 1930s and 1940s with their repercussions for the Algerian urban setting and the nascent Algerian nationalism and rebellion. The juxtaposition of urban and rural life enables Dib, on one hand, to tackle the problem of rural exodus attendant to a growing capitalism and its effects on the urban space, and on the other, to delve into that dual consciousness generated by the problems of colonialism. Ultimately the problems of the peasantry (read: the mass of the Indigenes) inform his narrative. Dib, unlike Camus views the social, economic, and political problems of Algeria as linked with her colonial structure.

The theme of dispossession, the colonized's alienation from his land is central to *L'Incendie* and *Le Métier à tisser*. Germaine Tillion's essay, *L'Algérie en 1957*, delves into the condition of the indigenous people in the 1950s and points out the peculiarities of the colonial process for which she coins the term "clochardisation." She contends:

> les deux tiers des Algériens ont eu le sort inverse des Français: leur
> malheur a voulu qu'ils se trouvent dans la zone d'ébranlement de la

révolution biologique moderne avant d'avoir atteint ce niveau de vie et de culture que je vous propose d'appeler 'niveau d'auto-protection.' Et c'est là qu'intervient, à mon avis, notre responsabilité.[18]

[Two-thirds of Algerians have lived a fate that is opposed to that of the French: their misfortune has been that they are caught in the unhinging zone of the modern biological revolution without having attained that level of life and culture which I propose to call "the level of self-protection." And, in my opinion, that is where our responsibility comes in.]

Tillion, an anthropologist, seeks to place the Algerian economic crisis within an international context—technological advancement, against which the indigenous culture presents a patent inadequacy. Western technology and civilization, according to her, are an overwhelming presence which underscores the Indigenes' perpetual dependency. Camus also points to this state of dependency, and in the same vein, registers his own admiration for Tillion's point of view. "L'Algérie purement arabe," Camus maintains, "ne pourrait accéder à l'indépendance économique sans laquelle l'indépendance politique n'est qu'un leurre . . . Je renvoie pour cette question et les problèmes qu'elle soulève, à l'admirable livre de Germaine Tillion" (*Essais* 1965, 1013). Camus paradoxically recognizes the existence of unjust colonial structures but refutes the thesis that the economic plight of the Indigenes is in any way linked with the various laws promulgated by the colonial government that invariably dispossessed the natives. Tillion sees the state of the Arab's sub-existence as a sequel of his "archaic" culture. Arguing that the misery of the indigenous population solicits "our" responsibility and not "our" guilt, she maintains that Algeria's present plight is an inevitable result of the confrontation between an archaic society and "the prodigious monster of World Civilization."

From both Camus's and Tillion's political point of view, "independence is pernicious" to Algeria. Her stage of "infancy" vis-à-vis the monster of technology demands careful nurturing of a "mother country," France. From a different perspective however, famine and plague attendant to French colonialism is not so much the product of economic crisis in Algeria nor the inadequacies of the indigenous culture vis-à-vis France's developed cultural patterns. Rather, famine is the result of the laws promulgated by France right after the conquest of Algeria, laws that regulated the spoliation of lands. Bennoune rightly asserts that the processes that led to what Tillion terms "clochardisation," evolved from the assimilation of the indigenous land.[19] He notes that the French settler understood the project of assimilation foremost as an appropriation of the communal lands of the native population. The target of the settler is thus to assimilate the land and not the Indigenes into French culture (1974, 421). The introduction of this new phenomenon, privatization of property, however, upset the local pre-existing structures. Dib's writings register the various abuses of the French laws and the resulting spoliation of the indigenous population.

Un monstre insaisissable, vorace, emportait à l'instant où ils s'y attendaient le moins de grands lambeaux dans sa gueule d'ombre, de cette terre qu'ils avaient arrosée de leurs sueurs et de leur sang. C'était la Loi. De quelque côté qu'ils se soient tournés la Loi les avait frappés. Ils seront toujours en faute au regard de la Loi [...] La Loi ouvre une route qui passe dans leurs cultures comme une roue à travers leur corps. La Loi leur conteste la propriété de leurs terres. La Loi a changé, leur dit-on. Il y a une nouvelle Loi. Et les anciens titres deviennent-ils caducs et nuls? Et nul l'héritage des ancêtres? Oui, mon petit père, nuls! [...] C'est comme ça qu'un pays a changé de main, que le peuple de cette terre, pourchassé, est devenu étranger sur son propre sol. (1954, 76–77)

[When they least expected it, a voracious and elusive monster was swallowing up into its shadowy mouth huge parcels of the lands they had watered with their sweat and blood. It was the Law. Whichever way they turned, they were hit by the Law. They would always be guilty where the Law was concerned. {...} Like a wheel running across their bodies, the Law opens a road through their culture. The Law contests the ownership of their lands. The Law has changed, they are told. There is a new Law. And have the old land titles become null and void? And are the inheritances of their ancestors equally void? Yes, my little father, void! {...} That is how a country has changed hands; that is how the native who is hunted has become a stranger on his own land.]

French capitalist greed presented metaphorically here as a monster points to the attendant starvation and famine. French law is presented in the image of a rapist ("[la loi] ouvre une route qui passe dans leurs cultures comme une roue à travers leur corps"). Not only does it leave behind a series of defilement but also inverts the paradigm of insider and outsider, since through its various manifestations the colonized becomes the outsider.

Such a presentation also undermines the concept of civilization as associated with French culture. The colonial laws, components of the assimilationist theory effected a negative impact on what Tillion labels as an "archaic" culture, since they served to undermine ethnic structures. French capitalism, by introducing the notion of private property (for the purpose of colonial settlements) in an hitherto communal society precipitated the collapse of the traditional system of collective ownership. *Le Métier à tisser* articulates this collapse, the transformation of the traditional society into a vagrant one. Thus, the French not only failed in their mission of promoting the "indigenous" into the French culture, but also turned the colonized into a vagrant population.

The query, "mais ne sommes-nous pas comme des étrangers dans notre pays?" (*L'Incendie* 1954, 53) points to the colonial politics which reversed positions and redefined the terms of "indigenous" and "foreigner." Dib thus re-examines the ideals of the "mission civilisatrice," the promotion of French culture, to bring out what is rather a truism, namely the disintegration of a social system which had hitherto fostered a sense of community. Dib's writings undercut Tillion's assertion that the Algerian problem is that of a cross-cultural dilemma resulting from the indigenes' inability to adapt, by pointing to a set of colonial laws that set and maintained cultural and political barriers against the assimilationist endeavor.

Both Camus and Dib put on their fictional stage the evils of political ideologies. Camus's *La Peste* allegorizes among other evils the Nazi threat to the "order of the world." The fight put up by Rieux and his sanitary team postulates a hope in the idea of change, yet a sense of nihilism and futility permeates the team's endeavor since the plague here is given both religious and political resonances, creating thus a discursive overlap. Such an overlap allows Camus to stress the Church's collusion with Fascist ideology. Doctor Rieux and his team of fighters are "free lords," "godless saints," in an "île sans avenir." The word "île (island)" coupled with the phrase "sans avenir (without a future)" naturally underscores the isolation and sense of futility in Rieux's struggle against plague. It has been noted that the metaphor carries also a religious significance in the work of Camus (Haddour 1989, 171). On an existential plane, the notion of "l'île sans avenir" conveys God's dethronement and its attendant enthronement of man "in a kingdom of exile." As a political space, France was in a state of exile during the Nazi occupation of Europe. Hence the walled city of Oran becomes a symbol of France's political alienation. France assumes the position of the colonized in her own colony. Rieux and his fighters enact microcosmically France's acclaimed position as the purveyor of the notion of freedom, equality and fraternity.

Dib's trilogy presents a different political image of the combatants of the plague as oppressors. The metaphor of "l'île sans avenir," the kingdom of exile articulates therefore the political space of the colonized Algerians in their native land. In *Le Métier à tisser*, the lives of the inhabitants of Tlemcen dramatize a state of exile, despair and anguish. Just as thousands of rats invade the streets of Oran, thousands of hitherto unknown creatures invade the streets of Tlemcen. On closer look, however, these turn out to be not rats but beggars. One immediate point of commonalty is that both appearances disturb the order of the cities. The parallel between the two narratives is striking; apart from the similarity of their topographical location (department of Oran), both writings have as optical target one form of imperialism and its ills.

Rather transparently, Dib represents the exile, deprivation and anxiety of the beggars. The latter presented in the animalistic image of rats, emerged literally from the ground, creating a great deal of concern.

> Sans relâche, l'armée grouillante des meur-de-faim affluait à travers rues et venelles. Elle soulevait le sol, aurait-on pensé, pour déboucher de profondeurs inconnues. Honteuse cohue qui s'épouillait en plein air, étalait ses membres épuisés, ses escarres purulentes, ses yeux trachomateux. Une cendre froide saupoudrait ces êtres sans identité. [...] Ils [les mendiants] surgissaient du crachin, ternes et diffus, un instant, puis y retournaient. Ils semblaient être vomis par le néant humide. (*Le Métier à tisser* 1957, 17)

> [Without respite, the teeming army of affamished people flocked to the streets and alleys. One would have thought they were lifting the ground in order to emerge from some unknown depths. A shameful mob which was delousing itself in open air, spreading out its exhausted bodies, purulent scabs, and trachomatic eyes. Cold ashes covered this throng of humanity without identity. {...} Drab and without form, they [the beggars] crept up from the drizzle for a moment, and disappeared. They seemed to be spewed up by the humid nothingness.]

These dehumanized beings are presented as a mirror of the entire indigenous population who are not necessarily beggars.

> Ces espèces d'humanité dépenaillés, au sombre aspect de bêtes des bois! plaisantaient des facétieux.
> Et les mêmes arguaient à la décharge de ces lamentables créatures:
> - Ce n'est rien de grave [...] Ce ne sont que les nôtres. Hé! Regardez-les; comme un miroir, ils vous renverront notre propre reflet. L'image la plus fidèle de ce que nous sommes, ils vous la montrent! (ibid)

[This sort of tattered humanity, with the dismal look of beasts of the wild! joked a humorous few. And the same argued for the discharge of these lamentable creatures:
- It's nothing serious {...} They are only our people. Hey, look at them; like a mirror, they will reflect back an image of ourselves. They are showing the most accurate picture of what we are.]

As with the emergence of the rats and the plague in *La Peste*, the appearance of the beggars creates a disarray, an awakening. The physical presence of the beggars, as that of the final certitude of the "fléaux" on the somnambulant cities (Oran and Tlemcen) draws the sleeping population from its lethargy. "Plagues [les fléaux] are, indeed, a common thing, but they are hard to believe when they hit you in the face. There have been in the world as many plagues as there are wars. And yet plagues and wars always take people by surprise" (*La Peste* 1947, 40).

If *La Peste* points symbolically to the presence of political evil within a selective context, Dib's *Le Métier à tisser*, using the beggars as a "miroir" projects abject poverty (clochardisation) and misery. *La Peste* is careful to conceal this reality. The evils of the plague presented as an impersonal problem threatens "humanity." This humanity is defined by Camus as French; while the same entity (French humanity) is divulged by Dib as the generative source of oppression and the penury of the indigenous population. Dib's trilogy, revealing the plague of "colonial famine and vagrancy," uncovers a layer of discourse camouflaged by the allegorical structure of *La Peste*.

Echoing Doctor Rieux's attempt to fight the plague, the government officials seek means of overcoming the threat of the human plague. *Le Métier à tisser* describes the daily deportation of the vagrants. Such an endeavour recalls the initial attempts in *La Peste* to rid the city of the rats; both moves amount to scratching the surface of the problem while ignoring the deep causes.

Un adjoint de la commission spéciale établie par le gouvernement de Vichy survint. [...] [Il] voulut tout d'abord apprendre d'où sortaient ces mendiants. Les choses se révélèrent aussitôt plus compliquées qu'on ne l'eût soupçonné. Personne ne se proposa pour éclaircir cette énigme. [...] L'adjoint décréta qu'il les ferait reconduire... Oui, il en débarrasserait la ville... Il était indispensable qu'on extirpât cette vermine.[...] A chaque pas fait dans la rue, on avait le sentiment qu'on encourait les plus graves dangers. (1947, 79-81)

[The assistant to the Special Investigation Commission, set up by the Vichy government, arrived. {...} First of all, he wanted to know where these beggars came from. Things turned out to be more complicated than we first expected. No one volunteered to shed light on this enigma. {...} The deputy decreed that he would have them sent away... Yes, he would rid the city of them... It was crucial that one rooted out this vermin. {...} With each step one took in the streets, one had the feeling of being in grave danger.]

The official decision to tackle what is really a symptomatic manifestation of the colonial problem by rendering invisible the problem of the displaced rural emigrants articulate its own impotency.

In both *La Peste* and *Le Métier à tisser*, the sanitary measures taken reveal themselves as ineffectual. The rural dispossessed, described in Dib's novel, return incessantly to infiltrate the town like the rats in Camus's narrative. "On aurait dit que plus on se hâtait de [les] refouler et plus il[s] échouai[en[t sur la ville. C'était tous les jours, à recommencer" (*Le Métier* 1957, 83). The official policy of camouflaging the problem of the beggars ironically replicates the narrative exclusion of the indigenous population from the discursive space of *La Peste*. Both Camus and Dib make use of a metonymic structure (repulsiveness of plague or vermin) to articulate their condemnation of political imperialism. For Camus, the plague and the presaging rats symbolize German Nazism, while Dib presents French colonialism in the metaphor of vermin, and famine as its outward manifestation.

The double optique of Dib's presentation is interesting. From the French "adjoint's" perspective one sees no further than the presence of the beggars. Myopic, he proposes no solution that goes beyond ridding the city of the "indésirables." The indigenous optique within the narrative allows however to see not a mere presence of beggars, but the generative source as well. "Croyez-moi bien, ... notre misère n'existe pas d'aujourd'hui, elle vient de loin. ... Il fallait avant tout remonter à l'origine de cet extraordinaire fourmillement de vagabonds" (*Le Métier* 1957, 82–83). The originality of Dib's narrative resides in his ability to maintain a dual perspective which allows him to present the concept of civilization within two different contexts dependent on the point of view assumed: "Tout cela avait l'air d'être le vrai visage de l'Algérie, mais n'était que simple surface; ce visage lui avait été façonné par la colonisation-et l'Algérie a un million d'autres visages" (*L'Incendie* 1954, 88).

The allegorical structure of *La Peste* exploits the simple surface which seems to be the authoritative face of Algeria, without however delving into the various deeper layers of her reality. Dib however reveals this reality as permeated by colonial politics of segregation. Tlemcen as a colonial space violated by beggars, presents some similarities with Oran of *La Peste*, the town submerged by rats. Both spaces prior to the plague, present a facade of tranquility, the proverbial calm preceding a storm.

> La ville [de Tlemcen] [...] paisible, de tout temps la plus parfaite civilité [...] aujourd'hui troublé[e] par la faute de ces individus [ces mendiants]. (*Le Métier* 1957, 84)

> [The city [of Tlemcen] {...} peaceful, at all times a model of the most perfect civilities, {...} is in turmoil today, thanks to these individuals [these beggars].]

> Notre petite ville, si tranquille jusque-là, et bouleversée en quelques jours, comme un homme bien portant dont le sang épais se mettrait tout d'un coup en révolution! (*La Peste* 1947, 22)

> [Our little town, so calm till then, and turned upside down within a few days, like a healthy man whose thick blood suddenly began a revolution!]

G. Kateb in his reading of *La Peste* points to "a split" within Camus's narrative. The novel as he argues, adopts a discontinuous allegorical structure, "a *freistimmig* style." In other words, "an allegory that may be picked up and dropped again at pleasure."[20] While acknowledging the various significations of the symbol of the plague, Kateb refuses to attribute to it (the symbol) any didactic motive or political potency because of the very inconsistencies involved in the allegory. "You must try to kill bacilli so that men may live. The enemy is not human. ... But if the agent of suffering and death were human," Kateb contends, "then ... the moral situation becomes more complicated" (1963, 293). In Kateb's estimation the evil (plague) preying on the city of Oran is not necessarily "foreign." The "city contains within itself the constant threat of having sick rats come up from its bowels to announce the spread of the disease" (ibid., 299). The comparison used by Camus "Comme un homme bien portant dont le sang épais se mettrait tout d'un coup en révolution" (1947, 22), points to an illusion of order which once prevailed in Oran. Both *La Peste* and *Le Métier à tisser* articulate the ineffectiveness of "clinical" measures taken by the authorities to curtail the plague. For in both cases these measures are based on a superficial apprehension of the situation. Nevertheless, the dissenting view of Doctor Rieux and the seemingly ubiquitous indigenous voice of Dib's narrative suggest a deeper layer and thereby a certain hopelessness.

> [Ces mendiants] nous montrent [notre] plaie [...] qui est là depuis des années. On la voit mieux à présent, c'est tout. [...] Le genre

humain avait été tenu dans l'ignorance du mal, semblait-il, jusqu'alors, et voilà que la vie se remplissait de tableaux abominables, d'incidents incohérents. (*Le Métier* 1957, 82–83)

[[These beggars] are showing us [our] wounds {...} which have been there for years. One sees them better now, that is all. {...} Mankind had been kept in ignorance of the evil, it seemed, till then; and now life was becoming full of atrocious pictures, with incoherent incidents.]

As observed, the religious meaning manifested with plague as divine wrath emphasizes potently the futility of the various sanitary measures. The religious authority in *La Peste* represented by Père Paneloux, choses to "combat" the evil purportedly brought on by God, by invoking the same God, who Camus conceives of as a mere ghost. Paneloux suggests as a remedy an attitude of penitence and submission to divine authority. Paneloux's call for submission to divine wrath produces a discomfort and disquietude in Rieux who refuses to bow down before "a lie," or a dethroned God. To Paneloux's haranguing proclamation, "Mes frères, vous êtes dans le malheur, mes frères, vous l'avez mérité" (*La Peste* 1947, 91), with all that it comports of fatality, Rieux opposes action, however minimal the impact might be. "Il fallait lutter de telle ou telle façon et ne pas se mettre à genoux" (1947, 92). While Paneloux's rhetoric points to the enemies of God, Rieux evidently regards God as the enemy of man. For Rieux, inaction and submission advocated for by moralists in the face of the inevitable are but manifestations of the absurd. Such a submission commanded by political and religious tyrannies epitomizes an intellectual humiliation against which Rieux revolts. Camus conflates religious tyranny and political injustice in his condemnation of history and ideology, viewing both the Church and political ideology as responsible for contemporary history and for World War crises. Dib points out that the very arbitrariness and tyranny condemned in Nazism and in the Church are the ruling principles of the French in Algeria.

Dib and the Plagues of Imperialism

As has been argued, despite the multi-symbolism of *La Peste*'s narrative, its scope seems limited, then, to addressing the issue of evil as confronting the Western mind. Within the allegory of the plague, the rats and what they stand for occupy a more central place in the mental energies of the combatants than the problem of the indigenous population which is clearly silenced. As in *L'Etranger, La Peste* exploits the colonial context of Algeria to articulate the problem of evil as manifested within the specificities of Western ideologies and counter-ideologies. In using Oran as a neutral ground, he is also able to distance religious and political problems from their specificities, in order to give room for "objectivity." In the first place, the plague, as stated, distanced from its biblical context, and given a certain "pagan" neutrality, is made to express the situation of man in a "post-Christian universe." In the second place, from the particular context of Fascism, the combat against evil is given universal resonances; the notion of evil seemingly subsumes various Western political intrigues. Hence the novel pre-refutes Quilliot's interpretation of "the rats [as] victims of colonialism and its oppressions" ("Albert Camus's Algeria" 1962, 42). Camus's "exclusive vision" precludes such a reading. Camus's narrative which transposes the Algerian colonial context into a Western political context clearly does not articulate the colonized Algerians' combat against French tyranny. Our contention this far has been that Camus remains on one side of the wall in a highly compartmentalized context. Dib's more penetrating vision of Oran as a Manichean space, using the very metaphor of the hospital to represent a colonized Algeria at grips with different types of plagues, not only points to the intertextual relationship between his work and Camus's, but also reveals the latter's depoliticization of the colonial context, resulting from an aestheticisation. Camus and Dib may be said to illustrate the two sides of an aesthetic experience: the one, a "disinterested" contemplation of its object without reference to reality; the other "involved" perhaps emotionally in the very object it contemplates. Such a distinction purporting to account for the two writers' attitude toward art is, however, simplistic, if not naive, for the obvious reason that the two tendencies (distance and involvement) overlap to greater or lesser degree in both authors.

La Peste, as one may recall, postdates the 1945 crisis in Algeria; the crisis, manifestations of the first nationalist feelings, has as its immediate impulse the economic conditions of the indigenous population, the central theme of Dib's writings. The various rebellions that broke out were accurately analyzed by Camus as resulting from economic distress. The nationalist impetus of the rebellion was overlooked, however, and its political motives misinterpreted. It is only by refuting one of the two components of the rebellion, namely Algerian nationalism, that Camus is able to advocate continued French domination. In all fairness, Camus admits the "bankruptcy of colonialism" but insists that France maintains its imperialist link with Algeria. This position of both recognizing the evils of colonialism and implicitly advocating its continuance is rather contradictory, since imperialism and colonialism are, by essence, bedfellows. "En Algérie," Camus insists, "Français et Arabes sont condamnés à vivre ou à mourir ensemble" (*Essais* 1965, 971). But as he maintains also, although he is vehemently opposed to French injustice in Algeria, he refuses to provide an alibi to the rebels, "[le fou criminel qui jettera sa bombe sur la foule innocente où se trouvent les miens" (*Actuelles III* 1958, 892). The epithet of "fou criminel" that Camus gives to the rebels suggests a misunderstanding of the driving force underlying the rebellion. Characteristically, Camus proposes that France improve the economic conditions of the Arabs, "si l'on veut sauver ces populations malheureuses et si l'on veut empêcher que des masses affamées, excitées par quelques fous criminels, recommencent les massacres de Sétif" (ibid.). This tendency to see the rebellion as a kind of juvenile manifestation exonerates France from its political culpability. Camus's interpretation of the Sétif events is in itself peculiar if not erroneous. As the chronicles records, the repressions in Sétif are he act of the French police in response to a peaceful demonstration (cf. chapter 2). The subsequent acts of violence and terrorism on the part of Algerian rebels were in themselves responses to a violent system, the product of a colonialist culture. The exploitation and oppression inherent in colonialism make it an essentially violent structure. France, which imposed and fueled such a structure, has a share of responsibility in what Camus calls terrorist acts engineered by mad criminals. The refusal to denounce France's role, one may say, stems from the author's refusal to give an "alibi" to the Algerian rebels. Camus's position ultimately obsfucates two fundamental facts, which are: 1. the so-called terrorism is basically a war between colonized and colonizer, a conflict of ideologies and power; 2. the "fous criminels" are Rieux-like figures, combatants of the plague of colonialism, and freedom fighters, who like Rieux refuse to genuflect before a certain lie (here the colonial lie of French supremacy). Interesting within Camus's rhetoric is the double standard of application of certain vocabularies. Camus's political discourse in the Algerian debate—like the "politicized" narrative of *La Peste*—is partisan in its denunciation of the Algerian nationalists as "fous criminels."

Dib's writing, notably *Le Métier à tisser*, which reads as a fiction-alization of Camus's *Misère de la Kabylie*, gives the colonized Arabs the political voice denied them in *La Peste*. Clearly, the beggars—those rat-like figures that invade the colonizer's space—point not only to economic distress but to a nascent movement of protestation.

Bientôt, aucun obstacle ne fut en mesure d'endiguer l'inlassable poussée qui conduisait leur horde vers les quartiers les plus récents, les artères commerçantes, les parties nobles de la cité. On ne discernait toujours pas ce que ce peuple errant gagnait à fréquenter de pareils endroits. Ils n'étaient pas faits pour lui, ne pouvaient lui convenir. Le réalisait-il au moins? [...] Il bafouait le monde de l'ordre et des riches qu'il côtoyait. (*Le Métier* 1957, 14–25, 83–84)

[Soon, there was no obstacle capable of ckecking the tireless force that drove this mob towards the newest neighborhoods, the commercial centers, the noble quarters of the city. One could still not tell what these vagabond people gained from frequenting such places. They were not made for them, they could not fit in. Did they realize this at least? {...} They baffled the world of order and rich people they were rubbing shoulders with.]

It should be noted that two important ideological events inform Dib's work, namely the political setting that his novels articulate (1930s) and the actual political setting in which the work is conceived and written (1940s). The two moments converge in the attitude of rebellion (latent or manifested) against the French political structure. The problem of the beggars thus mediates an economic crisis and a nationalist awakening. For, these beggars caught in the "vortex of economic depressions" and the nascent Algerian nationalism of the 1930s and the 1940s express the underlying revolutionary impulse of the 1945 uprising. The conflating of economic crisis and nationalism provide a potent narrative space. Both factors (economic problems and nationalist uprising) point to the nefariousness of the French economic, political and cultural structure. Ultimately then, the presence of the beggars "[qui] bafouaient le monde de l'ordre et des riches," articulates not only the radicalism of Algerian nationalism, but also the failure of the French civilizing mission. Theoretically, France's proposed mission is to "enlighten" the "dark continent," but Dib presents France as purveyor of gloom and "darkness." Menoune, a young child-wife, repudiated by her husband who is unable to provide for her, laments prior to her death:

Étrange est mon pays où tant
De souffles se libèrent [...]
-Terre brûlée et noire, Mère fraternelle,
Ton enfant ne restera pas seule
Avec le temps qui giffle le coeur;
Entends ma voix Qui file dans les arbres
Et fait mugir les boeufs.
(*La Grande Maison* 1952, 47)

[Strange is my country where so many
inspirations are rising {...}
-Burned and blackened land, Fraternal mother,
Your child will not remain alone
With time striking at the heart;
Hear my voice which moves in the trees
And which makes the cows moo.]

This is not so much the voice of a dying woman but that of an awakening consciousness amid the pervading images of despair and death. The voice of Menoune will be replicated in a much more prosaic manner by another character of the trilogy, Bensalem Adda, on whose "figure osseuse, affleura toute la misère de l'Algérien dépossédé" (*L'Incendie* 1954, 106). This last novel articulates concurrently with the themes of pervading famine, nationalist consciousness, the falseness of the ideals of the French civilizing mission.

La civilisation n'a jamais existé; ce qu'on prend pour la civilisation n'est qu'un leurre. Sur ces sommets, le destin du monde se réduit à la misère. Les fantômes d'Abd El Kader et de ses hommes rôdent sur ces terres insatisfaites. (ibid., 8)

[Civilization has never existed; what we take for civilization is only a deception. On these summits, the destiny of the world is reduced to misery. The ghosts of Abd El Kader and his men roam these discontented lands.]

The invocation of Abd El Kader's ghost here is interesting. Algeria's first nationalist hero, he and his group of followers fought and resisted the French conquest of Algeria in 1830. The idea of "terres insatisfaites [où] rôdent les fantômes d'Abd El Kader" is highly significant for it points to the link between the early resistance movement led by El Kader and the present insurgence. For the army of ragged ghosts (beggars) carry with them, not only the plague of famine, but also in its dormant state, the idea of national insurgence, both of which threaten to divulge the myth of the French mission and to undermine the colonial presence. El Kader obviously represents Algerian nationalism which though subdued by the French, was never entirely eradicated. Thus. the memory of this nationalist (his ghost) constitutes a driving force. His memory infuses hopefulness, and emerges as a potent symbol of defiance, providing the substance of a national myth that propels the nationalist movement into the orbit of Algeria's eventual political independence. The figure of El Kader as a symbol dissipating despair is made all the more obvious through the introduction within the narrative of *L'incendie*, of a myth of rebirth. This rebirth is presented through the personnage of Comandar, an Algerian veteran of the great war to which he lost both his legs.

> Comandar tirait son nom d'une longue carrière militaire, qui lui avait valu l'amputation des jambes. Depuis qu'on l'appelait Comandar, son vrai nom s'était perdu dans les mémoires. Il avait vu le feu de près à la Vieille guerre. Il était resté trois jours et trois nuits sous un amoncellement de corps. Il avait lutté; il avait hurlé trois jours et trois nuits. [...] Seul il avait vaincu la mort. Mais il avait perdu les deux jambes. (*L'Incendie* 1954, 15)

> [Commander owed his name to a long military career that cost him the amputation of his legs. Ever since they started calling him Commander, his real name had been lost in memory. He had witnessed at close range, the Great War. He had remained for three days and three nights buried under a pile of dead bodies. He had struggled, and howled for three days and three nights. {...} Alone, he had conquered death. But he had lost both legs.]

The appropriation of the Christian symbolism of death and resurrection, may be surprising since it derives from the colonialist cultural symbolism; but its usage here epitomizes the idea of rebirth of a nation in the midst of death. Thus in the dark, and gloom of Algeria, there germinates the seed of revolt; a revolt that will subsequently vanquish death itself. Another source of originality in Dib's narrative resides in the highly complex signification of "darkness," his ability to endow the term with oppositional meanings, whereby the image of darkness refers at once to colonial oppression and the "incubation of nationalist ideology," a rebirth.

The colonial culture, with its attendant challenges, as Haddour notes, provides interesting intertextual echoes in Camus and Dib. A substantial part of the trilogy as we have noted, reads as a dramatization of Camus's *Misère de la Kabylie*. *L'Incendie* shares the same political setting (1939) as that of Camus's essay. "Pour aujourd'hui," Camus writes "J'arrête ici cette promenade à travers la souffrance et la faim d'un peuple. On aura senti du moins que la misère ici n'est pas une formule ni un thème de méditation. Elle est. Elle crie et elle désespère" [I stop here my walk through the suffering and hunger of a people. One will have felt at least that misery here is neither a formula nor a theme for meditation. It exists. It howls and it despairs.] (*Essais* 1965, 909). "Crise en Algérie" which replicates the major themes of "Misère," views the political malaise of Algeria as a consequence of the failure of the colonial institution to promulgate the French principle of democracy. France thus, needs to rethink her "universal" democratic principles (ibid., 951). The political problem of Algeria, as Camus correctly sums up, antedates the economic crisis. He overlooks, however, the fact that the underlying political structure precludes any serious attempt at promoting French democracy.

L'Exile et Le Royaume is without doubt Camus's most direct approach in his fictional writing to the political and economic crisis of Algeria. Nonetheless, the stories, notably "L'Hôte" (which will be analyzed in Chapter five) circumvent any causal link, and present the underlying themes of famine and vagrancy of the Arab population as a natural disaster.

> Ils serait difficile d'oublier cette misère, *cette armée de fantômes haillonneux errant dans le soleil, les plateaux calcinés mois après mois, la terre recroquevillée peu à peu, littéralement torréfiée, chaque pierre éclatant en poussière sous le pied.* [...] *Ces terres ingrates, habitées seulement par des pierres.* Parfois, des sillons faisaient croire à des cultures, mais ils avaient été creusés pour mettre au jour une certaine pierre [...] On ne labourait ici que pour récolter des cailloux. [...] C'était ainsi, le caillou seul couvrait les trois quarts de ce pays. (*Théâtre, Récits, Nouvelles* 1962, 1610, 1615; emphasis added)

> [It would be hard to forget this misery, *this army of ghosts in rags, in the sun, roaming the sun-baked plateaus months after months, the shrivelled, and literally roasted land, each stone bursting into dust under the feet.* {...} *These unproductive lands, inhabited only by stones.* Sometimes, some furrows made one think of farming, but they had only been dug to bring out a certain stone. {...} One farmed here only to harvest rocks. {...} It was this way; three quarters of this country is covered by rocks only.]

"L'Hôte" presents the economic problems of Algeria as a natural calamity. Camus's "armée de fantômes haillonneux errant dans le soleil" (ibid.), is an intertextual echo of Dib's beggars, "[cette] armée grouillante des meurt-de-faim, . . . ces espèces d'humanité dépenaillées" (*Le Métier* 1957, 17–18). Both texts published during the Algerian war use the same image of "army of ragged [ghosts]." Within both texts, Algeria is presented as "a mummified space." Dib's narrative however unfolds the processes of vagrancy as those underlying the establishment of European hegemony, while Camus's writing maintains a double standard of vision. If *La Peste* presents the plague as the evil of German imperialism, "L'Hôte" and his essays in contrast, depict colonial plague of famine as a natural phenomenon. Such an attribution is tantamount to a deification of Nature, the latter becoming an absolute force, an aloof Godhead. Camus's presentation echoes Paneloux's sermon; the priest's concern with justifying God inhibits any efficacious action and creates a sense of imprisonment," inducing "passivity and conformity" (Tarrow 1985, 126).

Both Camus's and Dib's writings are informed by a shared perception of the artist/writer as a social critic. "Une oeuvre ne peut avoir de valeur que dans la mesure où elle est enracinée, où elle puise sa sève dans le pays auquel on appartient, où elle nous introduit dans un monde qui est le nôtre avec ses complexités et ses déchirements" (Dib 1960, 66). Thus, it behooves us to see their works against the backdrop of prevalent issues of the day.

A political re-reading of *La Peste* in the light of Camus's essays on Algeria, and of Dib's trilogy, reveals a paradoxical divergence and convergence of the novelist and the essayist. Camus's imaginative writing transposes the colonial context of Algeria; his essays, while addressing the various economic problems of Algeria, aestheticize as to the source of economic and political ills. *La Peste* exploits the Bubonic Plague to illustrate the repulsiveness of German imperialism. However, the German and the French imperialistic enterprises, informed by the same guiding principles of establishing their supremacy, converge in their oppressive manifestations. The combatants of the German "plague" carry in themselves a plague. The association of the plague with the German Occupation may not be exhaustive, and as Camus himself insists, its meaning must be extended beyond the immediate historical scene. Admittedly the plague represents hypothetically any form of tyranny. "Je veux exprimer au moyen de la peste l'étouffement dont nous avons tous souffert et l'atmosphère de menace et d'exil dans laquelle nous avons vécu. Je veux du même coup étendre cette interprétation à la notion d'existence en général" [I wish to express by means of the plague, the suffocation we all suffered and the climate of threat and exile in which we lived. I wish by the same token to extend this interpretation to the notion of existence in general].[21]

Camus and Dib, sharing the same political setting, are confronted with Algeria's process of decolonization, the de-establishment of the colonial order, and the rebellion of a famished army of ragged beggars. Such an intertextuality reveals, however, two different narrative visions. The colonized's absence from the political setting of *La Peste* illustrates an attempt to decontextualise the colonial arena. Dib's narrativization of the political malaise, interprets famine, one of the plagues of the colonial presence, showing it as a menacing force. The beggars of Tlemcen reenact microcosmically the evils of an appalling economic condition, undergirded by racial and class politics within a structure of apartheid.

Notes

1. Quoted as epigraph in Camus, *La Peste* (Paris: Gallimard, 1947). Further references to *La Peste* are to this edition.
2. Raymond Stephanson, "The Plague Narratives of Defoe and Camus," *Modern Language Quarterly* 43, no.4 (September 1987): 224.
3. Susan Sontag, *Illness as Metaphor* (New York: Straus and Giroux, 1977), 58.
4. Max Byrd, *London Transformed: Images of the City in the Eighteenth Century* (New Haven: Yale University Presss, 1978), 39, quoted in Raymond Stephanson, "The Plague Narratives of Defoe and Camus," *Modern Language Quarterly* 43, no.4 (September 1987): 225–26.
5. Antonin Artaud, "The Theater and the Plague," *The Theater and Its Double*, trans. Mary Caroline Richards (New York: Grove Press, 1958), 27, quoted in Raymond Stephanson, "The Plague Narratives of Defoe and Camus," *Modern Language Quarterly* 43, no.4 (September 1987): 226.
6. Elwin F. Sterling, "Albert Camus' La Peste: Cottard's Act of Madness," *College Literature* 13 no. 2 (Spring 1986): 177.
7. Jacqueline Lévi-Valensi, "Le temps et l'espace dans l'oeuvre romanesque de Camus: une mythologie du réel," *Albert Camus*, edited by Raymond Gay-Crosier (Gainesville: University of Florida Press, 1980), 64.
8. Mair E. Verthuy and Jennifer Waelti-Walters, "Critical Practice and the Transmission of Culture," *Neohelicon* 14 (1987): 405
9. Mohammed Dib, *La Grande Maison* (Paris: Seuil,1952); *L'Incendie* (Paris: Seuil, 1954); *Le Métier à tisser* (Paris: Seuil, 1957) All references to these three books are to these editions.
10. Laurence Porter, "From Chronicle to Novel: Artistic Elaboration in Camus's La Peste, " *Modern Fiction Studies* 28.4 (Winter 1982) 589.
11. Serge Doubrovsky "The Ethics of Albert Camus," *Camus: A Collection of Critical Essays*, edited by Germaine Brée (Englewood Cliffs, N.J.: Prentice-Hall, 1962), 81
12. Albert Camus, *Fragments*, quoted by S. Tarrow, *Exile from the Kingdom: A Political Rereading of Albert Camus* (The University of Alabama Press, 1985), 127.
13. Camus's Carnets cites the sources of his story. Prominent among them is the reference to several books of the Bible. See Lionel Cohn, "Motifs bibliques dans l'oeuvre d'Albert Camus," Biblical patterns in Modern Literature, ed David H. Hirsch and Nehama Aschkenasy (California: Scholars Press, 1984), 105–114.
14. Cf. the book of *Exodus*, chapters 7–11.
15. Such an analogy did not go unnoticed by Camus himself. Commenting elsewhere on French repressions in Madagascar and Algeria, he writes: "Le fait est là, clair et hideux comme la vérité: nous faisons, dans ces cas-là, ce que nous avons reproché aux Allemands de faire." *Combat* (10 mai 1947).

16. Pol Gaillard, *La Peste. Analyse critique* (Paris: Hatier, 1972), 33.

17. Mohammed Dib, *Au Café* (Paris: Sindbad, 1984), 56.

18. Germaine Tillion, *L'Algérie en 1957* (Paris: Les Éditions de Minuit, 1957), 67.

19. M. Bennoune, "Une analyse socio-économique de l'expérience coloniale algérienne: 1830–1954," *XXIVèmeCongrès Internationale de Sociologie* (Alger: Office des Publications Universitaires, 1974), 421.

20. G. Kateb, "Camus's La Peste: A Dissenting View," *Symposium* 17.4 (1963): 298.

21. Albert Camus, *Carnets Janvier 1942–mars 1951* (Paris: Gallimard, 1964), 72.

Chapter 5

The Dialogical Conclusion: A Breakdown of the Univocal Vision and Exile From the Kingdom

La beauté isolée finit par grimacer, la justice solitaire finit par opprimer. Qui veut servir l'une à l'exclusion de l'autre ne sert personne, ni lui-même, et, finalement sert deux fois l'injustice. Un jour vient où, à force de raideur, plus rien n'émerveille [...] C'est le temps de l'exil, de la vie sèche, des âmes mortes. (Albert Camus)

[Isolated beauty ends in grimaces, solitary justice in oppression. Anyone who seeks to serve the one to the exclusion of the other serves no one, not even himself, and in the end is doubly the servant of injustice. A day comes when, because we have been inflexible, nothing amazes us anymore. {...} It is a time of exile, dry lives, dead souls.][1]

Introduction

Camus's lyrical essay, *Retour à Tipassa*, from which the above passage is taken, is central to the collection of tales contained in *L'Exil et le Royaume* (1957).[2] In a series of polar oppositions typical of Camusian thought, *Retour à Tipasa* expresses the inherent dangers in what the author calls "an exclusive attention and service to human misery," or an equally narrow focus on beauty and sensual pleasure. The two poles of the human dichotomy solicit the artist's attention. An exclusive focus on one or the other of these polarities could lead to "dryness, artifice, oppression, and spiritual death" (Ellison 1990, 173–4). The subsequent opposition of exile and kingdom, as the underlying structure of the short stories, derives from the new lesson apprehended amid the ruins of Tipasa; it is that human existence is itself a balancing between two extremes in which "the stasis of a perfectly achieved equilibrium is, by definition, impossible" (ibid., 176). One—especially the artist—must remain faithful to the tension created by the interweaving of the threads of misery and beauty, for such is the human condition. Such a conviction is that which ultimately "inhabits the final literary texts of Albert Camus" (ibid.).

On a different level, *L'Exil et le Royaume* inscribes itself within the author's impasse in the political arena. The state of aporia was compounded by the intellectual (and not so intellectual) quarrel over *L'Homme Révolté*. It was a time when the author's political vision became the focus of both Left-wing and Right-wing intellectuals of the 1950s. For both camps, he was, at best, an intellectual whose political views rested on undefined premises. His reactionary position on the central issue of Algerian independence was a source of embarrassment to his admirers (Tarrow 1985, 195). But unlike the evasiveness of earlier fictional writings, Camus's confrontation with the Algerian chaotic political scene finds articulation within the fragmented narrative of *L'Exil et le Royaume*.

This collection of short stories is, without doubt, according to O'Brien, Camus's most direct approach in his imaginative writing, to the political situation in Algeria (1970, 70). The impermeability of *L'Etranger* and *La Peste* to Algerian political conflicts, the suppression of the indigenous voice gives way to a recognition of Otherness—a rewriting of the initial universalist vision. Rosemarie Jones views the short stories as moving towards unearthing a point of view which could have been, but has deliberately been suppressed. "The stories in *L'Exil et le Royaume* tend . . . to move towards a statement which appears as judgment, encapsulation, attitude, or summary in relation to what has gone before."[3] This opening up to a new totality registers a certain discomfort within the "kingdom." Jones's assertion that the narratives of Camus's collection are permeated with a certain "aphorism" is not only interesting, but valuable as well, pointing as it does to the new elements of Camus's vision. "The aphorism" the critic maintains, "expresses *multum in parvo*, condensing into a minimal formulation a point which could be, but has deliberately not been discussed more exhaustively" (ibid.). *L'Exil et le Royaume*, it seems, inserts a discontinuity in the overall Camusian vision of the kingdom. The choice of short stories as format has the advantage of presenting us with a variety of optiques of the disintegration of Camus's classical view of man and his inherent solitary consciousness. The partial points of view presented by each story become a fragmented whole in their interaction with one another. The format of the stories allows for a relativity that was somehow non-existent in earlier works. The ubiquitous theme of exile constitutes the *fil conducteur*, linking together the otherwise isolated islands of stories.

One preliminary question here might well be what exactly constitutes "exile." McCarthy points out that "diversity is more apparent than real in *L'Exil et le Royaume*" (1982, 303), and that the various "religious experiences" of the characters depicted, are "thoroughly Camusian." "Behind all these stories are the few images that run through Camus's life and work: the dream of oneness, the Arab, the violence of the Algerian war" (ibid.). The estrangement felt by Janine ("La Femme Adultère"), Daru ("L'Hôte") is registered within a consciousness at grips with an alien presence, that of the Arab. So that "exile" appears both as a cosmic experience and as an existential plight. Janine's sense of alienation and her subsequent "act of adultery" with the starry night desert is closely linked with her discovery of the Arabs. Camus, Erickson writes, "chooses the figure of the Arab as an objective correlative for the inner movement of his main character" (1988, 82). Through these personages, Camus reconstructs the world from the exile's point of view (McCarthy 1982, 305). The touristic detachment from the Algerian space formulated in earlier fictional writings gives way to a new resonance—that of the colonial reality of the Algerian setting. The characters presented in these narrative islands perceive their existential alienation primarily within a socially defined context. I propose to read the theme of exile against a political background—a context of "muted political language"—which rewrites Camus's earlier presentation of exile and estrangement.

These dialogical narratives reflect the collapse of the monological point of view prevalent in the Algerian settings of his fiction. The short stories, on the one hand, disrupt such a univocal vision by creating a context of colonial malaise, the alienation of the protagonists within such a colonial setting, and on the other hand, articulate Camus's own "fall" into colonial politics, concurrent with his political exile in the 1950s when he sought refuge in metropolitan France. The fragmented narratives of *L'Exil et le Royaume* reconstitute a "transient kingdom from which Camus is exiled politically" (Haddour 1989, 191). Three of the short stories, "La Femme Adultère," "Les Muets," and "L'Hôte," which will be the focus of this study, are seen as mediating a peculiar kind of exile. The idea of "l'exil," I insist, is not primarily a religious metaphor, but a political one. I shall however begin by exploring the classical Camusian view of the estranged hero, in order to point out the ways in which the stories of *L'Exil et le Royaume* present a dissenting view from earlier narratives. In this mature work, Camus, according to Amoia, seems to have "overcome" the violence of the war and postwar years, and to acknowledge "a possibility of transcending the crippling limitations of every day life, . . . a free and naked way of life."[4] However, the possibility of such a "kingdom" is itself threatened by political violence generated by colonial politics in the author's homeland. As Conilh rightly asserts, "Cet enfer du présent ne pouvait [pas] être un royaume [this present hell could not be a kingdom]" (1958, 674). The feeling of exile—which is neither new nor alien to the fictional and philosophical settings of the author—remains thus prevalent in the mature work of Camus, but as pointed out again, and much earlier, by Conilh,

> [ce sentiment de l'exil] se trouve tout naturellement réamorcé à une source pour ainsi dire plus charnelle, plus humaine. Le mal, la souffrance, la violence historique qui supprime toute indifférence et toute innocence, réalités dont *le Mythe de Sisyphe* nous était apparu dangereusement allégé, deviennent la matière principale de [*l'Exil et le Royaume*]. (ibid.)

> [[this feeling of exile] is naturally taken up again, linked this time to a more carnal and humane source. Evil, suffering, and historical violence which suppress all indifference and all innocence, realities that *The Myth of Sisyphus* appeared too dangerously to take lightly, become the main theme of [*Exile and the Kingdom*].]

The question with which Camus never ceases to grapple is at the root of the ever-widening gap between his theoretical positions and his values, and finds articulation within *L'Exil et le Royaume*. "Is it possible, legitimate, to be in history while using as points of reference values that go beyond history" (*Carnets II* 1964, 202)? Both Jonas and Daru register their frustration in attempting to transcend history and political debates.

Albert Camus's "Exile" and "The Kingdom"

The loneliness of the individual, his lack of relatedness to his environment, or the sense of foreignness in one's own land constitute one underlying theme of the six short stories that make up Camus's *L'Exil et le Royaume*, and provide the thematic continuities that link them together (Ellison 1990, 176). Each of the stories in its own way "illustrate[s] the same theme, thus giving unity to [the] collection, beneath the diversity of expression" (Maquet 1955, 170). North Africa "the land from which Camus has constantly drawn his best inspiration" (ibid.), provides the setting for four of the stories, but at a certain level the setting itself does not seem to impose a geographical necessity, merely furnishing, it would seem, the ambiance for the inner drama of the characters.

"La Femme adultère" as one instance, narrates Janine and her husband Marcel's journey into the Saharan territories of Algeria. The voyage to the interior is also a voyage into Janine's inner self. Her confrontation with the silent Arabs, "ces seigneurs sans royaumes," and the arid desert reveal her own solitude and servitude. She is fascinated by these nomads, wanderers without respite, who possessed nothing, but who served no one, miserable yet free lords of a strange realm. Their apparent freedom, Janine gleaned intuitively, could have been hers; it had been promised her from the beginning of time, but she had missed it somehow, perhaps through her marriage, through a life crowded with the pursuit of material comfort. But perhaps she can recapture for a brief moment, symbolically at least, that complete pantheistic communion that the Arabs appear to enjoy. Hours later, "[répondant] à un appel qui lui sembla tout proche" (1962, 1571), she leaves her husband; with the sound of voices drifting from the Arab village, she flees into the night to yield herself to the possession of the starry night:

> Pressée de tout son ventre contre le parapet, tendue vers le ciel en mouvement, elle attendait [...] Les dernières étoiles des constellations laissèrent tomber leurs grappes un peu plus bas sur l'horizon du désert, et s'immobilisèrent. Alors avec une douceur, l'eau de la nuit commença d'emplir Janine, [...] monta peu à peu du centre obscur de son être et déborda en flots ininterrompus jusqu'à sa bouche pleine de gémissement. L'instant d'après, le ciel entier s'étendait au-dessus d'elle, renversée sur la terre froide. (1962, 1572–3)

> [Her whole belly pressed against the parapet as she strained toward the moving sky. She was {...} waiting. {...} The last stars of the constellations dropped their clusters a little lower on the desert horizon and became still. Then with unbearable gentleness, the water of night began to fill Janine, {...} rose gradually from the hidden core of her being and overflowed in wave after wave, rising up even to her mouth full of moans. The next moment, the whole sky stretched out over her, fallen on her back on the cold earth.][5]

However, following her cosmic experience, her "adulterous" moment, Janine returns to her husband, to her life of material comfort and mediocrity, her "exile." She does so with apparent regret, as evidenced by her tears. "Elle pleurait, de toutes ses larmes, sans pouvoir se retenir" (ibid.) [She was weeping copiously, unable to restrain herself]. Retrospectively, "La Femme adultère" can be said to illustrate a point of departure of Camus's thought espoused in *L'Etranger*, namely man's unrelatedness to his environment. The short story situates the principal character at the center of a spectacle. In contrast with Meursault's lack of introspection, Janine consciously registers the strange music which penetrates her progressively. As Maquet rightly underlines, however, it is "a music of discordant tonalities, expressing both plenitude and emptiness" (1955, 30–31). "La Femme adultère" recapitulates the vision of *L'Envers et l'Endroit* (1937), which is that of a complete divestiture allowing for a profound journey, that of the soul. Janine and Marcel's life so far is made of "the humdrum of daily routine, with its habits and techniques" (Maquet 1955, 31). These have woven around them a soft cocoon. The attendant lethargy has abolished all objective responsiveness to their own existence, until the bus ride. The movement of the fly ("une mouche maigre [qui] tournait, depuis un moment" [1962, 1557]) in the bus transporting the couple into the interior desert reflects their own existence prior to the voyage. Voyage is an important theme here. It drags the couple from their comfort zone. It is the moment when the familiar decor crumbles ("les décors habituels s'écroulent"). With the collapse of the inner and outer décor, Janine is able to confront her veritable self. At the horizon of her introspection lies anguish. Janine's self-confrontation begins with an attempt at re-discovering her husband.

> Janine regarda son mari. Des épis de cheveux grisonnants plantés bas sur un front serré, le nez large, la bouche irrégulière, Marcel avait l'air d'un faune boudeur. A chaque défoncement de la chaussée, elle le sentait sursauter contre elle. Puis il laissait retomber son torse pesant sur ses jambes écartées, le regard fixe, inerte de nouveau, et absent. Seules, ses grosses mains imberbes, rendues plus courtes encore par la flanelle grise qui dépassait les manches de chemise et couvrait les poignets, semblaient en action. Elles serraient si fortement une petite valise de toile, placée entre ses genoux, qu'elles ne paraissaient pas sentir la course hésitante de la mouche. (1962, 1557)

> [Janine looked at her husband. With wisps of graying hair growing low on a narrow forehead, a broad nose, a flabby mouth, Marcel looked like a pouting faun. At each hollow in the pavement she felt him jostle against her. Then his heavy torso would slump back on his widespread legs and he would become inert again and absent, with a vacant stare. Nothing about him seemed active but his thick hairless hands, made even shorter by the flannel underwear extending below his cuffs and covering his wrists. His hands were holding so tight to a little canvas suitcase set between his knees that they appeared not to feel the fly's halting progress.] (1958, 3)

In the course of this examination what is revealed to her eyes or inner eyes is a life of boredom and her husband's greed suggested by the "hands . . . holding so tightly to a little canvas suitcase. The discord that Janine perceives between her and the man she has married becomes quickly that of her life in general; a life marked by inertia. This is driven home even more forcefully as she progresses in her voyage, and is soon stripped of the illusions which have given her support and the pretense of a universe of familiar perceptions and gestures. What she feels now is a certain opaqueness, even heaviness, symbolized not only by her husband's "heavy torso slump[ed] back," but by her own physical "lourdeur." "Elle ne pouvait se baisser, en effet, sans étouffer . . . Au collège pourtant, elle était première en gymnastique, son souffle était inépuisable. Y avait-il si longtemps de cela? Vingt-cinq ans" (1962, 1558) [She could not stoop over without gasping . . . Yet in school she had won the first prize in gymnastics and hadn't known what it was to be winded. Was that so long ago? Twenty-five years. (1958, 5–6)]. Confronted with her own heaviness, itself a symbol of a now impenetrable universe, Janine the traveler feels lost in the glaring light of her own consciousness, raised to a high level of awakeness. Within the newly acquired alertness, each reality, even that of the fly is endowed with a unique fact of existence, its own "miraculous worth" (Maquet 1955, 32). Paradoxically, however, it is also a lucidity that excludes Janine from the images she now confronts, reducing her life to solitude and exile. "Ce divorce entre l'homme de [sic] sa vie, l'acteur et son décor," Camus writes in *Le Mythe de Sisyphe*, "c'est proprement le sentiment de l'absurdité" [This divorce between man and his life, between the actor and his setting, this is, strictly speaking, the sentiment of absurdity.] (1943, 18). Thus Janine's voyage, a rather prosaic business trip, divests her of her habitual decor leaving her to confront both the alienness of her new surroundings and her own alienation from such a decor.

Of much more interest to us is the presence of the Arab which triggers in the character the consciousness of her own malaise. For this very presence engenders a certain break in the Camusian monological presentation of the universe of exile, thus conferring upon the term a new dimension. It would be noted that Janine and Marcel as characters present a certain palpability—a novelty from the more abstract characters of *La Peste*. They are, as Tarrow underlines, "creations of flesh and blood" (1985, 177). Their experience of the desert acquires thus a tangibility. Janine and Marcel's life prior to the voyage has been a relatively comfortable one in the relative security of the coastal area of Algeria. The economic crisis following the World War Two has made it necessary for Marcel to sell directly to retailers, thus avoiding middle men. Their journey to the interior is thus in response to economic exigencies. The hostility and fear they experience in their new environment stems from an "exposure to a strange land with undefined parameters" (ibid., 175).

In a reversal of roles, Marcel finds himself bowing to the whims of the Arabs whose patronage he has come to solicit. Also the necessity of expressing himself in Arabic strips him of the position of dominance held in the city where French is the language of the dominant class (ibid.). Typically, Marcel's fear manifests itself in racist insinuations. "Ils [les Arabes] se croient tout permis, maintenant [They think they can get away with anything now]," he remarks, following an encounter with a majestically dressed Arab who almost tramples over them, seemingly oblivious to their presence. Janine, on the other hand, "détestait la stupide arrogance de cet Arabe et se sentait tout d'un coup malheureuse. Elle voulait partir, elle pensait à son petit appartement. . . Et son malaise, son besoin de départ augmentaient. "Pourquoi suis-je venue?" (1962, 1566) [She loathed that Arab's stupid arrogance and suddenly felt unhappy. She wanted to leave and thought of her little apartment . . . "Why did I come?"] (1958, 20-21). Janine and Marcel's position here is that of solicitors; their linguistic inadequacy, moreover, puts them in the subservient role usually played by the Arab in the city.

Added to, and reinforcing, their security is the reversal of role they experience on this trip. Marcel, the pied-noir, is presented as "a whore" showing off his "goods." This position naturally put him at the mercy of the Arab.

> Alors il [Marcel] ouvrait la malle, montrait les étoffes et les foulards, poussait la balance et le mètre pour étaler sa marchandise devant le vieux marchand. Il s'énervait, haussait le ton, riait de façon désordonnée, il avait l'air d'une femme qui veut plaire et qui n'est pas sûre d'elle. (1962, 1565)

> [Then he [Marcel] opened the trunk, exhibited the wools and the silks, pushed back the scale and yardstick to spread out his merchandise in front of the old merchant. He got excited , raised his voice, laughed nervously, like a woman who wants to make an impression and is not sure of herself. (1958, 18)]

Neither is Janine exempt from a certain form of "prostitution." Her experience in the desert, one might recall, is explicitly presented as adulterous. In the sexual attraction she feels for the Arab, she discovers herself and the fragility of her life.

Underlying their insecurity is also a certain attraction for the way of life of the Arab. Janine for instance is drawn toward the autonomy enjoyed by these nomads who seem not to have a care for material comforts. The servile attention the Arab usually gives to the French dominant group is totally lacking in these vagrant lords who seem to ignore the very existence of the couple.

> Des Arabes les croisaient [...] sans paraître les voir, ramenant devant eux les pans de leurs burnous. Elle leur trouvait, même lorsqu'ils portaient des loques, un air de fierté que n'avaient pas les Arabes de sa ville. (1962, 1564)

> [They encountered Arabs who stepped out of their way without seeming to see them, wrapping themselves in their burnooses. Even when they were wearing rags, she felt they had a look of dignity unknown to the Arabs of her town.] (1958, 16)

Indeed the dignity ascribed to the Arab here is alien to the throng of Arabs, affamished and in rags, who invade the city of Tlemcen (*Le Métier à tisser* 1957, 17). As stated earlier, what Janine confronts in the desert is the collapse of the habitual décor of her life, a décor made up of her language, her frenchness, the Arab's servile dependency on the Europeans for his living. In this desert, the Arabs, despite their rags, are the sovereign lords. Janine and Marcel are literally out of their element on several levels, and excluded from the vastness of the desert. Janine's encounter with the desert awakens her from a life of lethargy, to come to grips with "the benign indifference" of the desert, but also with her own position as a social misfit. The following sections will examine the theme of exile within a political context to demonstrate that the narratives of *L'Exil et le Royaume*, encapsulating moments of social and political estrangement, disrupt Camus's earlier representation of existential exile.

"Exile" and "The Kingdom" Reconsidered

For the sake of chronological order, let us recapitulate a little here, by pointing out that *La Chute*, initially conceived as part of the collection, but subsequently published separately a year earlier than *L'Exil et le Royaume*, contains the seminal disintegration of Camus's "utopian vision of the Kingdom projected unto the Mediterranean." Clamence's physical and mental solitude finds deeper echo in the physical exile of Camus's subsequent characters. The "adulterous" Janine, the frustrated Daru, the defeated Yvars find themselves estranged from their "kingdom" which Camus located in the Mediterranean landscapes and North-African deserts. The plight of the various protagonists stems from an inability to live in what Camus refers to as "l'île sans avenir" untainted by religious or political ideologies. The characters' predicament is articulated within a clearly defined political context. The feeling of solitude expressed by Daru, Janine and Yvars translates as their alienation from the Mediterranean kingdom invaded by colonial violence.

Camus's work on two of the stories, "La Femme adultère," and "Le Rénégat" coincided with a particular stage in Camus's involvement with Algeria (1954). Following the painful controversy over *L'Homme Révolté*, Camus finding himself increasingly estranged from the Parisian intellectual scene, turned to his homeland seeking inspiration and a rediscovery of the source of his artistic production. The "spiritual" quest resulted in a trip to Algiers, specifically Tipasa, a "pelerinage aux sources," to which we owe the lyrical essay *Retour à Tipasa*.[6] The modification in political outlook, the fall into colonial politics find articulation in the tale of Jonas. "Jonas" more than any other of the collection reenacts the political argument with Sartre over Camus's tendency to withdraw from concrete reality. More importantly, the tale articulates a certain revisionist move by which the author apparently arrives at a new understanding of the work of the artist.

The tale, obviously, is framed upon the biblical rendition of "Jonah," a prophet sent out to warn the citizens of Nineveh of impending doom if they do not turn from their sins. Jonah, unwilling to carry out the mission, escapes on a boat, experiences a near-ship wreck, spends three days and three nights in the belly of a whale, and finally sobers up to the necessity of his duty.[7] Camus draws upon two important aspects of the biblical narrative to illustrate the position of the modern writer: 1. Jonah's attempt to flee from God's calling (i.e., his duty) and 2. the necessity of facing the demands of society. The full title of the story, "Jonas ou l'artiste au travail (Jonas or the artist at work)," points to a divine call placed on the artist/writer, but also throws a dissenting note in the collection of short stories. The tale, transparently autobiographical, is the only one of the six stories that takes place in Europe (Paris most likely). There is in Jonas a certain affinity with Voltaire's Candide. As the leitmotif, "tout est pour le mieux dans le meilleur des mondes," that runs through the Voltairean tale, so is Jonas's firm belief in the infaillibility of his "star." The latter is in its place, and all is well in Jonas's world.

The ironic distance from which Camus views his protagonist is rather interesting, since the story relates Camus's own experience as an artist. Just as Voltaire set out to deflate his hero's excessive optimism, Camus also chose to crowd his protagonist's life with various peripetias, mostly in the form of intrusions from family, friends, disciples, who finally reduced him to a state of non-productivity. Camus, in loading his hero with the demands of a hectic modern-day world, "was tracing his own self portrait and was detailing the confrontation between his own naive optimism and the calamities that beset the [artist] in the twentieth century" (Ellison 1990, 201). As the story moves to its conclusion, the artist, wallowing more and more in the adulation of friends and disciples and facing miscellaneous demands from family and society at large, becomes increasingly sterile. This creative sterility, recalling Camus's own "writers's block" after the publication of *L'Homme Révolté*, propels the artist into what one might call an "existential anguish." The less creative he becomes, the more he attempts to grapple with the puzzles of existence. The ultimate solution he comes up with is to construct a loft within the apartment, thus isolating himself from the outside world. The confinement, however, does not lead to the expected creative rejuvenation. He collapses besides his canvas on which he has been able to scribble only one word—a word that can be deciphered as either *solitaire* or *solidaire*. The ambiguity of the word reflects perhaps the impossibility of choosing between the privilege of artistic solitude on the one hand, and the necessity of solidarity with fellow humans on the other. The optimistic ending (The doctor pronounced Jonas's physical collapse, unalarming: "ce n'est rien, . . . dans une semaine, il sera debout [It's nothing, . . . in a week, he will be on his feet]" [1962, 1652]) would seem to suggest however that the artist has found a solution to the problem, which lies in reconciliation: to be creative, he needs the inspiration of the world of men as well as the solitary cell. "His duty is a double one, and the balance must be constantly reassessed and reasserted" (Tarrow 1985, 189). "Jonas" presages the fundamental problem articulated in "L'Hôte" where Daru is faced with a choice between a solitary life outside human conflicts, and solidarity with his human fellows. Jonas and Daru are both denied "the luxury of self-involved isolation" beyond the cares of human fellowship and the attendant conflicts (I shall return to this presently, in my reading of "L'Hôte").

The tale of the artist at work can be said to illustrate on a broader level Camus's relationship with the Marxist metropolitan intelligentsia and ultimately the author's solitude. Camus, as remarked, rejected the notion of history in the Marxist eschatology. "Jonas" reveals, however, the impossibility of transcending history and political debates. The political quarrel with Sartre and the increasing colonial violence of the

Algerian situation shatter the myth of the Mediterranean outside history and politics. The language of hatred that permeates the narratives of *L'Exil et le Royaume* involves a breakdown in the former univocal narrative of *L'Etranger* and *La Peste*. In "Le Rénégat," for instance, the missionary falls under the power of the idol-worship inhabitants of the desert, "une armée de méchants" (1962, 1579), thereby propelling the tale into a historical moment.

The collection of short stories unfolds thus new dynamics of the colonial landscape. The Other, entering into the dialogue, reveals a fissure. For, as stated by Haddour, as long as the "Other" is peripheral, fossilized as a feature of landscape, marginalised or completely excluded, univocal texts, like *L'Etranger*, or *La Peste* can sustain a coherent vision (1989, 193). But the presence of the alien element in certain narratives of *L'Exil et le Royaume* fetters this vision, reflecting a collapse of Camus's "monological point of view" prevalent in the Algerian settings of earlier fiction. Such a monological view, as I argued in earlier chapters, symbolized an attempt to withdraw from "the closure of colonial discourse." The "loft" that Camus constructs against exposure to colonial politics, collapses, thus propelling him into brutal human conflicts. Although *L'Exil et le Royaume* inscribes itself within Camus's passionate pilgrimage to Tipasa, the collection lacks the vital elements of joy and freedom attendant on the sun-and-sea bathed atmosphere of pagan sensuality of earlier essays and of *L'Etranger*— "La Femme adultère" and "L'Hôte" are set in the harsh climate of the mountainous zones of Algeria. Thody remarks that the inspiration provided by the Mediterranean setting "is no longer the revelation of happiness. . .; it is the realization that those whom he . . . described as happy barbarians in *L'Eté à Alger* are now ordinary human beings faced with the twin problems of growing old and of facing a terrible political situation" (1961, 184–5). The explosiveness of the Algerian political situation seems to compel Camus out of his dialogue between stone and flesh, his contemplation of beauty and nature. *L'Exil et le Royaume* reveals a significant modification in his novelistic regard for the Algerian setting (Erickson 1988, 82). The landscape of *L'Etranger*'s lucid vision becomes a landscape permeated with confusion as Camus himself fails to formulate a viable political position consistent with the earlier univocal, "universal discourse."

The modification in Camus's mediterranean landscape can primarily be seen in the dialectics of hatred as they are played out and shifted from narrative to narrative. The power relations between Arabs and pieds-noirs is rather revealing. As remarked, the presence of the Arabs as in the case of Janine, le Rénégat and Daru serves as catalyst to an inner voyage. In a reversal of roles, the mostly silent Arabs here assume the position of power. These nomads, "free and miserable lords," extensions of the desert, hold for Janine an attraction akin to that of a predator. In his critical review of the story, McCarthy asserts that Janine's seeming irritation with the Arabs "contains a fascination and her mystical experience of the desert is a sublimation of the sexual attraction she feels for them. The Arabs live with the country whereas she has been living against it; they are authentic whereas she is not; their bodies have the lithe grace of dancers or soccer-players" (1982, 304). The Algeria one gleans from the narrative of "La Femme Adultère" appears as a far cry from the golden cities of Louis Bertrand. It is here, a bleak, gloomy country which, however, elicits two different set of responses. Onimus points to the touch of humor in the juxtaposition of the reaction from the European couple and that from the Arabs.[8] More than humor, however, the juxtaposition—on the one hand, the settled, sedentary and lethargic couple, and on the other the gaunt nomads with proud souls—brings out the precariousness of the Europeans' hold over the barren land. Compounding the panorama of anguish is the underlying insecurity of their life in an alien world.

"L'Hôte": A Political Landscape

Camus's political position provides yet again a context to an understanding of the colonial complex as articulated in "L'Hôte." I would, however, like to interject here a new voice, that of Jules Roy who provides another inside perspective to the ossified political view of Camus. Roy's *La Guerre d'Algérie* (1960) and *Etranger à mes frères* (1982) engage retrospectively, one might say, Camus's political essays in a dialogue. Roy, faced with the "infernal dialectics of violence" in Algeria, and viewing in retrospect Camus's hesitation, writes:

> Pour moi, j'ignore, Camus, si je suis comme toi capable de placer ma mère au-dessus de la justice. Comment oserais-je parler de cela? [...] Il ne s'agit pas de préférer sa mère à la justice. Il s'agit d'aimer la justice autant que sa propre mère.
> Ce que je sais seulement, c'est qu'au-dessus de la justice, je placerai toujours le royaume de Dieu où les enfants légitimes n'ont pas forcément rang sur les bâtards. [9]

> [As for me, I do not know, Camus, if I am capable, like you of placing my mother above of justice. How could I talk of that? {...} It is not a question of preferring one's mother to justice. It is a question of loving justice as much as one's own mother.

All I know is that above justice, I will always place the kingdom of God where the legitimate children are not necessarily ranked above the illegitimate ones.]

The distinction posited here between "enfants légitimes" and "bâtards" displays the racist context in which even many of the well-intentioned intellectuals, such as Jules Roy himself, were brought up. Notable however, is the latter's attempt to transcend the colonialist attitude inherited. *La Guerre d'Algérie*, let us keep in mind, is Roy's response to the Algerian political crisis, and a indirect response to Camus's various reports of the crisis. *La Guerre d'Algérie* expresses Roy's disillusionment with France and the peculiar nature of her political endeavors in his native country Algeria. Roy was not without recognising the ambiguities of his own position, which is that of a former anti-Nazi combatant, now serving the causes of colonialist France in Indochina. He was acutely aware of himself as a "bourreau" in Indochina, and perhaps more, as a "victim" of France's political contradictions. His relative lucidity allowed him to dismiss Camus's idea that France was defending her humanist ideals in Algeria.

We may recall that in Algeria, as well as in Indochina, Camus viewed the process of decolonisation primarily as a "Marxist threat" to the West. The demand for independence, specifically that of Algeria, was for him a manifestation of a new Arabic imperialism. As Roy remarks, this anti-nationalist fixation smacks of colonialist paranoia. Algerian nationalism may very well carry marxist undertones; but it is primarily an anti-colonial movement. In *Étranger à mes frères*, Roy points again to Camus's colonial "conformism" as complicitous with French tyranny in Algeria, thereby casting doubt on Camus's claim to objectivity.[10] Roy deconstructs Camus's hypothetical scenario, "je défendrai ma mère avant la justice;" Camus, according to Roy, surrenders to the judgments of his heart "afin de déguiser la réalité en mensonge [in order to disguise reality in lies]" (*La Guerre d'Algérie* 1960, 222). Roy seeks to undermine both Camus's emotional attachment to "French brotherhood" at the expense of justice, and the notion of justice upheld in *Lettres à un ami allemand*. The principles of justice as expounded to the fictitious German friend, and as fought for in the World War Two do not apply in colonized Algeria (ibid., 157-8). In *Actuelles III*, Camus reiterates his earlier replique given to the Algerian student at Stockholm (cf. chapter two): "ceux qui continuent de penser héroïquement que le frère doit périr plutôt que les principes, je me bornerai à les admirer de loin. Je ne suis pas de leur race [I can only admire from a distance those who continue to believe heroically that the brother must perish rather than principles]" (*Essais* 1965,

892–93). *La Guerre d'Algérie* points out that the "brotherhood" as envisaged by Camus is not one relating colonizer and colonized, but one that seeks to build a protective wall around his "frères de sang" shielding them from the Arabs:

> Nos frères ne sont pas seulement nos frères mais tous ceux qui souffrent de l'iniquité, et nous ne pouvons pas leur préférer ceux qui nous sont unis par les liens de sang quand ceux-là mangent à leur faim et sont relativement heureux alors que les autres crèvent en se débattant contre le malheur.
> Qu'on ne prétende pas non plus que je tue mon frère en réclamant du pain et la paix pour ceux qui meurent. Qu'on n'abuse pas d'une confusion facile. (1960, 219)

> [Our brothers are not only our brothers, but all those who suffer from inequity; and we cannot prefer our own blood brothers to them, when our own eat to their contentment and are relatively happy while others die and struggle against misfortune.
> Let us not pretend either, to kill our brothers while demanding bread and peace for those who are dying. We should not indulge in a simplistic confusion.]

For Roy, the victimization of the French "brother" in the process of decolonisation is purely hypothetical; so by setting up an entire discursive defense of the colonizer based on a hypothetical injustice from which the latter might suffer, Camus debunks the universal applicability of the concept of justice. The choice of his "mother" at the expense of justice places him at the side of the colonialist, for the "mother"—*la mère patrie*—in Algeria presents the characteristics of the "bourreau." The idea of "mother" is itself impregnated with colonial ideology. As natural as Camus's hesitations between" . . . son amour filial et le souci de la justice [filial love and the concern for justice]" are, it is also highly problematic; for, within the highly polarized and tragic political situation of Algeria, the distinction he posits between his "mother" and "justice" loaded as it is with emotion, is unacceptable as a "rational political statement." Roy continues,

> Camus aurait rejoint ce qu'il croyait être l'innocence—sa mère—; il aurait eu cette noblesse. Après tout, peut-être l'aurais-je imité si ma mère avait été en vie. Si j'ai été plus loin que lui, c'est parce qu'il m'a ouvert les yeux. Lui s'est arrêté en route, il a fait pour moi comme l'instituteur de *L'Exil et le Royaume*. Après avoir libéré l'Arabe qui lui a été confié comme prisonnier, l'instituteur le met sur le chemin et lui dit: "De ce côté-là c'est les gendarmes; de l'autre côté, c'est la liberté," et il ne s'en occupe plus.

Je dois avouer qu'il n'y a pas d'injustice qu'on puisse réparer sans commettre d'autres injustices. Toutes les injustices se tiennent les unes aux autres, dans un enchaînement dont on ne sort pas. Que faire? Comment choisir? Si on agit, d'une façon ou d'une autre, il y a toujours un moment où on se le reproche. Dans la religion judaïque, le même mot désigne justice et charité, et la justice passe toujours avant la mère. (*Etranger à mes frères* 1982, 128)

[Camus would have sided with what he believed to be innocence— his mother—; he would have been that noble. After all, perhaps I would have done the same if my mother had been alive. If I went further than he did, it is because he opened my eyes. He, Camus, stopped mid-way; to me, he acted like the schoolteacher in *Exile and the Kingdom*. After freeing the Arab prisoner who was entrusted to him, the schoolteacher places him on the road and tells him: "On this side is the police; on the other is freedom;" and he washes off his hands.
I must confess that one cannot redress an injustice without committing others. All injustices are linked in a chain from which one cannot escape. What can one do? How does one choose? Whether one acts in one way or another, there is always a moment when one reproaches oneself for the choice. In Jewish religion the same word designates justice and charity, and justice always comes before one's mother.]

The comparison Roy establishes between Camus and the schoolteacher in "L'Hôte" points to Camus's inability to transcend his attachment to his mother country, to "violate the colonialist taboo [associated] with his mother." Roy's reading of Camus is of great importance to us here, bringing yet a fresh appraisal of the writer's political position, which has been the focal point of this study. Camus's *Crise en Algérie* not only gives voice to the Algerian political crisis as stated, but engages in a political combat on behalf of the Arab. The combat, however, is never carried out to its conclusion. Like Daru, Camus points to the existence of the "colonial prison" and the way to justice for the colonized Arab, but fails to follow it up.

As has been insisted upon throughout this study, one cannot claim that Camus ever explicitly condoned colonial injustices. Theoretically he was vehemently opposed to their various manifestations. As a leitmotif, running through his essays on Algeria, was the cry for an end of injustice, "la disparition des injustices qui empoisonnent le climat politique de l'Algérie" (*Essais* 1965, 952). "L'Hôte" unfolds the author's conflict between "amour filial et le souci de la justice." His failure to overcome the complex of "le sang des races" constitutes a formidable block to any effectual action on behalf of the colonized. Like Daru, Camus is limited to pointing the way to justice.

Daru recognizes his fraternal tie with the Arab. However, aside from short term measures such as sharing bread with his guest or putting him on the path to momentary liberty, he is unable to offer much because of a stronger tie with the colonial institution, a tie which he seeks to disavow. The short story thus replicates Camus's own conflicting structure of feeling. Daru's attempt to disengage himself from the political problems attendant on the colonial setting is foiled by the Arab's choice—the path to colonial justice. The setting of the story, the Eastern desert of Algeria, is highly charged with political conflicts. Both the host and the guest as representatives of the conflicting groups are unable to shelter themselves from colonial politics. The setting has a political significance in the history of Algeria, having been the seat of the 1945 and 1954 uprisings and rebellion. Politically, the southern territory (the Oran of *La Peste*) and the eastern territory (of "L'Hôte") are in open hostility. "Ça bouge," says Balducci, the gendarme, "on parle de révolte. Nous sommes mobilisés, dans un sens" (1962, 1612) [Things are brewing, it appears. There is talk of a forthcoming revolt. We are mobilized, in a way. (1958, 92)][11]

As stated, Daru's attempt to disengage from politics and to construct a "racial brotherhood" with the Arab fails. Daru's initial reaction when ordered to deliver the prisoner is refusal. "Ce n'est pas mon métier," he declares; to which Balducci replies "A la guerre, on fait tous les métiers" (1962, 1612). Turning his back on politics, Daru seeks a shared communion in the breaking of bread with the Arab outside political conflicts. Daru seeks to de-politicize his encounter with the Arab. However, the latter's invitation to Daru to join their cause ("Viens avec nous" [1962, 1617]) circumvents the effort. Daru's attempt at neutrality or indifference is further undermined by the gendarme's instruction to deliver the Arab to justice. His crime, the murder of his cousin over a theft of grain, points to economic distress. The connection between famine, revolutionary politics, and colonial politics is "crystallized" in the figure of the Arab. Although the latter is not explicitly presented as a revolutionary, the threat on the blackboard ("tu as livré notre frère, tu paieras [ibid., 1621] [You handed over our brother. You will pay for this]" [1958, 109].) speaks of a collective hostility that goes beyond the specificities of the issue at hand here. The threat significantly written across the geo-political map of France on the blackboard of Daru's classroom reveals a solidarity of men striking against a political system and against Daru as a representative of colonial history and power.[12] Within such a confrontational context,

Daru is bound by implication to take a position (Haddour 1989, 204), which preempts any communion with the Other in a shared religion or racial brotherhood. This failure heralds a message of despair permeating Camus's "desert" or the "Mediterranean." Cryle interprets the story as an "affrontement symbolique entre l'homme civilisé et l'homme primitif."[13]

It is worth insisting, however, on the political nature of the confrontation which takes its impulse from the colonial climate of the 1950s in which Camus's vision of a Mediterranean unity breaks down, to show a "desert" very much under political siege. Cryle correctly points to Camus's nostalgic attempt to re/capture the harmony of a desert already invaded by colonial violence and hatred.

> Nous avons déjà dit qu'il est possible de résumer les relations complexes de Daru et de l'Arabe en parlant d'un affrontement symbolique de l'homme civilisé et de l'homme primitif. Cet affrontement n'aurait pas été nouveau pour l'auteur, qui, dans ses premiers ouvrages, parle avec admiration de la simplicité de ses compagnons algériens. [...] *Mais devant les atrocités de la guerre algérienne, il ne s'agissait plus sans doute pour Camus d'éprouver une simple nostalgie pour l'unité de cet état primitif: n'étaient-ce pas ceux-mêmes dont il avait admiré l'amoralité pure qui maintenant, se livraient sans arrière-pensée à des actes d'une cruauté brutale?* (1973, 135–6; emphasis added.)

> [We have already stated that it is possible to sum up the complex relationship between Daru and the Arab by speaking of the symbolic confrontation between the civilized man and the primitive man. Such confrontation would not have been new to the author who, in his first works, talks with admiration about the simplicity of his fellow Algerians. {...} *but face with the atrocities of the Algerian war, it was no longer for Camus, no doubt, a simple yearning for the harmony of this primitive state: was it not the same people whose pure amorality he admired, who were now engaged in acts of cruel brutality?*]

Camus's desert, or "l'unité d[un] état primitif" of the Mediterranean become contextual fields under siege and invaded by a language of hatred. So the symbolical confrontation Cryle alludes to must primarily be interpreted within the context of the political climate generated by the crisis of the 1950s. "L'Hôte" illustrates "the failure of a stand that refuses total commitment to either side" in a conflict (Tarrow 1985, 185). On a personal level, Daru's humanitarian gesture towards the prisoner is entirely laudable; politically, however, it is a tacit withdrawal from commitment, at best an ambiguous stand that leaves itself to condemnation from both sides. To the French administration his act is a treacherous one; to the Arabs, his inability to take any effectual action on their behalf marks him off as a traitor. The tale clearly illustrates the sterility of Daru's ambiguous stand, an echo of the author's own ambivalences during the polemics of the 1950s. For failing to choose "between black and white" in such a highly polarized situation as that of the Algerian political scene, he, like Daru, became a suspect to both sides. He was, in his own words, attacked "sur sa droite et sur sa gauche, forcé de poursuivre sa route sans satisfaire personne" (Lottman 1978, 629).

The Dialectics of Violence
in "Les Muets" and "L'Hôte"

"L'Hôte" as stated, unearths the latent antagonism which lurked behind "the limpid narratives" of *L'Envers et L'endroit, Noces, L'Etranger,* and *La Peste.* I have argued in my earlier chapters on *L'Etranger* and *La Peste* that the peculiar absence or representation of the colonized indigenous population in these narratives constitute an effort to suppress the colonial malaise evoked by the landscape. The representational "void" suppressed the dialectics of hatred inherent in a colonial setting. This section endeavors to read "Les Muets" and "L'Hôte" from the narrative point of view of *Crise en Algérie.* This essay written to point out the various crises in Algeria, focuses mainly on the issue of famine. It is also a prevalent theme of the two short stories. Both narratives, embodying a political resonance, seem to give flesh to the ossified political stance of Camus formulated in his political essays. A reading of the two stories in the light of *Crise en Algérie* reveals that both narratives, while replicating the Camusian effort to revoke the colonial dilemma, unfold what is clearly a malaise generated by a "language of violence" which overwhelms the "Mediterranean" and forces the writer to relinquish the former "lyricism" upheld throughout the narratives of *L'Etranger* and *La Peste.*

Camus's report on the 1945 political revolt, which forms the nexus of the essays, is summarized by him as follows:

Si grave et si urgente que soit la pénurie économique dont souffre l'Afrique du Nord, elle n'explique pas, à elle seule, la crise politique algérienne. Si nous en avons parlé d'abord, c'est que la faim prime tout. Mais, à la vérité, le malaise politique est antérieur à la famine. Et lorsque nous aurons fait ce qu'il faut pour alimenter la population algérienne, il nous restera encore tout à faire. C'est une façon de dire qu'il nous restera à imaginer enfin une politique. [...] La politique algérienne est à ce point déformée par les préjugés et les ignorances que c'est déjà faire beaucoup pour elle, *si l'on en présente un tableau objectif par le moyen d'une information vérifiée. C'est ce tableau que je voudrais entreprendre.* (*Essais* 1965, 950; emphasis added.)

[As serious and as urgent as the economic crisis of North Africa is, it does not explain all alone the Algerian political crisis. If we have primarily spoken about it, it is because hunger takes precedence over everything else. But the truth is that the political malaise comes before the famine. After we have done what we must to feed the Algerian population, we will still have everything left to accomplish. It is a way of saying that it will still remain for us, ultimately, to imagine a politics. {...} Algerian politics are at this moment so deformed by prejuduces and ignorance that it is already a great help *to present an objective picture by means of verifiable information. Such is a the picture I would like to present.*]

Having pertinently delineated the underlying causal structure of the Algerian political situation, Camus proceeds, however, to mystify the political revolt by diffusing the nationalist structure of feeling that informs the uprising. Quilici, rightly no doubt, objects to Camus's claim to presenting "un tableau objectif" and rejects the report on the ground of its "insuffisance . . . à vouloir connaître la situation nord-africaine après trois semaines d'enquête."[14] The presentation of the case in "Crise en Algérie," one may say, is teleological, for the argument is presented, seemingly with the sole purpose of positing one solution: France must endeavor to reconquer the confidence of the Arabs. This can be done if France "attribuait à ses principes démocratiques une valeur universelle pour qu'elle pût les étendre aux populations dont elle avait la charge" (*Essais* 1965, 951). France, as Camus insists, must begin to lend some credibility to her project of assimilation which so far has remained purely theoretical. As Camus acknowledges himself, merely addressing the question of famine is not itself enough if the underlying injustice of the system is not attended to.

"Crise en Algérie" concurrently articulates the author's call to redress the economic injustices prevalent in the system, and aims at uniting the two conflicting parties in Algeria. More importantly, it reflects the author's belief in integration as the only viable solution to the Algerian political problem. Indeed, assimilation at the time had become an "inaccessible reality." Ferhat Abbas, the leader of "Amis du Manifeste," sums up the assimilationist project at the time as "une réalité inaccessible et une machine dangereuse mise au service de la colonisation" (ibid., 955). Camus's political vision for Algeria, as I

have already argued, quite apart from overlooking the contradiction of
the politics proposed, constituted an anachronism even at the time
(1945). Camus's position in the 1950s—despite his anti-colonial
claims—appears as supportive of an orthodox colonialist position.
Both Sartre and Roy view such a position as reflecting the author's
political short-sightedness. Such myopia is, however, not entirely
without justifications. Underlying the author's discourse that puts
forward assimilation is the desire to reconcile the opposed parties and
to avoid at all costs, if possible, a violent clash. The subsequent war
would prove the futility of the attempt. Also, Camus's physical
absence from the Algerian scene (Camus had fully integrated—at least
physically—Parisian life in the 1950s), made him review the crisis of
the 1950s in the light of aspirations (assimilationist) prevalent in the
1940s. The unpleasant reality of the fifties was that the "Mediterranean"
"où l'Orient et l'Occident cohabitent" was already overwhelmed by the
"dialectics of exclusion," the logical consequence of colonial co-
habitation. As analyzed in previous chapters, in Camus's *La Maison
de la culture*, Algeria emerges as a pre-historic symbol of primitive
innocence, binding together a humanity in its original state of
innocence, of natural morality untouched by "adult civilizations." The
political crisis of the 1950s makes it clear however, that the
Mediterranean is not a melting pot of the races, but a conflictual spot
governed by at least two distinctive xenophobias. The marriage of the
"Same" and the "Other" sought by Camus passes quickly from one of
"convenances" ("ce n'est pas par l'Orient que l'Orient se sauvera
physiquement, mais par l'Occident, qui, lui-même, trouvera alors
nourriture dans la civilisation de l'Orient" [*Essais* 1965, 979]), to one
where "les deux populations algériennes se dress[ent] l'une contre
l'autre, dans une sorte de délire xénophobe et tent[ent] de se massacrer
mutuellement" (ibid., 981). "Les Muets" conveys what Haddour terms
the "closure of [Camus's] colonial discourse, [his] denunciation of his
former mytho-poetics" (1989, 201). It will be interesting to observe
how this text both articulates and resists Camus's confrontation with
decolonisation.

"Les Muets" narrates the revolt of a small factory's workers against
the growing force of industrialization. Here again, Algeria as a
landscape is the seat of economic distress displacing earlier idealism.
Yvars, the main character, articulates the contours of this new
landscape.

> [Il] avait perdu peu à peu l'habitude de ces journées violentes qui le
> rassasiaient. L'eau profonde et claire, le fort soleil, les filles, la vie
> du corps, il n'y avait d'autre bonheur dans son pays. Et ce bonheur

passait avec la jeunesse. [...] Il n'avait rien à faire qu'à attendre, doucement, sans trop savoir quoi. [...] Les matins [...] il n'aimait plus regarder la mer, toujours fidèle au rendez-vous. (1962, 1596)

[Little by little he had lost the habit of those violent days that used to satiate him. The deep, clear water, the hot sun, the girls, the physical life—there was no other form of happiness in this country. And that happiness disappeared with youth. {...} He had nothing to do but wait quietly, without quite knowing for what. {...} He didn't like to look at the sea. Though it was always there to greet him.] (1958, 64)

Within the conflictual violence of the period, Algeria loses her image of untouched youth, the idealism of *Jeunesse de la Méditerranée* with its cult of physical pleasure. In fact, both "Les Muets" and "L'Hôte" are devoid of the intense hedonist feelings of Meursault in *L'Etranger*, of the Cagayous of "L'Eté à Alger." They reflect rather the colonial conflicts and the existential future of the "pied-noir" community. The problems of death and age that confront Yvars take on at this moment a cosmic dimension, "souligne[ant] la solidarité des hommes, que tout ailleurs sépare, devant la mort" ("Notes et variantes" 1962, 2037). However, and more so, the conflicting feelings of the character towards life and death as he contemplates the other side of the Mediterranean, acquire a political signification, due to the insertion of the narrative within the concrete reality of industrial labor.

In his commentary on the text, Quilliot points to Camus's attempt at realism, which makes it hard to admit the text within the general framework of the collection. Camus, he writes, "entendait prouver, ou se prouver à lui-même, qu'il était capable de traiter du monde ouvrier, où avait baigné son enfance. Comme il me le disait un jour par boutade, j'ai voulu faire, moi aussi, du réalisme socialiste" ("Notes et variantes" 1962, 2036). However, Quilliot's conclusion that "Les Muets" is free from symbolic representations ("D'où, la facture réaliste de ce récit, quasiment libre de toute intention symbolique") (ibid.), is not entirely accurate. "Les Muets," although dramatizing the economic crisis of 1954, symbolically conveys a sense of shared brotherhood and communion. The narrative puts on stage a group of victims Yvars, the pied-noir, Esposito, the Spaniard and Saïd, the Arab. All three are helpless victims of the industrial machinery that reduces them to a state of destitution. Obviously the narrative, conflating "pied-noir" and "pieds-nus," silences the ideological conflict between colonized and colonizer, reconciling the hardship of Saïd the Arab who subsists on "figs" and that of Yvars the pied-noir who could only afford a cheese sandwich.

[Yvars] commençait de manger lorsque, non loin de lui, il aperçut Saïd, couché sur le dos dans un tas de copeaux, le regard perdu vers les verrières, bleuies par un ciel maintenant moins lumineux. Il lui demanda s'il avait déjà fini. Saïd dit qu'il avait mangé ses figues. Yvars s'arrêta de manger. Le malaise qui ne l'avait pas quitté depuis l'entrevue avec Lasalle disparaissait soudain pour laisser seulement place à une bonne chaleur. Il se leva en rompant son pain et dit, devant le refus de Saïd, que la semaine prochaine tout irait mieux. "Tu m'inviteras à ton tour," dit-il. Saïd sourit. Il mordait maintenant dans un morceau du sandwich d'Yvars. (1962, 1603)

[[Yvars] was beginning to eat when, not far from him, he noticed Saïd lying on his back in a pile of shavings, his eyes looking vaguely at the window made blue by a sky that had become less luminous. He asked him if he had already finished. Saïd said that he had eaten his figs. Yvars stopped eating. The uneasy feeling that hadn't left him since the interview with Lassalle suddenly disappeared to make room for a pleasant warmth. He broke his bread in two as he got up and, faced with Saïd's refusal, said that everything would be better next week. "Then it'll be your turn to treat," he said. Saïd smiled. Now he bit into the piece of Yvars's sandwich. (1958, 77)]

Yvars's symbolic gesture of breaking bread with Saïd is not without recalling Daru's gesture in "L'Hôte." In both narratives, the act posits fraternal ties, what Camus terms a freemasonry. The act recalls Camus's political activities in the late 1950s which were reduced to private interventions on behalf of individuals, mostly Moslem nationalists. "All the power of science today" he writes, "is aimed at strengthening the state. Not one scholar has thought of directing his research towards the defense of the individual. But that is where a freemasonry would have some meaning" (*Carnets II* 1964, 328). In "L'Hôte" human solidarity takes the form of an interracial brotherhood transcending political and racial barriers. "Les Muets" on the other hand, collapses economic barriers existing between colonized and colonizer. Yvars's assumption that "la semaine prochaine tout irait mieux" carries within it a certain utopianism in the face of the economic crisis of 1954, and silences as Haddour rightly puts it, "the ideological voice of the *va-nu-pieds* colonized" (1989, 202). Yvars's gesture towards his co-worker the Arab, reflects Camus's own moral scruples, his sentiment of "fraternal warmth" interpenetrate with colonial paternalism. Cryle, however, rejects an attribution of paternalism to Yvars's compassion for the Arab: "Il ne s'agit pas là de charité paternaliste mais de chaleur fraternelle [It is not a matter of parternalist charity but of brotherly warmth]" (1973, 107). The two sentiments, I believe, are not mutually exclusive.

Seen in the light of Dib's trilogy, the poverty of the Arab is directly linked with the colonial process. Famine and dispossession are factors that lend impulse to the Algerian war. "L'Hôte" rightly articulates the revolt of the vagrant Arabs as linked with the problem of famine, setting a context to interpret the political symbolism latent in the narrative of "Les Muets." Concurrently, however, "L'Hôte" de-emphasizes the importance of colonial famine in the revolt so as not to provide an alibi for decolonisation (Cryle 1973, 107). It can thus be said that both "L'Hôte" and "Les Muets" narrativise the political malaise of 1954; both texts also resist a total rendition ("condamnation totale? Non" [*La Peste* 1947, 18–19]). If "L'Hôte" correctly exposes economic destitution as the cause of uprising, it fails to present the economic crisis as mishaps of colonial rule. The 1954 Algerian revolution which forms the backdrop of "L'Hôte"[15] is exposed as a sequel of misery and famine, just as *Crise en Algérie* presented earlier an ossified view of the 1945 uprisings purported to arise from economic predicaments.

"L'Hôte" as a narrative is clearly caught in a dialectics of exposure and suppression. It must be said however, that "L'Hôte" expresses the problems of colonial Algeria with much more depth than *Misère de la Kabylie* (1939) and *Crise en Algérie* (1945). Both essays fall short of "a full investigation," and somehow both misrepresent the underlying impulse of the Algerian political uprisings. In presenting famine as the cause of the revolt in "L'Hôte," Camus only tells a partial story, failing yet again to delve into the deeper layer of structure of the nascent Algerian nationalism. The author evades political polemics in his failure to present the Arab's agitations as rebelliousness against French domination. This is not to imply that Camus was oblivious to the underlying cause of the uprising, but rather that he accords a peripheral recognition to the political dimension of the misery of the indigenes. This is again reflected in Daru's comments on the lot of the Arabs, and the French administration's efforts to provide for the needs of impoverished families hit by poor harvest.

> Il [Daru] avait [...] les sacs de blé qui encombraient la petite chambre et que l'administration lui laissait en réserve pour distribuer à ceux de ses élèves dont les familles avaient été victimes de la sécheresse. En réalité, le malheur les avait tous atteints puisque tous étaient pauvres. Chaque jour, Daru distribuait une ration aux petits. [...] Il fallait faire la soudure avec la prochaine récolte, voilà tout. Des navires de blé arrivaient maintenant de France, le plus dur était passé. Mais il serait difficile d'oublier cette misère, cette armée de

fantômes haillonneux errant dans le soleil, les plateaux calcinés
mois après mois, la terre recroquevillée peu à peu, littéralement
torréfiée, chaque pierre éclatant en poussière sous le pied. (1962,
1610)

[He [Daru] had {...} a room cluttered with bags of wheat that the
administration left as a stock to distribute to those of his pupils
whose families had suffered from the drought. Actually they had all
been victims because they were all poor. Every day Daru would
distribute a ration to the children. {...} It was just a matter of
carrying them over to the next harvest. Now shiploads of wheat
were arriving from France and the worst was over. But it would be
hard to forget that poverty, that army of ragged ghosts wandering in
the sunlight, the plateaus burned to a cinder month after month, the
earth shriveled up little by little, literally scorched, every stone
bursting into dust under one's foot. (1958, 87–88)]

Daru's "le plus dur était passé [the worst was over]," echoes Yvars's
optimistic rejoinder to Saïd that "tout irait mieux [la semaine
prochaine]" (1962, 1603). Yvars's gesture of sharing his lunch with his
Arab co-worker replicates symbolically France's help to her colony in
forms of "ravitaillement" for the famished Arabs. Both Daru and Yvars
overlook the deeper structure of the system, a myopia not far removed
from that exhibited by Camus who clings to his belief of justice and
reparation (in the form of charity) for the indigenous population: "Des
centaines de bateaux de céréales . . . c'est ce que nous demandons
immédiatement. . . ." (1965, 949), "Des navires de blé arrivaient
maintenant de France, le plus dur était passé" (1962, 1610). The
continued economic dependency advocated here implies an imperialist
conformism, a continued Western hegemony in Algeria, uncovering
thus, the inherent contradiction in Camus's position which calls for an
end to colonialism, while supporting implicitly a continuance of
France's imperialism.

The Renegade and the "Language of Hatred"

The narrative of the renegade recalls that of *La Chute*. The excessive
verbosity of both narratives weaves "a devious rhetorical web in which
[the protagonists] attempt to enmesh [the] reader" (Ellison 1990, 183).
An added element in "Le Rénégat" is its "meandering confusion." The
rhetoric of *démesure*, in its excess and "anti-Cartesian context"(ibid.)
totally subverts Camus's notion of enlightened (or "solar") thought
associated with the Mediterrenean, "la pensée de midi." For the "solar

narrative" that Camus appropriates here is not only anti-logical, but it also presents a profoundly destructive resonance. The monological narrative evolving on two simultaneous temporal levels ressembles that of "La Femme adultère." It advances both on the level of the protagonist's present life in the desert and on that of his past life, his youth to the present. An enthusiastic Catholic, the protagonist sets off across the Sahara to convert the pagan inhabitants of Taghâza, thus fulfilling the overriding ambition of his youth: "aller aux sauvages et leur dire: 'Voici mon Seigneur, regardez-le, il ne frappe jamais, ni ne tue, il commande d'une voix douce, il tend l'autre joue, c'est le plus grand des seigneurs, choisissez-le. . . .'" (1962, 1578). One explicit underlying drive is also that of mastery and domination. Concurrent with the desire to convert is also that of total power. "Je subjuguerais ces sauvages, comme un soleil puissant. Puissant, oui, c'était le mot que sans cesse, je roulais sur ma langue, je rêvais du pouvoir absolu, celui qui fait mettre genoux à terre, qui force l'adversaire à capituler" (ibid., 1579). He is, however, unable to penetrate the cultural and linguistic space of these pagans and succumbs ultimately to the religion of the barbarous; it is he who bows his knees in adoration of his new masters who, to obtain total subservience from their new convert, cut out his tongue, a gesture which symbolically destroys "the word" of the Gospel. The brutality of the act, as Ellison correctly underlines, appears "to be a literalization of the renegade's own dreams of total domination, an ironical turnabout whereby one form of absolutism is simply replaced by another" (ibid.). The forced con-version of Camus's protagonist comes about with a progressive loss of clarity. His new religion is presented as one of confusion and fanaticism involving a systematic destruction of logical distinctions.

In a reversal of roles, the Fetish he earlier sought to eradicate is promoted to a position of absolute power.

> Salut, il [le fétiche] était le maître, le seul seigneur, dont l'attribut indiscutable était la méchanceté, il n'y a pas de maîtres bons. [...] je m'abandonnai à lui et approuvai son ordre malfaisant, j'adorai en lui le principe méchant du monde. [...] Je reniai la longue histoire qu'on m'avait enseignée. On m'avait trompé, seul le règne de la méchanceté était sans fissures. (1962, 1587)

> [Hail! he [the Ferish] was the master, the only Lord, whose indisputable attribute was malice, there are no good masters. {...} I surrendered to him and approved his maleficent order, I adored in him the evil principle of the world. {...} I repudiated the long history that had been taught me. I had been misled, solely the reign of malice was devoid of defects. (1958, 53–54)]

It can be inferred that the story of the renegade articulates the two sides of what Camus refers to as "modern nihilism," namely mastery and servitude. One distinctive feature of such a nihilism is the tendency to succumb to absolutes, to totalities that negate all shades and nuances. Camus's protagonist ultimately comes to the realization that Evil by dint of consistency is preferable to all other forms of absolutism that he had adhered to (i.e., his former Catholic faith). "Sans fissures," it pushes itself to its logical conclusion, which is absolute evil. "Seul le mal peut aller jusqu'à ses limites et régner absolument, c'est lui qu'il faut servir pour installer son royaume visible. . . ." (1962, 1588). As Ellison asserts again, one can read in this disjointed tale, the author's indictment of totalitarian solutions that expel compromises necessary to the democratic process, that erect the absolutes of ideology above the constitutive limitations of the human condition (1990, 187). The tale of the renegade's mad descent from one form of absolutism into another conveys the author's cautionary rejoinder. The protagonist's mind, capable of apprehending life only in absolute terms, is a fertile ground for the evils of political totalitarianism. The tale is, to borrow Ellison's words, a disconcerting "elaboration of absolutism and nihilism carried to their limits in a monomaniacal imaginative frenzy" (ibid., 190).

It has also been suggested that the underlying confusion of the renegade echoes the political confusion of the 1950s (Haddour 1990, 216), a confusion that informs the various essays of Camus's grouped under *Actuelles III*. An underlying thrust of these essays, is the author's own recognition of bankruptcy of the French colonial mission in Algeria, "[cette] politique de démission" (*Actuelles III* 1960, 976–7). The apt subtitle given to the story, "Un esprit confus," articulates not only the political confusion engendered by colonial politics, but also the attendant violence. The missionary (le rénégat) goes to the savages with the purpose of civilizing and subjugating them. His failure and subsequent conversion to the "faith" of the people he sought to transform, is an ironical rendition of the bankrupt project which generated the 1950s violence, in the midst of which Camus opted for neutrality: "ne plus participer aux incessantes polémiques qui n'ont eu d'autre effet que de durcir en Algérie les intransigeances aux prises et de diviser un peu plus une France déjà empoisonnée par les haines et les sectes" (ibid., 891–2). In a fictional mode, however, Camus projects onto the setting of "Le Rénégat" the language of hatred that dominates the political arena both in Algeria and metropolitan France. The renegade's bleak desert heralds a message of political despair. In the dialectics of Same and the Other, political violence and fanaticism translate into a drive for absolute domination illustrated by the two extreme positions upheld successively by the renegade. If indeed the *denouement* (ending) of the story hints at the failure of the colonial mission to conquer the Other, it also suggests the imposition of the Other as absolute power. The inevitable confrontation and violence are put forward in the critical account of the original text of "L'Hôte": "sur cette terre implacable, les hommes, les races, les religions s'affrontaient sans se mêler, sans pouvoir reconnaître de règle commune ou saluer le même dieu" ("Notes et variantes" 1962, 2044). Ultimately, it seems, the question of "l'envers et l'endroit (wrong and right)" becomes irrelevant since both can present the face of destructive totalitarianism. "S'ils ont tort ou raison, ce n'est pas la question. Pour discuter un jour, il faut ne pas être égorgé aujourd'hui" (ibid., 2041).

"Le Rénégat" as an allegory of the colonial experience, symbolizes the violence and "political fanaticism" that permeate both Algerian nationalism and right-wing politics. Camus's presentation of the colonial malaise in religious terms (Haddour 1989, 217) is interesting in terms of its political symbolism. The denouement of the tale narrativises the failure of the colonial mission to conquer the Other. Such a failure is translated mostly through a physical malaise on the part of Camus's characters. The missionary's confrontation with the impenetrable desert is felt on a very physical level by both Janine ("La Femme adultère") and Daru ("L'Hôte"). One source of Janine's discomfort, one remembers, is the hostile natural environment. The desert, contrary to her romantic dreams, turned out be all stone and dust. "Elle voyait à présent que le désert n'était pas cela, mais seulement la pierre, la pierre partout, dans le ciel où régnait encore, crissante et froide, la seule poussière de pierre, comme sur le sol où poussaient seulement, entre les pierres, des graminées sèches" (1560). In contrast to Janine's physical distress, the Arabs seem in total harmony with the arid desert, even indifferent to the jostle of the unpleasant bus ride. "[Les] Arabes . . . faisaient mine de dormir, enfouis dans leurs burnous . . . Ils semblaient au large, malgré leurs amples vêtements, sur les banquettes où son mari et elle tenaient à peine" (1962, 1558–59). So also, Daru's rapport with the desertic landscape sheds light on the ambiguity of the title of the tale (Tarrow 1985, 178–9). Indeed the word "l'hôte" meaning "guest" also, could very well apply to the school teacher. As other pieds-noirs of the same generation, Daru was born and raised on Algerian soil. "[Il] était né sur cette terre recroquevillée . . ., littéralement torréfiée, chaque pierre éclatant en poussière sous le pied. Partout ailleurs, il se sentait exilé" (1962, 1611). The narrative emphasizes Daru's love of his natural environment despite its harshness. Rather transparent here, and structuring the narrative, is a contrast between exile (*l'exil*) and kingdom (*le royaume*). Daru's kingdom is threatened not solely by the irruption of colonial politics as earlier specified, but also by the destructive potential of the natural landscape. The harmony which he believes exists between himself and the Algerian landscape turns out to be mere illusion (Tarrow 1985, 179). For instance, his initial exaltation at the appearance of the sun turns into discomfort as it quickly dries up the melting snow and transforms the hilly landscape into a rocky and harsh land. "Le soleil était maintenant assez haut dans le ciel et commençait de lui dévorer le front. . . Quand il parvint à la petite colline, il ruisselait de sueur. Il . . . s'arrêta essoufflé . . . Sur la plaine, à l'est, une bueur de chaleur montait déjà" (1962, 1621). The physical attack of the mineral element on Camus's protagonist is a presage to the threat of the rebels he finds scribbled on the blackboard later on. Obviously, the Algerian sun, mostly a source of physical pleasure to the Mediterranean, is presented here as deadly. One recalls that a similar presentation is accorded the solar element in *L'Etranger*. Meursault at one crucial moment, registers an acute discomfort in the torrential heat on the beach, and this, in direct contrast to the flute playing Arabs who seem perfectly absorbed into their natural surroundings. Meursault, Roland Barthes observes, "est un homme charnellement soumis au soleil . . . Il faut entendre cette soumission dans un sens un peu sacral . . . Le soleil est ici expérience si profonde du corps, qu'il en devient destin; il fait l'histoire, et dispose dans la durée indifférente de Meursault, certains moments générateurs d'actes." The sun as vital element, is, during the three strategic moments of Meursault's life (i.e., the mother's burial, the killing of the Arab, his own trial) viewed by the protagonist in entirely negative terms. "Le soleil débordant qui faisait tressaillir le paysage le rendait inhumain et déprimant." Naturally, the same inhuman sun beats down on the Arabs without however producing in them the same sense of "physical disarray, of jangling nerves and assaulted senses" (Tarrow 1985, 180). In fact the latter experience none of the inhumanness. "Couchés dans leurs bleus de chauffe graisseux ils avaient l'air tout à fait calmes et presque contents" (1962, 1163). The juxtaposition of discomfort and contentedness foreshadows similar polar oppositions in *L'Exil et le royaume*. The various characters' permeability to their surroundings is undermined by a certain fixity. The natural elements as sources of joy, carry within both a "kingdom" and an "exile." Their confrontation with the landscape is as threads interwoven into a rope, and stretched to a breaking point. The resulting tension between beauty and exile is, Camus asserts, "faithful to the human condition" (*Retour à Tipasa* 1962, 870).

On a different level, we may say that the representation of these various characters as misfits in an alien landscape stands in contradiction to Camus's political inclusionary vision. The author's intellectual and cultural interests as stated, favored an Algeria in which the two communities of French and Arabs could live together in harmony. As we have already ascertained, his opposition to Algerian independence is, however, not entirely objective, clouded as it is by the fear of expulsion for his people—the million or so French Algerians. Yet his fictional European characters appear as "uncomfortable strangers in a country they regard as theirs" (Tarrow 1985, 181). "L'Hôte" for instance, presents Daru's position as precarious. Despite the "warm human bond" that ties him to the Arabs, despite his love for the land, Daru is an unwelcome guest threatened by both the harshness of the barren plateau and by the irruption into his life, of colonial politics. "Dans ce vaste pays qu'il avait tant aimé, il était seul" (1962, 1621).

The desert, with which Daru feels such an affinity—despite its cruelty ("le pays était ainsi, cruel à vivre")—is a colonial space. Though Daru attempts to keep it untrammeled by politics, politics explode in the "sheltered" life of his plateau, permeate the dramatic monologue of "le renégat" and pollute the romantic idyll of "La Femme adultère." The violence articulated by these various narratives is concomitant with the intrusion of the Other into the colonial text. Such a presentation registers Camus's confrontation with a historical scene.

It is rather interesting that Camus uses specifically the desert as a setting for these tales. In colonial rhetorics, the desert symbolizes an empty space for occupation. Emptied of every "alien" presence, the desert offered itself for a systematic exploitation, a colonial space in which the Other "assumed the fixed status of an object frozen once and for all in time by the gaze of Western percipients (Saïd, "Orientalism reconsidered" 1985, 16). The Other as a "frozen object" becomes an "adjunct feature of the colonial wilderness;" in other words, he is never an involved subject, "an interlocutor in the colonial discourse but a silent Other" (ibid., 17). Thus, the desert as a metaphor does not only point to a concrete referent (the Sahara) but "also constitutes a discourse within which the Other assumes a residual status" (Haddour 1989, 219). Camus's earlier univocal narratives of *L'Etranger* and *La Peste,* for instance, articulate the relegation of the Other outside history, culture and civilization. *La Peste* more explicitly replicates the desertification of the colonial space, the absence of the Other, while *L'Etranger* presents the Other as an extension of the colonial landscape, which is clearly "assimilated into the dominant culture." The entry of the Other into the narratives of *L'Exil et le royaume*, reflects historical moments, an "alien" presence in the arena of history and politics, which disrupts the "empty tableau where the Other figured as a phantasmagorical appearance" (ibid.). Both the characters of Daru and the renegade are significant in their roles as school teacher and missionary, two components of the French civilizing mission. In this desert which they sought to conquer, they face the adversities of decolonisation.

The "voyeuristic" narrative of *L'Etranger*, as stated, embodies a colonial vision which fossilizes and suppresses the Other. However, the irruption of violence tangential to the process of decolonisation—articulated in *L'Exil et le Royaume*—fragments such a vision, and deconstructs the "Cagayous" harmonious images which Camus discovered in his literary settings. As Lekehal notes, the disintegration of these settings "porte témoignage de l'état d'esprit de la dernière génération d'artistes français nés en Algérie."[16] The various fictional characters of Janine, the renegade, and Daru carry with them a certain nostalgic vision of colonial harmonies. Invariably they all sustain a colonial dream of empty and peaceful deserts. Such a perspective collapses, however, in these narratives which reconstruct a space haunted by Arab nomads, free and miserable lords "d'un étrange royaume," and fetish-worshippers—generators of violence. This dialectics of violence, as analyzed, stems from the machinery of decolonisation already in place. The political tension of the 1950s necessitated a movement away from romanticism and poetics to the language of violence in *L'Exil et le Royaume*. The narrativisation deconstructs Camus's earlier monological vision of Algeria outside history and politics, as it registers the author's own descent into colonial politics.

Notes

1. I adopt here Ellen Kennedy's translation. *Albert Camus, Lyrical and Critical Essays*, edited and with notes by Philip Thody, translated by Ellen Conroy Kennedy (New York: Alfred A. Knopf, 1968), 165.

2. All references to L'Exil et le Royaume are from *Théâtre, Récits, Nouvelles*, edited with Introduction and Notes by Roger Quilliot (Paris: Gallimard, 1962).

3. Rosemarie Jones, "Camus and the Aphorism: L'Exil et le Royaume," *The Modern Language Review* 72.2 (April 1983): 306.

4. Alba Amoia, "Albert Camus's Exile and the Kingdom," *Dalhousie French Studies* 19 (1990): 43.

5. *Albert Camus, Exile and the Kingdom*, trans. Justin O'Brien (New York: Alfred A Knopf, 1958), 33. Unless indicated otherwise, all translations of L'Exil et le Royaume are taken from this edition.

6. Ellison remarks on the rejuvenating effect of the visit on Camus: "it appears that [the] short visit to his native land constituted a welcome if momentary relief from the frustrations of the Parisian limelight. He came back to France convinced that the source of his literary creativity still lay in the sun, the sea, and the ancient stones of Algeria" *Understanding Camus* (n.p.: University of South Carolina Press, 1990), 168.

7. Cf "Jonah," King James Version (n.p.: Oxford University Press, 1967) 941-3.

8. Jean Onimus, "Camus, the 'Adulterous Woman,' and the Starry Sky," *Essays on Camus's Exile and the Kingdom*, edited by Judith D. Suther. *Romance Monographs, Inc.* No. 41 (1980): 107.

9. Jules Roy, *La Guerre d'Algérie* (Paris: Julliard, 1960), 227–8.

10. Jules Roy, *Étranger à mes frères* (Paris: Stock, 1982), 127.

11. The original manuscript of "L'Hôte" articulates more clearly the violence and racial antagonism that permeate the eastern desert:
"Sur cette terre implacable, les hommes, les races, les religions s'affrontent sans se mêler jamais, sans pouvoir reconnaître de règle commune ou saluer le même dieu. Seul le plus fort imposait ici ses lois et y pliait tous les autres hommes. Lui, Daru, faisait partie des plus forts et cependant il reconnaissait en regardant cette terre couverte maintenant de pierre et de neige la faiblesse fondamentale qui l'empêchait d'exercer cette force. Il ne reconnaissait pas non plus les lois de sa propre tribu et ne voulait saluer que la loi ou le Dieu qui serait celui de tous, et ne le connaissant pas, il voulait seulement attendre que ce désert une voix s'élève, une rosée (comment?) du matin. Peut-être le silence seul lui répondait, peut-être mourait-il dans ce désert toujours (?) mais il ne voulait plus dire non, ni juger, ni détruire, ni humilier personne ou lui-même. Et c'est pourquoi il maudissait ces hommes qui lui envoyaient ce criminel et celui-ci aussi dont le crime le dégoûtait. Mais à ce moment il revit l'expression de peur et de violence qu'avait eue l'Arabe" ("L'Hôte, " "Notes et variantes," 2042).
That the violence depicted in the earlier draft was toned down suggests that the narrative of "L'Hôte" is "self conscious of its political setting." Commenting on the changes in the manuscript, Quilliot states:" La tournure prise par les évènements [en Algérie] a ... modifié le détail de son propos. La misère et ses effets sont moins brutalement soulignés dans l'édition définitive. . . . Sans doute ne voulait-il rien dire qui pût être utilisé par l'un ou par l'autre des camps en présence" ("Présentation," "Notes et variantes," 2039).

12. The original version of "L'Hôte" makes more explicit the Arabs' attack as targeting the school, the very seat of the values of the French civilizing mission. "Tu a livré mon frère, Ton école brûlera, et toi avec." "Notes et variantes," 2042.

13. Peter Cryle, *Bilan critique: L'Exil et le Royaume d'Albert Camus* (Paris: Lettres Modernes Minard, 1973), 135.

14. François Quilici, "Le 8 mai 1945: élément pour une analyse des positions de Camus face au nationalisme algérien," ed. *Camus et la Politique* (Paris: Harmattan, 1985), 160.

15. Roger Quilliot in his "presentation" of "L'Hôte" points to the author's increasing anxiety with the political scene in his homeland, a preoccupation which may have informed the short story, in fact motivated the story: "Dès cette époque [1952], l'évolution politique de l'Algérie préoccupait assez Camus pour que son projet de nouvelle porte la marque de ses inquiétudes. Il n'ignorait rien de la révolte qui couvait. Avant même qu'il eût rédigé "L'Hôte," en Juillet 1954, il avait écrit dans le numéro I de Libérons les condamnés d'Outre-Mer un article intitulé "Terrorisme et amnistie" qui traduit son angoisse. C'était quelques mois avant que la guerre ne devienne ouverte. Aussi peut-on supposer qu'il a tenu à définir ici, concrètement et symboliquement à la fois, son attitude dans le conflit naissant." "Notes et variantes" (*Essais*, 2039).

16. A. Lekehal, "Aspects du paysage algérien. Étude du fantastique dans le Rénégat ou un esprit confus," *Cahiers Algériens de Littérature Comparative* 3 (1968): 16.

Index

Amash 84–85, 118
Amrouche 34–35, 38–39, 65,
   67, 109, 112
Artaud 122, 155
Ashcroft xxxiii, 39
Audisio xxii, 32, 34, 36–38,
   40–41, 43, 49, 51, 65, 67
Barrière 5, 25
Barthes xvi, 116, 122,
   136–37
Bertrand xiv, xxi, xxxv,
   xxxvii, 1, 14, 16–19, 22,
   27, 36–38, 40–42, 49, 56,
   90, 103–4, 173
Bonn 113
Braun 44, 58, 61–63, 66–67,
   69, 76, 94, 121, 125
Brée xxvi, 38, 158
Byrd 124, 158
Camus xiii, xvi–xxvi,
   xxviii–xxxii, xxxiv–xxxix,
   1, 9, 23, 27, 29–32, 34–36,
   41–69, 71–72, 74–77,
   80–81, 83–84, 86–90,
   92–99, 102–3, 105–6, 108,
   110–11, 114–15, 117–40,
   142–43, 145, 147, 149–52,
   155–59, 161–64, 166–67,
   170–74, 176–81, 183–85

Carrol 38
Chute, La 131, 139, 170, 186
Cruickshank 128
Cryle 178–79, 184–85
De Man 39
Dejeux xxiv, xxxvi, xxxviii,
   16, 18, 27
Dib xxiv–xxv, xxxii, xxxiv,
   8, 20, 26, 123, 126,
   140–45, 147–53, 155–59,
   184
Doubrovsky 127, 158
Durand 44–45, 66, 68
During xix, 25, 89, 100, 129
Ellison 85, 121, 161, 165,
   171
Erickson xxxi, xxxv, xxxix,
   30, 89, 126, 137–38, 163,
   173
Fanon xxvi–xxvii, 7, 65,
   106–7
Fayad 88–89, 122
Feraoun xxiii–xxv, xxxii,
   xxxiv, 35, 71, 74, 98, 101,
   108, 110–12, 114–16,
   118–19, 122
Gallup 16, 18, 24–25, 27
Gillespie 26
Girard 84, 87, 121

Gordon 25, 65, 67
Gourdon xxxvii, 34, 92, 102
Grenier 32, 45, 50–55, 67–68
Haddour xx, xxii–xxiii,
    xxxvii, 1, 13–14, 20, 23,
    27, 40, 42, 52, 65, 67–68,
    72, 80, 86, 88, 98, 106,
    110, 113–14, 117, 126,
    130, 132, 134–36, 142,
    145, 155, 163, 172, 178,
    182, 184
Hargreaves xx, 2, 8–9, 11,
    25–26, 30–31, 48
Ibrahim 87, 93, 122
Irele xxxii, xxxiv–xxxv,
    xxxix
Isaac xvi, xix, 37, 63
JanMohamed xxv,
    xxvii–xxviii, xxxiii,
    xxxvii–xxxviii, 2, 7, 47
Joyaux 19, 27, 98
Kateb 149, 159
Kellman xvii, xxv, xxxvii
Kessous 133
Kirsch xiv, xxxvi, 113
Kréa 91
Kritzman 38
Lecoq 14, 27
Lekehal 192, 194
Lottman xvi, 44, 179
Mammeri xxii–xxiv, xxxi,
    xxxiii, 69, 72, 95, 99,
    100–103, 105, 107,
    116–17, 119

Maquet 77–78, 165–67
Masters 80
McCarthy 37–38, 45–46, 68,
    163, 173
Memmi xiii–xv, xxv,
    xxviii–xxix, xxxiii, xxxvi,
    xxxviii, 6, 12, 26, 103, 105
Merad 2, 105
Monego xiv, xxxvi
Nora 32, 49, 83, 90, 92, 122
O'Brien xvii, xx, xxiii, xxvi,
    xxviii–xxx, 47, 87, 94,
    110, 137, 140, 162
Pommier xxxvii, 21, 27
Quillot 45, 59
Quinn 91
Roy 66–67, 174–77, 181
Saïd xvi, xx, xxv, xxx, xxxi,
    37, 39, 89, 94, 183–84,
    186
Sartre xvi, xix, xxviii, xxxiii,
    xxxviii, 7, 26, 31, 61, 66,
    72, 76, 78–79, 81, 117,
    170, 172, 181
Scott 68
Sontag 123, 158
Sprintzen 75, 121
Stephanson 124, 130, 158
Tarrow xx, xxx, 39, 45–47,
    66, 68, 73, 81, 87, 120,
    127–28, 156, 158, 162,
    168, 172, 179
Thody 66–67, 72, 129, 173
Tillion xxxvii, 139–42, 156

Selected Bibliography

Primary Sources

Camus, Albert. *L'Etranger*. Paris: Gallimard, 1942.
_____. *La Peste*. Paris: Gallimard, 1947.
_____. *L'Exil et le Royaume*. Paris: Gallimard, 1957.
_____. *Théâtre, Récits, Nouvelles*, edited with Introduction and Notes by Roger Quilliot. Paris: Gallimard, 1962.
_____. *Essais*, edited with Introduction and Notes by Roger Quilliot. Paris: Gallimard, 1965.
Dib, Mohammed. *La Grande Maison*. Paris: Seuil, 1952.
_____. *L'Incendie*. Paris: Seuil, 1954.
_____. *Le Métier à tisser*. Paris: Seuil, 1957.
Feraoun, Mouloud. *La Terre et le Sang*, Paris: Seuil, 1953.
_____. *Le Fils du Pauvre*. Paris: Seuil, 1954.
_____. *Les Chemins qui montent*. Paris: Seuil, 1957.
Mammeri, Mouloud *La Colline oubliée*. Paris: Librairie Plon, 1952.
_____. *Le Sommeil du Juste*. Paris: Librairie Plon, 1956.

Secondary Sources

Abun-Nasr, Jamil. *History of the Maghrib*. Cambridge: n.p., 1971.
Achour, Christiane. *Mouloud Feraoun, une voix en contrepoint*. Paris: Silex, 1986
Amrouche, Jean. *L'Eternel Jugurtha, 1906-1962*. Marseille: Archives, 1985.
Arnaud, Jacqueline. *Hommage à Mohammed Dib*. Alger: Office des publications universitaires, 1985.

Ashcroft, Bill, Gareth Griffiths, and Helen Tiffin.*The Empire Writes Back.Theory and Practice in Post-Colonial Literatures*. London: Routledge, 1989.

Audisio, Gabriel. *Jeunesse de la Méditerranée*. Paris: Gallimard, 1935.

_____. *Sel de la mer*. Paris: Gallimard, 1936.

Belhadj-Kacem, Nourredine. *Le thème de la dépossession dans la "trilogie" de Mohammed Dib*. Alger: Entreprise nationale du livre, 1983.

Bertrand, Louis. *Le Mirage Oriental*. Paris: Perrin, 1910.

_____. *Les Villes d'or*. Paris: Fayard, 1921.

Bonn, Charles. *La Littérature Algérienne de langue Française et ses lectures*. Ottawa: Naaman, 1974.

Bouguerra, Tayeb. *Le dit et le non-dit: a propos de l'Algérie et de l'Algérien chez Albert Camus*. Alger: office des publications universitaires, 1989.

Braun, Lev. *Witness of Decline, Albert Camus: Moralist of the Absurd*. Associated University Presses, Inc., 1974.

Brée, Germaine ed. *Camus: A Collection of Critical Essays*. Englewood Cliffs, N.J.: Prentice-Hall, 1962.

_____. *Camus and Sartre. Crisis and commitment*. New York: Dell Publishing Company, Delta series, 1972.

Brunschwig, Henri. *Mythes et Réalités de l'Impérialisme Colonial Français, 1871–1914*. Paris: n.p., 1960.

Camus, Albert.*Le Mythe de Sisyphe*. Paris: Gallimard, 1943.

_____. *Lettres à un ami allemand*. Paris: Gallimard, 1948.

_____. *L'Homme Révolté*. Paris: Gallimard, 1951.

_____. *La Chute*. Paris: Gallimard, 1956.

_____. *Actuelles III, Chroniques algériennes 1939-1958*. Paris: Gallimard, 1958.

_____. *Resistance, Rebellion and Death*. Translated by Justin O'Brien. New York: Alfred A. Knopf. Inc.,

_____. *Carnets Janvier 1942-mars 1951*. Paris: Gallimard, 1964.

Césaire, Aimé. *Discourse on Colonialism*. Trans. by Joan Pinkham. New York: Monthly Review Press, 1972.

Charles-André, Julien. *History of North Africa*. Trans. John Petrie. New York: n.p., 1960.

Cheze, Marie Helene. *Mouloud Feraoun*. Paris: Seuil, 1982.

Chikhi, Beida. *Problématique de l'écriture dans l'oeuvre romanesque de Mohammed Dib*. Alger: Office des publications universitaires, 1989.

Conrad, Joseph. *Heart of Darkness* with *the Congo Diary*, edited with an Introduction and Notes by Robert Hampson. London: Penguin Books, 1995.

Cruickshank, John. *Albert Camus and the Literature of Revolt*. Oxford University Press, 1959.

Cryle, Peter. *Bilan critique: L'Exil et le Royaume d'Albert Camus*. Paris: Lettres Modernes Minard, 1973.

Dejeux, Jean. *La Littérature Algérienne Contemporaine*. Paris: Presses Universitaires de France, 1975.

_____. *Bibliographie de la littérature "algérienne" des Français*. Paris: Éditions du Centre national de la recherche scientifique, 1978.

Derrida, Jacques. *Monolingualism of the Other*. Trans. Patrick Mensah. Stanford, California: Stanford University Press, 1998.

Dib, Mohammed. *Au Café*. Paris: Sindbad, 1984.

Dupuy, Aimé. *L'Algérie dans les Lettres d'expression Française*. Paris: Editions Universitaires, 1957.

Durand, Anne. *Le Cas Albert Camus*. Paris: n.p., 1961.

El Houssi, Majid. *Albert Camus: un effet spatial algérien*. Rome: Bulzoni editore, 1992.

Ellison, David. *Understanding Camus*. University of South Carolina Press, 1990.

Fanon, Frantz. *The Wretched of the Earth*. Trans. Constance Farrington. New York: Grove Press, Inc., 1963.

_____. *A dying colonialism*. Trans. Haakon Chevalier. New York: Grove Press, Inc., 1965.

Feraoun, Mouloud. *L'Anniversaire*. Paris: Seuil, 1972.

Fitch, B. T. *Narrateur et narration dans L'Étranger d'Albert Camus*. Paris: Minard, 1968.

Gadourek, K. *Les innocents et les coupables*. The Netherlands: Mouton, 1963.

Gaillard, Pol. *La Peste. Analyse critique*. Paris: Hatier, 1972.

Gallup, Dorothea M. "The French Image of Algeria: its origin, its place in Colonial Ideology. Its effect on Algerian Acculturation." Ph.D. diss., Los Angeles: University of California, 1973.

Gillespie, Joan. *Algeria: Rebellion and Revolution*. New York: n.p., 1960.

Gleyze, Jack. *Mouloud Feraoun*. Paris: L'Harmattan, 1990.

Gordon, David C. *The passing of French Algeria*. London: Oxford University Press, 1968.

Grenier, Jean. *Inspirations Méditerranéennes*. Paris: Gallimard, 1961.

_____. *Albert Camus*. Paris: Gallimard, 1968.

Guérin, Jeanyves, ed. *Camus et la Politique Actes du colloque de Nanterre 5–7 juin 1985. Nanterre*. Paris: L'Harmatan, 1986.

Haddour, Azzedine. "Camus: The Other as an Outsider in a Univocal Discourse." Ph.D. diss., The University of Sussex, 1989.

Hargreaves, Alec G. *The Colonial Experience in French Fiction*. New York: The Macmillan Press Ltd., 1981.

Irele, Abiola. *The African Experience in Literature and Ideology*. London: Heinemann, 1981.

JanMohamed, Abdul R. *Manichean Aesthetics*. Amherst: University of Massachusetts Press, 1983.

Kellman, Steven G. *The Plague: Fiction and Resistance*. New York: Twayne Publishers, 1993.

Khadda, Naget. *Mohammed Dib romancier: esquisse d'un itinéraire*. Alger: Office des publications universitaires, 1986.

Khatibi, Abdelkébir. *Roman Maghrébin*. Paris: n.p., 1968.

King, Adele.*Camus*. New York: Capricorn Books., n.d.

King, Jonathan H. *Albert Camus. Selected Political Writings*. London: Methuen & Co., 1981.

Knapp, Bettina L., ed. *Critical Essays on Albert Camus*. Boston: G. K. & Co. Boston, 1988.

Lacheraf, Mostefa. *Littératures de combat: essais d'introduction, étude et préfaces*. Alger: Éditions Bouchene, 1991.

Laroui, Abdallah. *The History of the Maghrib: An Interpretative Essay*. Translated by Ralph Manheim, Princeton: n.p., 1977.

Lebel, R. *Histoire de la littérature coloniale en France*. Paris: Larose, 1931.

Leconte, Daniel. *Les Pieds-noirs*. Paris: Seuil, 1980.

Lecoq, Louis. *Anthologie des écrivains maghrébins d'expression française*. Paris: Présence Africaine, 1965.

_____. *Anthologie des Ecrivains Français du Maghreb*. Paris: Présence Africaine, 1969.

Lenzini, José. *L'Algérie de Camus*. La Calade, Aix-en-Provence: Edisud, 1988.

Lewis, A. W. *Philosophy and the Modern World*. Bloomington: n.p., 1959.

Lottman, Herbert. *Albert Camus*. Translated by Marianne Véron. Paris: Editions du Seuil, 1978.

McCarthy, Patrick. *Camus, A Critical Study of his Life and Work*. London: Hamish Hamilton, 1982.

_____. *Camus: "The Stranger"*. Oxford: Cambridge University Press, 1988.

Mahood, M. M. (Molly Maureen). *The Colonial Encounter. A reading of six novels*. New Jersey: Rowman and Littlefield, 1977.

Maquet, Albert. *Albert Camus ou l'invincible été*. Paris: Editions Debresse, 1955.

Masters, Brian. *Camus: A Study*. n.p.: Heinemann, 1974.

Memmi, Albert. *Portrait of the Colonizer.* n.p.: The Orion Press, Inc., 1965.

Merad, Ghani. *La Littérature Algérienne d'expression Française.* Paris: Pierre Jean Oswald, 1976.

Monego, Joan P. *Maghrebian Literature in French..* Boston: Twayne Publishers, 1984.

Nora, Pierre. *Les Français d'Algérie.* Paris: Réné Julliard, 1961.

Nouschi, A. *Le Nationalisme algérien.* Paris: Minuit, 1962.

O'Brien, Conor Cruise. *Albert Camus of Europe and Africa.* New York: The Viking Press, 1970.

Oxenhandler, Neil. *Looking for heroes in postwar France.* Hanover, Dartmouth College: University Press of New England, 1996.

Pierce, Roy. *Contemporary French Political Thought..* London and New York: Oxford University Press, 1966.

Quillot, Roger. *La Mer et les prisons: Essai sur Albert Camus.* Paris: Gallimard, 1956.

_____. *Théâtre, Récits, Nouvelles.* Paris: Gallimard, 1957.

Roblès, Emmanuel. *Les Hauteurs de la ville.* Paris: Seuil, 1960.

Ross, Stephen D. *Literature and Philosophy. An Analysis of the Philosophical Novel.* New York: Appleton-Century Crofts, 1969.

Roy, Jules. *La Guerre d'Algérie.* Paris: Julliard, 1960.

_____. *Étranger à mes frères.* Paris: Stock, 1982.

Saïd, Edward W. *Orientalism.* n.p.: Vintage Books Edition, 1979.

_____. *Culture and Imperialism.* New York: Alfred A. Knopf, 1993.

Scott, Nathan A. *Albert Camus.* New York: Hilary House Publishers, 1969.

Showalter, English Jr. *Exiles and Strangers.* Columbus: Ohio State University Press, 1984.

Sprintzen, David. *Camus: a Critical Examination.* n.p.: Temple University Press, 1988.

Tarrow, Susan. *Exile from the Kingdom: A Political Rereading of Albert Camus.* The University of Alabama Press, 1985.

Thody, Philip. *Albert Camus, 1913–60.* London: Hamish Hamilton, 1961.

Tillion, Germaine. *France and Algeria: Complementary Enemies.* New York: Alfred A. Knopf, 1961.

Valensi, Lucette.*On the eve of Colonialism: North Africa before the French Conquest.* Translated by Kenneth J. Perkins. New York: n.p., 1977.

Verthuy Mair E. and Jennifer Waelti-Walters. "Critical Practice and the Transmission of Culture." *Neohelicon* 14 (1987): 405–414.

Weyembergh, Maurice. *Albert Camus, ou, la mémoire des origines.* Bruxelles: De Boeck Université, 1988.

Willhoite, Fred H. *Beyond Nihilism: Albert Camus's Contribution to Political Thought.* Baton Rouge: Louisiana University Press, 1968.

Woelfel, James. *Albert Camus on the Sacred and Secular: An Introduction to His Thought.* Lanham: University Press of America, 1987.